ALSO BY ROBERT BYRNE

NONFICTION

McGoorty, A Pool Room Hustler
Byrne's New Standard Book of Pool and Billiards
Byrne's Treasury of Trick Shots in Pool and Billiards
Byrne's Advanced Technique in Pool and Billiards
Byrne's Wonderful World of Pool and Billiards
The 637 Best Things Anybody Ever Said
The Other 637 Best Things Anybody Ever Said
The Third—and Possibly the Best—637 Best Things Anybody Ever Said
The Fourth—and by Far the Most Recent—637 Best Things Anybody Ever Said
The Fifth and Far Finer than the First Four 637 Best Things Anybody Ever Said
Writing Rackets
Cat Scan: All the Best from the Literature of Cats (editor)
Every Day is Father's Day (editor)

FICTION

Thrill
Byrne's Book of Great Pool Stories
Mannequin
Skyscraper
Always a Catholic
The Dam
The Tunnel
Memories of a Non-Jewish Childhood

THE
2,548

BEST THINGS ANYBODY EVER

SAID

ROBERT BYRNE

A FIRESIDE BOOK

PUBLISHED BY SIMON & SCHUSTER

NEW YORK   LONDON   TORONTO   SYDNEY   SINGAPORE

FIRESIDE
Rockefeller Center
1230 Avenue of the Americas
New York, NY 10020

The 637 Best Things Anybody Ever Said
copyright © 1982 by Robert Byrne
The Other 637 Best Things Anybody Ever Said
copyright © 1984 by Robert Byrne
*The Third—and Possibly the Best—637 Best Things
Anybody Ever Said* copyright © 1986 by Robert Byrne
*The Fourth—and by Far the Most Recent—637 Best Things
Anybody Ever Said* copyright © 1990 by Robert Byrne

These titles were originally published individually.

First Fireside Edition 2003

FIRESIDE and colophon are registered trademarks
of Simon & Schuster, Inc.

For information about special discounts for bulk purchases,
please contact Simon & Schuster Special Sales:
1-800-456-6798 or business@simonandschuster.com

Designed by William Ruoto

Manufactured in the United States of America

1   3   5   7   9   10   8   6   4   2

Library of Congress Cataloging-in-Publication Data

Byrne, Robert.
The 2,548 best things anybody ever said / Robert Byrne.
p.   cm.
Includes bibliographical references and indexes.
1. Quotations, English.   I. Title: The two thousand five hundred forty-
eight best things anybody ever said.   II. Byrne, Robert.

PN6081.A128 2003
082—dc21   2002029971

ISBN 0-7432-3579-7

CONTENTS

INTRODUCTION

The quotes you hold in your hand first saw the light of day as four separate collections of 637 each. Five years ago, the four appeared as an anthology of the 2,548 best things anybody ever said with four introductions and four indexes of sources, authors, and key words. If you were looking for something on a particular subject or by a favorite wag, if you were trying to track down a half-remembered line, you had four places to look. In this new edition, the introductions and reference lists have been combined into one and the quotes are numbered from 1 to 2,548, not four times from 1 to 637. The streamlining will enable many readers, writers, and speakers to more easily feign a sense of humor where none exists.

Why 2,548 quotes instead of, say, 2,547? I didn't want to leave a good one out. Why not 2,549? I didn't want any padding. The goal was simply to compile the best (funniest) things ever said (or written), zingers that can be used in everyday life without the odor of pomposity. Look elsewhere for rosy words of uplift or inspiration, unless you are uplifted and inspired by lines more appropriate for performers than pontificators. A serious attempt was made to eliminate the chaff and retain only the wheat, which is to say that you should be able to open the book to any page and be glad you did.

Many of the quotes are clustered by subject, but the subjects aren't ordered according to the alphabet. It struck me as logical, for example, to follow remarks about Love with those about Sex, Wedlock, Self-Abuse, Kids, Drink, and Death, in that order. In most books of this kind, Sex is followed by such unrelated topics as Shakespeare, Sickness, and Socialism and there is no category for Self-Abuse at all.

I feel bad about most of the quotes attributed to celebrities, for in almost every case, I'm willing to bet, the wit was supplied by a publicist or gagwriter. As a rule, celebrities aren't funny without help. Many non-celebrities are funny, though, at least once in a while, which is why there are so many lines in these pages from unknowns who took the time to send me contributions. One is a man who calls himself Strange de Jim. Should he appear in the Index of Authors under Strange or de? Then there is Hal Lee Luyah, who appears five times. Is that a pseudonym or did his parents call him that to have something to shout on Easter Sunday?

I quote myself a few times, too, which comes under the heading Abuse of Editorial Privilege. I apologize for that and other character flaws.

A word about the antique line cuts, since nobody asked. They are taken from several dozen collections, most of them published by Dover, totaling around 15,000 images. It's not easy matching up a drawing with a quote. Imagine my joy when I found the perfect one for Number 424, Nietzsche's observation that "only sick music makes money today."

Have fun. I did.

Robert Byrne
Dubuque, Iowa

THE

2,548

BEST THINGS ANYBODY EVER

SAID

1

Why don't you get a haircut? You look like a chrysan-
themum.

—*P. G. Wodehouse (1881–1975)*

2

How can I believe in God when just last week I got my
tongue caught in the roller of an electric typewriter?

—*Woody Allen*

3

If I had been present at creation, I would have given some useful hints.

—*Alfonso the Wise (1221–1284)*

4

The gods play games with men as balls.

—*Titus Maccius Plautus (254?–184 B.C.)*

5

He was a wise man who invented God.

—*Plato (427?–348? B.C.)*

6

Plato is a bore.

—*Friedrich Nietzsche (1844–1900)*

7

It is the final proof of God's omnipotence that he need not exist in order to save us.

—*Peter De Vries*

8

Man is a god in ruins.

—*Ralph Waldo Emerson (1803–1882)*

9

God has always been hard on the poor.

—*Jean Paul Marat (1743–1793)*

10

Man is certainly stark mad. He cannot make a worm, and yet he will be making gods by dozens.

—*Montaigne (1553–1592)*

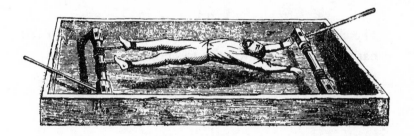

11

The good Lord never gives you more than you can handle. Unless you die of something.

—*Guindon cartoon caption*

12

If I had been the Virgin Mary, I would have said "No."

—*Margaret "Stevie" Smith (1902–1971)*

13

Few people can be happy unless they hate some other person, nation, or creed.

—*Bertrand Russell (1872–1970)*

14

Religions change; beer and wine remain.

—*Hervey Allen (1889–1949)*

15

The chicken probably came before the egg because it is hard to imagine God wanting to sit on an egg.

—*Unknown*

16

In England there are sixty different religions and only one sauce.

—*Francesco Caracciolo (1752–1799)*

17

Living with a saint is more grueling than being one.

—*Robert Neville*

18

He was of the faith chiefly in the sense that the church he currently did not attend was Catholic.

—*Kingsley Amis*

19

Everybody should believe in something; I believe I'll have another drink.

—*Unknown*

20

Under certain circumstances, profanity provides a relief denied even to prayer.

—*Mark Twain (1835–1910)*

21

The trouble with born-again Christians is that they are an even bigger pain the second time around.

—*Herb Caen*

22

I'm astounded by people who want to "know" the universe when it's hard enough to find your way around Chinatown.

—*Woody Allen*

23

It is better to know some of the questions than all of the answers.

—*James Thurber (1894–1961)*

24

It is only possible to live happily ever after on a day to day basis.

—*Margaret Bonnano*

25

I have a new philosophy. I'm only going to dread one day at a time.

—*Charles Schulz (1922–2000)*

26

I have a simple philosophy. Fill what's empty. Empty what's full. Scratch where it itches.

—*Alice Roosevelt Longworth (1884–1980)*

27

I know the answer! The answer lies within the heart of all mankind! The answer is twelve? I think I'm in the wrong building.

—*Charles Schulz (1922–2000)*

28

Life is like an overlong drama through which we sit being
nagged by the vague memories of having read the reviews.

—*John Updike*

29

There is more to life than increasing its speed.

—*Mahatma Gandhi (1869–1948)*

30

Life is like playing a violin in public and learning the in-
strument as one goes on.

—*Samuel Butler (1835–1902)*

31

Life is what happens while you are making other plans.

—*John Lennon (1940–1980)*

32

Life is a God-damned, stinking, treacherous game and nine hundred and ninety-nine men out of a thousand are bastards.

—*Theodore Dreiser (1871–1945)*
quoting an unnamed newspaper editor

33

There is no cure for birth and death save to enjoy the interval.

—*George Santayana (1863–1952)*

34

Why is it that we rejoice at a birth and grieve at a funeral? It is because we are not the person involved.

—*Mark Twain (1835–1910)*

35

The cost of living is going up and the chance of living is going down.

—*Flip Wilson (1933–1998)*

36

Is life worth living? That depends on the liver.

—*Unknown*

37

Dying is one of the few things that can be done as easily lying down.

—*Woody Allen*

38

I'm not afraid to die. I just don't want to be there when it happens.

—*Woody Allen*

39

Perhaps there is no life after death . . . there's just Los Angeles.

—*Rick Anderson*

40

Death is nature's way of saying "Howdy."

—*Unknown*

41

The best way to get praise is to die.

—*Italian proverb*

42

There is no such thing as inner peace. There is only nervousness and death.

—*Fran Lebowitz*

43

In the long run we are all dead.

—*John Maynard Keynes (1883–1946)*

44

The patient is not likely to recover who makes the doctor his heir.

—*Thomas Fuller (1608–1661)*

45

After I'm dead I'd rather have people ask why I have no monument than why I have one.

—*Cato the Elder (234–149 B.C.)*

46

For three days after death hair and fingernails continue to grow but phone calls taper off.

—*Johnny Carson*

47

I wonder if anybody ever reached the age of thirty-five in
New England without wanting to kill himself.

—Barrett Wendell (1855–1921)

48

I have had just about all I can take of myself.

—S. N. Behrman (1893–1973)
on reaching the age of 75

49

When you don't have any money, the problem is food.
When you have money, it's sex. When you have both, it's
health. If everything is simply jake, then you're frightened
of death.

—J. P. Donleavy

50

Most people would sooner die than think; in fact, they
do so.

—Bertrand Russell (1872–1970)

51

Early one June morning in 1872 I murdered my father—
an act which made a deep impression on me at the
time.

—*Ambrose Bierce (1842–1914?)*

52

One murder makes a villain, millions a hero.

—*Beilby Porteus (1731–1808)*

53

If once a man indulges himself in murder, very soon he
comes to think little of robbing; and from robbing he next
comes to drinking and Sabbath-breaking, and from that
to incivility and procrastination.

—*Thomas De Quincey (1785–1859)*

54

A murderer is one who is presumed to be innocent until
proven insane.

—*Unknown*

55

Either this man is dead or my watch has stopped.

—*Groucho Marx (1890–1977)*

56

There is no money in poetry, but then there is no poetry in money, either.

—*Robert Graves (1895–1985)*

57

This poem will never reach its destination.

—*Voltaire (1694–1778)*
on Rousseau's Ode to Posterity

58

I hope that one or two immortal lyrics will come out of all this tumbling around.

—*Poet Louise Bogan (1898–1970)*
on her love affair with
poet Theodore Roethke

59

I write poetry not for publication but merely to kill time. Airplanes are a good place to write poetry and then firmly throw it away. My collected works are mostly on the vomit bags of Pan American and TWA.

—*Charles McCabe*

60

The writing of more than 75 poems in any fiscal year should be punishable by a fine of $500.

—*Ed Sanders*

61

Show me a poet and I'll show you a shit.

—*A. J. Liebling (1904–1963)*

62

The human mind treats a new idea the way the body treats a strange protein; it rejects it.

—*Biologist P. B. Medawar (1915–1985)*

63

The intelligent man finds almost everything ridiculous, the sensible man hardly anything.

—*Johann Wolfgang von Goethe (1749–1832)*

64

The difference between genius and stupidity is that genius has its limits.

—*Unknown*

65

The only reason some people get lost in thought is because it's unfamiliar territory.

—*Paul Fix*

66

Only the mediocre are always at their best.

—*Jean Giraudoux (1882–1944)*

67

I'm going to speak my mind because I have nothing to lose.

—*Semanticist S. I. Hayakawa (1906–1992)*

68

I live in the crowd of jollity, not so much to enjoy company as to shun myself.

—*Samuel Johnson (1709–1784)*

69

For every ten jokes, thou has got an hundred enemies.

—*Laurence Sterne (1713–1768)*

70

Wit is educated insolence.

—*Aristotle (384–322 B.C.)*

71

Seriousness is the only refuge of the shallow.

—*Oscar Wilde (1854–1900)*

72

He who laughs, lasts.

—*Mary Pettibone Poole (c. 1938)*

73

Man: An animal [whose] . . . chief occupation is extermi-
nation of other animals and his own species, which, however, multiplies with such insistent rapidity as to infest the
whole habitable earth and Canada.

—*Ambrose Bierce (1842–1914?)*

74

Woman: An animal . . . having a rudimentary susceptibil-
ity to domestication . . . The species is the most widely
distributed of all beasts of prey. . . . The woman is omniv-
orous and can be taught not to talk.

—*Ambrose Bierce (1842–1914?)*

75

Cabbage: A . . . vegetable about as large and wise as a man's head.

—*Ambrose Bierce (1842–1914?)*

76

Memorial Service: Farewell party for someone who has already left.

—*Robert Byrne*

77

Eunuch: A man who has had his works cut out for him.

—*Robert Byrne*

78

I hate definitions.

—*Benjamin Disraeli (1804–1881)*

79

The affair between Margot Asquith and Margot Asquith will live as one of the prettiest love stories in all literature.

—*Dorothy Parker (1893–1967)*
in a review of a book by Margot Asquith

80
To love oneself is the beginning of a life-long romance.
—*Oscar Wilde (1854–1900)*

81

Like all self-made men he worships his creator.

—*Unknown*

82

Egotist: A person . . . more interested in himself than in me.

—*Ambrose Bierce (1842–1914?)*

83

A narcissist is someone better looking than you are.

—*Gore Vidal*

84

Don't be humble. You're not that great.

—*Golda Meir (1898–1978)*

85

Stop crime at its source! Support Planned Parenthood.

—*Robert Byrne*

86

When turkeys mate they think of swans.

—*Johnny Carson*

87

Except during the nine months before he draws his first breath, no man manages his affairs as well as a tree does.

—*George Bernard Shaw (1856–1950)*

88

It is now quite lawful for a Catholic woman to avoid pregnancy by a resort to mathematics, though she is still forbidden to resort to physics or chemistry.

—*H. L. Mencken (1880–1956)*

89

Somewhere on this globe, every ten seconds, there is a woman giving birth to a child. She must be found and stopped.

—Sam Levenson (1911–1980)

90

To enter life by way of the vagina is as good a way as any.

—Henry Miller (1891–1980)

91

I have an intense desire to return to the womb. Anybody's.

—Woody Allen

92

To my embarrassment I was born in bed with a lady.

—Wilson Mizner (1876–1933)

93

My obstetrician was so dumb that when I gave birth he forgot to cut the cord. For a year that kid followed me *everywhere*. It was like having a dog on a leash.

—Joan Rivers

94

I knew I was an unwanted baby when I saw that my bath toys were a toaster and a radio.

—*Joan Rivers*

95

A child is a curly, dimpled lunatic.

—*Ralph Waldo Emerson (1803–1882)*

96

All children are essentially criminal.

—*Denis Diderot (1713–1784)*

97

A vegetarian is a person who won't eat anything that can have children.

—*David Brenner*

98

When I was a child what I wanted to be when I grew up was an invalid.

—*Quentin Crisp (1908–1999)*

99

Children of the poor should work for some part of the day when they reach the age of three.

—*John Locke (1632–1704) in 1697*

100

Of all the animals, the boy is the most unmanageable.
—*Plato (427?–348? B.C.)*

Plato is a bore.
—*Friedrich Nietzsche (1844–1900)*

101

Children are guilty of unpardonable rudeness when they spit in the face of a companion; neither are they excusable who spit from windows or on walls or furniture.
—*St. John Baptist de La Salle (c. 1695)*

102

Thank God kids never mean well.
—*Lily Tomlin*

103

Mothers are fonder than fathers of their children because they are more certain they are their own.
—*Aristotle (384–322 B.C.)*

104

There's nothing wrong with teenagers that reasoning with them won't aggravate.
—*Unknown*

105

Young people are more hopeful at a certain age than adults, but I suspect that's glandular. As for children, I keep as far from them as possible. I don't like the sight of them. The scale is all wrong. The heads tend to be too big for the bodies, and the hands and feet are a disaster. They keep falling into things. The nakedness of their bad character! We adults have learned how to disguise our terrible character, but children, well, they are like grotesque drawings of *us*. They should be neither seen nor heard, and no one must make another one.

—*Gore Vidal*

106

I tell you I can feel them! They're all around us! Young people! Getting closer and closer!

—*Hamilton cartoon caption*

107

The reason husbands and wives do not understand each other is because they belong to different sexes.

—*Dorothy Dix (1870–1951)*

108

There was a time when we expected nothing of children but obedience, as opposed to the present, when we expect everything of them but obedience.

—*Anatole Broyard*

109

The reason grandparents and grandchildren get along so well is that they have a common enemy.

—*Sam Levenson (1911–1980)*

110

I never met a kid I liked.

—*W. C. Fields (1880–1946)*

111

It is a good thing for an uneducated man to read books of quotations.

—*Winston Churchill (1874–1965)*

112

I hate quotations.

—*Ralph Waldo Emerson (1803–1882)*

113

If men could get pregnant, abortion would be a sacrament.

—*Florynce Kennedy*

114

Ever since the young men have owned motorcycles, incest has been dying out.

—*Max Frisch (1911–1991)*

115

Familiarity breeds attempt.

—Goodman Ace (1899–1982)

116

Sex drive: A physical craving that begins in adolescence and ends at marriage.

—Robert Byrne

117

Sex is the most fun you can have without smiling.

—Unknown

118

I would rather go to bed with Lillian Russell stark naked than Ulysses S. Grant in full military regalia.

—Mark Twain (1835–1910)

119

Last time I tried to make love to my wife nothing was happening, so I said to her, "What's the matter, you can't think of anybody either?"

—Rodney Dangerfield

120

If it weren't for pickpockets I'd have no sex life at all.

—Rodney Dangerfield

121

I've tried several varieties of sex. The conventional position makes me claustrophobic and the others give me a stiff neck or lockjaw.

—Tallulah Bankhead (1903–1968)

122

A woman occasionally is quite a serviceable substitute for masturbation.

—Karl Kraus (1874–1936)

123

Sex is nobody's business except the three people involved.

—*Unknown*

124

What men desire is a virgin who is a whore.

—*Edward Dahlberg (1900–1977)*

125

The orgasm has replaced the Cross as the focus of longing
and the image of fulfillment.

—*Malcolm Muggeridge (1903–1990)*

126

All this fuss about sleeping together. For physical pleasure
I'd sooner go to my dentist any day.

—*Evelyn Waugh (1903–1966)*

127

What a man enjoys about a woman's clothes are his fan-
tasies of how she would look without them.

—*Brendan Francis*

128

Women who miscalculate are called "mothers."

—*Abigail Van Buren*

129

Nothing is so much to be shunned as sex relations.

—*St. Augustine (354–430)*

130

I kissed my first girl and smoked my first cigarette on the same day. I haven't had time for tobacco since.

—*Arturo Toscanini (1867–1957)*

131

The only really indecent people are the chaste.

—*J. K. Huysmans (1848–1907)*

132

For the preservation of chastity, an empty and rumbling stomach and fevered lungs are indispensable.

—*St. Jerome (340?–420)*

133

I hate women because they always know where things are.

—*James Thurber (1894–1961)*

134

Sex is the biggest nothing of all time.
—Andy Warhol (1928?–1987)

135

Love is the delightful interval between meeting a beautiful girl and discovering that she looks like a haddock.
—John Barrymore (1882–1942)

136

Love is an ocean of emotions entirely surrounded by expenses.

—Lord Dewar

137

Love is a grave mental disease.
—Plato (427?–348? B.C.)

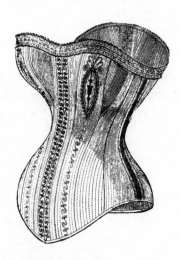

138

Whatever deceives seems to produce a magical enchantment.

—Plato (427?–348? B.C.)

Plato is a bore.

—Friedrich Nietzsche (1844–1900)

139

The heaviest object in the world is the body of the woman you have ceased to love.

—Marquis de Luc de Clapiers Vauvenargues
(1715–1747)

140

In expressing love we belong among the undeveloped countries.

—Saul Bellow

141

A man can be happy with any woman as long as he does not love her.

—Oscar Wilde (1854–1900)

142

Love will find a lay.

—Robert Byrne

143

It takes a woman twenty years to make a man of her son, and another woman twenty minutes to make a fool of him.

—*Helen Rowland (1876–1950)*

144

It is better to have loved and lost than never to have lost at all.

—*Samuel Butler (1835–1902)*

145

I sold my memoirs of my love life to Parker Brothers and they are going to make a game out of it.

—*Woody Allen*

146

The only solid and lasting peace between a man and his wife is doubtless a separation.

—*Lord Chesterfield (1694–1773)*

147

Marriage: A master, a mistress and two slaves, making in all, two.

—*Ambrose Bierce (1842–1914?)*

148

Marriage is not a word but a sentence.

—*Unknown*

149

Marriage is a great institution, but I'm not ready for an institution.

—*Mae West (1893–1980)*

150

If I ever marry it will be on a sudden impulse, as a man shoots himself.

—*H. L. Mencken (1880–1956)*

151

For the upper middle class, marriage is the only adventure left.

—*Unknown*

152

We want playmates we can own.

—*Jules Feiffer on marriage*

153

It was so cold I almost got married.

—*Shelley Winters*

154

At American weddings, the quality of the food is inversely proportional to the social position of the bride and groom.
—*Calvin Trillin*

155

I was married once. Now I just lease.
—*From the movie* Buddy, Buddy *(1981)*

156

I married beneath me. All women do.
—*Nancy, Lady Astor (1879–1964)*

157

An archeologist is the best husband a woman can have;
the older she gets, the more interested he is in her.

—*Agatha Christie (1891–1976),*
who was married to one

158

I tended to place my wife under a pedestal.

—*Woody Allen*

159

My mother-in-law broke up my marriage. One day my
wife came home early from work and found us in bed together.

—*Lenny Bruce (1926–1966)*

160

Divorce is the sacrament of adultery.

—*French proverb*

161

What scares me about divorce is that my children might
put me in a home for unwed mothers.

—*Teressa Skelton*

162

Take my wife . . . please!

—*Henry Youngman (1906–1998)*

163

A CURSE

May your soul be forever tormented by fire and your bones be dug up by dogs and dragged through the streets of Minneapolis.

—*Garrison Keillor*

164

My work is done, why wait?
> —*Suicide note left by Kodak founder*
> *George Eastman (1854–1932)*

165

All right, then, I'll say it: Dante makes me sick.
> —*Last words of Spanish playwright*
> *Lope de Vega on being assured on his*
> *deathbed that the end was very near*

166

I don't feel good.
> —*Last words of Luther Burbank*
> *(1849–1926)*

167

Don't let it end like this. Tell them I said something.
> —*Last words of Pancho Villa*
> *(1877?–1923)*

168

It is better to be a coward for a minute than dead for the rest of your life.
> —*Irish proverb*

169

The reverse side also has a reverse side.

—*Japanese proverb*

170

Tell the truth and run.

—*Yugoslavian proverb*

171

Do not insult the mother alligator until after you have crossed the river.

—*Haitian proverb*

172

Too clever is dumb.

—*German proverb*

173

The Irish ignore anything they can't drink or punch.

—*Old saying*

174

If God lived on earth, people would break his windows.

—*Jewish proverb*

175

It is nothing, they are only thrashing my husband.

—*Portuguese proverb*

176

When the cat and mouse agree, the grocer is ruined.

—*Persian proverb*

177

I do not say a proverb is amiss when aptly and reasonably applied, but to be forever discharging them, right or wrong, hit or miss, renders conversation insipid and vulgar.

—*Miguel de Cervantes (1547–1616)*

178

Wise men make proverbs but fools repeat them.

—*Samuel Palmer (c. 1710)*

179

Nobody has ever bet enough on the winning horse.

—*Overheard at a track by Richard Sasuly*

180

One of the worst things that can happen in life is to win a bet on a horse at an early age.

—*Danny McGoorty (1901–1970)*

181

Nobody ever committed suicide who had a good two-year-old in the barn.

—*Racetrack proverb*

182

It is morally wrong to allow suckers to keep their money.

—*"Canada Bill" Jones*

183

All life is six to five against.

—*Damon Runyon (1884–1946)*

184

Much as he is opposed to lawbreaking, he is not bigoted about it.

—*Damon Runyon (1884–1946)*

185

You might as well fall flat on your face as lean over too far backward.

—*James Thurber (1894–1961)*

186

Alexander III of Macedonia is known as Alexander the Great because he killed more people of more different kinds than any other man of his time.

—*Will Cuppy (1884–1949)*

187

Aristotle was famous for knowing everything. He taught that the brain exists merely to cool the blood and is not involved in the process of thinking. This is true only of certain persons.

—*Will Cuppy (1884–1949)*

188

All Gaul is divided into three parts: igneous, metamorphic, and sedimentary.

—*Geologist Wilson Hinckley (1928–1972)*

189

What a time! What a civilization!

—*Cicero (106–43* B.C.)

190

Oh, this age! How tasteless and ill-bred it is!

—*Catullus (87?–54?* B.C.)

191

How little you know about the age you live in if you think that honey is sweeter than cash in hand.

—*Ovid (43?* B.C.–A.D. *18)*

192

It is sometimes expedient to forget who we are.

—*Publilius Syrus (c. 42* B.C.)

193

There is no glory in outstripping donkeys.

—*Martial (40–102)*

194

The school of hard knocks is an accelerated curriculum.

—*Menander (342?–292?* B.C.)

195

There is nothing so absurd but some philosopher has
said it.

—*Cicero (106–43* B.C.*)*

196

A man with his belly full of the classics is an enemy of the
human race.

—*Henry Miller (1891–1980)*

197

Patriotism is the willingness to kill and be killed for trivial
reasons.

—*Bertrand Russell (1872–1970)*

198

Democracy substitutes election by the incompetent many
for appointment by the corrupt few.

—*George Bernard Shaw (1856–1950)*

199

America has been discovered before, but it has always
been hushed up.

—*Oscar Wilde (1854–1900)*

200

The 100% American is 99% an idiot.

—*George Bernard Shaw (1856–1950)*

201

A government which robs Peter to pay Paul can always depend on the support of Paul.

—*George Bernard Shaw (1856–1950)*

202

And that's the world in a nutshell—an appropriate receptacle.

—*Stan Dunn*

203

The remarkable thing about Shakespeare is that he really is very good, in spite of all the people who say he is very good.

—*Robert Graves (1895–1985)*

204

Crude, immoral, vulgar, and senseless.

—*Leo Tolstoy (1828–1910) on Shakespeare*

205

I know not, sir, whether Bacon wrote the works of Shakespeare, but if he did not it seems to me that he missed the opportunity of his life.

—*James Barrie (1860–1937)*

206

If Shakespeare had been in pro basketball he never would have had time to write his soliloquies. He would always have been on a plane between Phoenix and Kansas City.

—*Paul Westhead, basketball coach*

207

A team is a team is a team. Shakespeare said that many times.

—*Dan Devine, football coach*

208

A piano is a piano is a piano.—Gertrude Steinway

—*Unknown*

209

A manuscript, like a foetus, is never improved by showing it to somebody before it is completed.

—*Unknown*

210

Every journalist has a novel in him, which is an excellent place for it.

—*Russell Lynes*

211

Why authors write I do not know. As well ask why a hen lays an egg or a cow stands patiently while a farmer burglarizes her.

—*H. L. Mencken (1880–1956)*

212

Why do writers write? Because it isn't there.

—*Thomas Berger*

213

Never let a domestic quarrel ruin a day's writing. If you can't start the next day fresh, get rid of your wife.

—*One of Mario Puzo's rules
for writing a best-selling novel*

214

Every novel should have a beginning, a muddle, and an end.

—*Peter De Vries (1910–1993)*

215

Boy meets girl; girl gets boy into pickle; boy gets pickle
into girl.

—Jack Woodford (1894–1971) on plotting

216

Writing is easy. All you do is stare at a blank sheet of paper
until drops of blood form on your forehead.

—Gene Fowler (1890–1960)

217

With a novelist, like a surgeon, you have to get a feeling
that you've fallen into good hands—someone from whom
you can accept the anesthetic with confidence.

—Saul Bellow

218

Sometimes when reading Goethe I have a paralyzing sus-
picion that he is trying to be funny.

—Guy Davenport

219

The novelist, afraid his ideas may be foolish, slyly puts
them in the mouth of some other fool and reserves the
right to disavow them.

—Diane Johnson

220

He can compress the most words into the smallest idea of any man I ever met.

—*Abraham Lincoln (1809–1865)*

221

If a writer has to rob his mother he will not hesitate; the *Ode On a Grecian Urn* is worth any number of old ladies.

—*William Faulkner (1897–1962)*

222

In literature as in love, we are astonished at what is chosen by others.

—*André Maurois (1885–1967)*

223

It is a delicious thing to write, to be no longer yourself but to move in an entire universe of your own creating. Today, for instance, as man and woman, both lover and mistress, I rode in a forest on an autumn afternoon under the yellow leaves, and I was also the horses, the leaves, the wind, the words my people uttered, even the red sun that made them almost close their love-drowned eyes. When I brood over these marvelous pleasures I have enjoyed, I would be tempted to offer God a prayer of thanks if I knew he could hear me. Praised may he be for not creating me a cotton merchant, a vaudevillian, or a wit.

—*Gustave Flaubert (1821–1880)*

224

I'm a lousy writer; a helluva lot of people have got lousy taste.

—*Grace Metalious (1924–1964), author of* Peyton Place

225

A custom loathsome to the eye, hateful to the nose, harm-
ful to the brain, dangerous to the lungs, and in the black,
stinking fumes thereof, nearest resembling the horrible
Stygian smoke of the pit that is bottomless.

—King James (c. 1604) on smoking

226

I can write better than anybody who can write faster, and
I can write faster than anybody who can write better.

—A. J. Liebling (1904–1963)

227

I used to be treated like an idiot, now I'm treated like an idiot savant.

—*Martin Cruz Smith after his novel*
Gorky Park *became a bestseller*

228

Income tax returns are the most imaginative fiction being written today.

—*Herman Wouk*

229

Marry money.

—*Max Shulman's advice*
to aspiring authors

230

What is a writer but a shmuck with an Underwood?

—*Jack Warner (ascribed)*

231

There's no thief like a bad book.

—*Italian proverb*

232

A big book is a big bore.

—*Callimachus (c. 260 B.C.)*

233

Never read a book that is not a year old.

—*Ralph Waldo Emerson (1803–1882)*

234

The man who doesn't read good books has no advantage over the man who can't read them.

—*Mark Twain (1835–1910)*

235

Any ordinary man can . . . surround himself with two thousand books . . . and thenceforward have at least one place in the world in which it is possible to be happy.

—*Augustine Birrell (1850–1933)*

236

I have always imagined that Paradise will be a kind of library.

—*Jorge Luis Borges (1899–1986)*

237

Studying literature at Harvard is like learning about women at the Mayo Clinic.

—*Roy Blount, Jr.*

238

I wonder how so insupportable a thing as a bookseller was ever permitted to grow up in the Commonwealth. Many of our modern booksellers are but needless excrements, or rather vermin.

—*George Wither (1588–1667)*

239

It takes the publishing industry so long to produce books it's no wonder so many are posthumous.

—*Teressa Skelton*

240

In every fat book there is a thin book trying to get out.

—*Unknown*

241

No, I haven't read the New Testament, but I read the Old Testament, and I liked it very, very much.

—*One shepherd to another in a* New Yorker *cartoon*

242

What an ugly beast is the ape, and how like us.

—*Cicero (106–43 B.C.)*

243

Your life story would not make a good book. Don't even try.

—*Fran Lebowitz*

244

Drunkenness is the ruin of reason. It is premature old age. It is temporary death.

—*St. Basil (330?–379?)*

245

I drink no more than a sponge.

—*François Rabelais (1494–1553)*

246

They talk of my drinking but never my thirst.

—*Scottish proverb*

247

A drinker has a hole under his nose that all his money runs into.

—*Thomas Fuller (1608–1661)*

248

'Twas a woman who drove me to drink, and I never had the courtesy to thank her for it.

—*W. C. Fields (1880–1946)*

249

An Irishman is the only man in the world who will step over the bodies of a dozen naked women to get to a bottle of stout.

—*Unknown*

250

One more drink and I'll be under the host.

—*Dorothy Parker (1893–1967)*

251

I drink to make other people more interesting.

—*George Jean Nathan (1882–1958)*

252

Inflation has gone up over a dollar a quart.

—*W. C. Fields (1880–1946)*

253

Even though a number of people have tried, no one has yet found a way to drink for a living.

—*Jean Kerr*

254

I haven't touched a drop of alcohol since the invention of the funnel.

—*Malachy McCourt*

255

The less I behave like Whistler's mother the night before, the more I look like her the morning after.

—*Tallulah Bankhead (1903–1968)*

256

One reason I don't drink is that I want to know when I am having a good time.

—*Nancy, Lady Astor (1879–1964)*

257

I'd rather have a free bottle in front of me than a prefrontal lobotomy.

—*Unknown*

258

I hate to advocate drugs, alcohol, violence, or insanity to anyone, but they've always worked for me.

—*Hunter S. Thompson*

259

If you drink, don't drive. Don't even putt.

—*Dean Martin*

260

I tremble for my country when I reflect that God is just.

—Thomas Jefferson (1743–1826)

261

If you weren't such a great man you'd be a terrible bore.

—Mrs. William Gladstone to her husband

262

He speaks to me as if I were a public meeting.

—Queen Victoria (1819–1901) on Gladstone

263

Harding was not a bad man, he was just a slob.

—Alice Roosevelt Longworth (1884–1980)

264

The only man, woman, or child who ever wrote a simple declarative sentence with seven grammatical errors is dead.

—e. e. cummings (1894–1962)
on the death of Warren G. Harding, 1923

265

In 1932, lame duck President Herbert Hoover was so desperate to remain in the White House that he dressed up as Eleanor Roosevelt. When FDR discovered the hoax in 1936, the two men decided to stay together for the sake of the children.

—*Johnny Carson*

266

The Arabs are a backward people who eat nothing but camel dung.

—*Winston Churchill (1874–1965)*

267

Things have never been more like the way they are today in history.

—*Dwight David Eisenhower (1890–1969)*

268

John Foster Dulles.

—*Mort Sahl on being asked
to say something funny*

269

Listen, there is no courage or any extra courage that I know of to find out the right thing to do. Now, it is not only necessary to do the right thing, but to do it in the right way and the only problem you have is what is the right thing to do and what is the right way to do it. That is the problem. But this economy of ours is not so simple that it obeys to the opinion of bias or the pronouncements of any particular individual, even to the President. This is an economy that is made up of 173 million people and it reflects their desires, they're ready to buy, they're ready to spend, it is a thing that is too complex and too big to be affected adversely or advantageously just by a few words or any particular—say, a little this and that, or even a panacea so alleged.

—Dwight David Eisenhower (1890–1969) in response to the question: "Has government been lacking in courage and boldness in facing up to the recession?"

270

Nixon is a shifty-eyed goddamn liar. . . . He's one of the few in the history of this country to run for high office talking out of both sides of his mouth at the same time and lying out of both sides.

—Harry S Truman (1884–1972)

271

I don't give a shit about the Italian lira.
—President Richard M. Nixon (1913–1994) on
being asked by H. R. Haldeman if he wanted to
hear a report on the decline of the Italian lira

272

I would have made a good Pope.
—Richard M. Nixon (1913–1994)

273

How do you like that guy? Can't run six balls and he's
President of the United States.
—Pool hustler Johnny Irish on Nixon

274

Henry Kissinger may have wished I had presented him as
a combination of Charles DeGaulle and Disraeli, but I
didn't . . . out of respect for DeGaulle and Disraeli. I described him as a cowboy because that is how he described
himself. If I were a cowboy I would be offended.
—Oriana Fallaci

275

Jerry Ford is a nice guy, but he played too much football
with his helmet off.
—Lyndon Baines Johnson (1908–1973)

276

I never trust a man unless I've got his pecker in my pocket.
—*Lyndon Baines Johnson (1908–1973)*

277

No.

—*President Jimmy Carter's daughter Amy
when asked by a reporter if she had any
message for the children of America*

278

Sometimes when I look at my children I say to myself,
"Lillian, you should have stayed a virgin."
—*Lillian Carter, mother of Jimmy and Billy*

279

"Who's Virginia?"

—*Rose Kennedy (1890–1995) when asked why
her daughter-in-law Joan lived in Boston
while her son Ted lived in Virginia*

280

I see the world in very fluid, contradictory, emerging, in-
terconnected terms, and with that kind of circuitry I just
don't feel the need to say what is going to happen or will
not happen.
—*Former California Governor Jerry Brown*

281

Ronald Reagan is not a typical politician because he doesn't know how to lie, cheat, and steal. He's always had an agent for that.

—Bob Hope

282

Ronald Reagan is the Fred Astaire of foot-in-mouth disease.

—Jeff Davis

283

Never forget that the most powerful force on earth is love.
—Nelson Rockefeller (1908–1979)
to Henry Kissinger

284

Sure Reagan promised to take senility tests. But what if he forgets?

—Lorna Kerr-Walker

285

Ronald Reagan is the most ignorant president since Warren Harding.

—Ralph Nader

286

Ronald Reagan has held the two most demeaning jobs in the country—President of the United States and radio broadcaster for the Chicago Cubs.

—*George Will*

287

Nancy Reagan fell down and broke her hair.

—*Johnny Carson*

288

Well, I would—if they realized that we—again if—if we led them back to that stalemate only because that our retaliatory power, our seconds, or strike at them after our first strike, would be so destructive that they couldn't afford it, that would hold them off.

—*Ronald Reagan when asked if nuclear war could be limited to tactical weapons*

289

Nixon, Ford, Carter, Reagan—a Mount Rushmore of incompetence.

—*David Steinberg*

290

When I was a boy I was told that anybody could become President; I'm beginning to believe it.

—*Clarence Darrow (1857–1938)*

291

I'd rather entrust the government of the United States to the first 400 people listed in the Boston telephone directory than to the faculty of Harvard University.

—*William F. Buckley, Jr.*

292

The only thing that saves us from the bureaucracy is its inefficiency.

—*Eugene McCarthy*

293

We have a crisis of leadership in this country. Where are the Washingtons, the Jeffersons, and the Jacksons? I'll tell you where they are—they are playing professional football and basketball.

—*Unknown*

294

It is inaccurate to say I hate everything. I am strongly in favor of common sense, common honesty, and common decency. This makes me forever ineligible for any public office.

—*H. L. Mencken (1880–1956)*

295

What this country needs is more unemployed politicians.

—*Edward Langley*

296

All right, I will learn to read, but when I have learned, I never, never shall.
—*British novelist David Garnett at age 4, to his mother*

297

Henry James writes fiction as if it were a painful duty.
—*Oscar Wilde (1854–1900)*

298

Henry James chews more than he bites off.
—*Mrs. Henry Adams (c. 1880)*

299

Henry James was one of the nicest old ladies I ever met.
—*William Faulkner (1897–1962)*

300

Henry James would have been vastly improved as a novelist by a few whiffs of the Chicago stockyards.
—*H. L. Mencken (1880–1956)*

301

Henry James created more convincing women than Iris Murdoch put together.

—*Wilfred Sheed*

302

Go not in and out of court that thy name may not stink.

—*The Wisdom of Anii (c. 900 B.C.)*

303

A lawyer and a wagon-wheel must be well greased.

—*German proverb*

304

Law is a bottomless pit.

—*John Arbuthnot (1667–1735) (c. 1712)*

305

Lawyers, I suppose, were children once.

—*Charles Lamb (1775–1834)*

306

When men are pure, laws are useless; when men are corrupt, laws are broken.

—*Benjamin Disraeli (1804–1881)*

307

I became a policeman because I wanted to be in a business where the customer is always wrong.

—*Unnamed officer quoted by Arlene Heath*

308

The mistakes are all there waiting to be made.

—*Chessmaster Savielly Grigorievitch Tartakower (1887–1956) on the game's opening position*

309

Moral victories don't count.

—*Savielly Grigorievitch Tartakower (1887–1956)*

310

The only reason I would take up jogging is so that I could hear heavy breathing again.

—*Erma Bombeck (1927–1996)*

311

I don't jog. If I die I want to be sick.

—*Abe Lemons*

312

It was such a primitive country we didn't even see any joggers.

—*Hamilton cartoon caption*

313

Be careful about reading health books. You may die of a misprint.

—*Mark Twain (1835–1910)*

314

Old people shouldn't eat health foods. They need all the preservatives they can get.

—*Robert Orben*

315

A closed mouth gathers no feet.

—*Unknown*

316

Never eat more than you can lift.

—*Miss Piggy*

317

Punctuality is the thief of time.

—*Oscar Wilde (1856–1900)*

318

Platitudes are the Sundays of stupidity.

—*Unknown*

319

It is unbecoming for young men to utter maxims.

—*Aristotle (384–322 B.C.)*

320

They were such a progressive couple they tried to adopt a gay baby.

—*Unknown*

321

He who marries a widow will often have a dead man's head thrown in his dish.

—*Spanish proverb*

322

I don't know the key to success, but the key to failure is trying to please everybody.

—*Bill Cosby*

323

The brain is a wonderful organ; it starts working the moment you get up in the morning and does not stop until you get to the office.

—*Robert Frost (1874–1963)*

324

I have never seen a greater monster or miracle than myself.
—*Michel Eyquem de Montaigne (1533–1592)*

325

Until you walk a mile in another man's moccasins you can't imagine the smell.

—*Robert Byrne*

326

I don't have a warm personal enemy left. They've all died off. I miss them terribly because they helped define me.
—*Clare Boothe Luce (1903–1987)*

327

I'm lonesome. They are all dying. I have hardly a warm personal enemy left.

—*James McNeill Whistler (1834–1903)*

328

Nothing is said that has not been said before.

—*Terence (185–159 B.C.)*

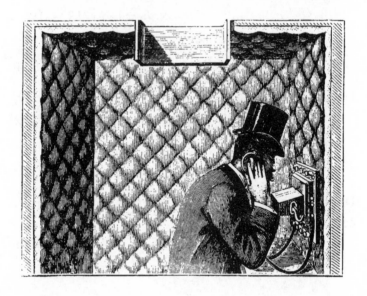

329

I'm in a phone booth at the corner of Walk and Don't Walk.

—*Unknown*

330

How come they picked you to be an astronaut? You got such a great sense of direction?

—*Jackie Mason*

331

Recipe (in its entirety) for boiled owl:
Take feathers off. Clean owl and put in cooking pot with lots of water. Add salt to taste.

—The Eskimo Cookbook *(1952)*

332

Do not make loon soup.

—*Valuable advice from* The Eskimo Cookbook

333

Fall is my favorite season in Los Angeles, watching the birds change color and fall from the trees.

—*David Letterman*

334

I met a guy once who was half Italian and half Chinese. His name was Video Pong.

—*Unknown*

335

My father never lived to see his dream come true of an all-Yiddish-speaking Canada.

—*David Steinberg*

336

That man has missed something who has never left a brothel at sunrise feeling like throwing himself into the river out of pure disgust.

—*Gustave Flaubert (1821–1880)*

337

Gary Cooper and Greta Garbo may be the same person. Have you ever seen them together?

—*Ernst Lubitsch (1892–1947)*

338

He had a God-given killer instinct.

—*Al Davis of the Oakland Raiders on George Blanda*

339

I was gratified to be able to answer promptly. I said I don't know.

—*Mark Twain (1835–1910)*

340

Few people know how to be old.

—*La Rochefoucauld (1613–1680)*

341

The enemy came. He was beaten. I am tired. Goodnight.

—*Message sent by Vicomte Turenne*
after the battle of Dunen, 1658

342

Byrne's Law: In any electrical circuit, appliances and wiring will burn out to protect fuses.

—*Robert Byrne*

343

McCabe's Law: Nobody *has* to do *anything*.

—*Charles McCabe*

344

Parker's Law: Beauty is only skin deep, but ugly goes clear to the bone.

—*from* Murphy's Law

345

Chamberlain's Law: Everything tastes more or less like chicken.

—*from* The Official Rules

346

A man can wear a hat for years without being oppressed by its shabbiness.

—*James Douglas*

347

Boozer's Revision: A bird in the hand is dead.
—*from* The Official Rules

348

Any fool can make a rule.

—*Henry David Thoreau (1817–1862)*

349

Happiness Is Seeing Lubbock, Texas, in the Rearview Mirror.

—*Song title*

350

The important thing in acting is to be able to laugh and cry. If I have to cry, I think of my sex life. If I have to laugh, I think of my sex life.

—*Glenda Jackson*

351

There are more bores around than when I was a boy.

—*Fred Allen (1894–1956)*

352

I've tried relaxing, but—I don't know—I feel more comfortable tense.

—*Hamilton cartoon caption*

353

I'm just a person trapped inside a woman's body.

—*Elayne Boosler*

354

I happened to catch my reflection the other day when I was polishing my trophies, and, gee, it's easy to see why women are nuts about me.

—*Tom Ryan*

355

What to do in case of emergency:
    1. Pick up your hat
    2. Grab your coat
    3. Leave your worries on the doorstep
    4. Direct your feet to the sunny side of the street.

—*Unknown*

356

Nolan Ryan is pitching much better now that he has his curve ball straightened out.

—*Joe Garagiola*

357

In many ways the saying "Know thyself" is lacking. Better to know other people.

—*Menander (342?–292? B.C.)*

358

Only the shallow know themselves.

—*Oscar Wilde (1854–1900)*

359

We all have the strength to endure the misfortunes of others.

—*La Rochefoucauld (1613–1680)*

360

There is no sweeter sound than the crumbling of one's fellow man.

—*Groucho Marx (1890–1977)*

361

It takes a great man to make a good listener.

—*Arthur Helps (1813–1875)*

362

In this business you either sink or swim or you don't.
—*David Smith*

363

I don't have a photograph, but you can have my foot-prints. They're upstairs in my socks.
—*Groucho Marx (1890–1977)*

364

I've always been interested in people, but I've never liked them.
—*Somerset Maugham (1874–1965)*

365

Are you going to come quietly or do I have to use ear-plugs?
—*From* The Goon Show

366

One of the symptoms of an approaching nervous break-down is the belief that one's work is terribly important.
—*Bertrand Russell (1872–1970)*

367

A little inaccuracy sometimes saves tons of explanation.

—*H. H. Munro (Saki) (1870–1916)*

368

It's really hard to be roommates with people if your suit-cases are much better than theirs.

—*J. D. Salinger*

369

Take most people, they're crazy about cars. I'd rather have a goddamn horse. A horse is at least *human,* for God's sake.

—*J. D. Salinger*

370

Three o'clock is always too late or too early for anything you want to do.

—*Jean-Paul Sartre (1905–1980)*

371

A reformer is a guy who rides through a sewer in a glass-bottomed boat.

—*New York Mayor Jimmy Walker*
(1881–1946) in 1928

372

The doctor can bury his mistakes but an architect can only advise his client to plant vines.

—*Frank Lloyd Wright (1869–1959)*

373

I wash everything on the gentle cycle. It's much more humane.

—*Unknown*

374

The breakfast of champions is not cereal, it's the opposition.

—*Nick Seitz*

375

There is nothing in the world so enjoyable as a thorough-going monomania.

—*Agnes Repplier (1858–1950)*

376

Virtue is its own revenge.

—*E. Y. Harburg (1898–1981)*

377

A good deed never goes unpunished.

—*Gore Vidal*

378
The curtain rises on a vast primitive wasteland, not unlike
certain parts of New Jersey.

—*Woody Allen*

379

Man is the only animal that laughs and has a state legislature.

—*Samuel Butler (1835–1902)*

380

Until a child is one year old it is incapable of sin.

—*The Talmud (c. 200)*

381

I wish people who have trouble communicating would just shut up.

—*Tom Lehrer*

382

A man is as young as the woman he feels.

—*Variously ascribed*

383

Toots Shor's restaurant is so crowded nobody goes there anymore.

—*Yogi Berra*

384

I don't care what is written about me so long as it isn't true.

—*Dorothy Parker (1893–1967)*

385

He can beat yourn with hisn and he can beat hisn with yourn.

—*Pro football coach "Bum" Phillips
on the merits of coach Don Shula*

386

More than any time in history mankind faces a crossroads. One path leads to despair and utter hopelessness, the other to total extinction. Let us pray that we have the wisdom to choose correctly.

—*Woody Allen*

387

It is dangerous to be sincere unless you are also stupid.

—*George Bernard Shaw (1856–1950)*

388

You can't steal second base and keep one foot on first.

—*An unnamed 60-year-old junior executive*

389

When something good happens it's a miracle and you should wonder what God is saving up for you later.

—*Marshall Brickman*

390

Cogito ergo spud. I think, therefore I yam.

—*Graffito*

391

If you want an audience, start a fight.

—*Gaelic proverb*

392

Everything hurts.

—*Michelangelo Antonioni*

393

I propose getting rid of conventional armaments and replacing them with reasonably priced hydrogen bombs that would be distributed equally throughout the world.

—*Idi Amin*

394
I like a woman with a head on her shoulders. I hate necks.
—*Steve Martin*

395

I don't know why people like the home run so much. A home run is over as soon as it starts . . . wham, bam, thank you, ma'am. The triple is the most exciting play of the game. A triple is like meeting a woman who excites you, spending the evening talking and getting more excited, then taking her home. It drags on and on. You're never sure how it's going to turn out.

—Baseball player George Foster

396

Working on television is like being shot out of a cannon. They cram you all up with rehearsals, then someone lights a fuse and—BANG—there you are in someone's living room.

—Tallulah Bankhead (1903–1968)

397

Talk is cheap because supply exceeds demand.

—Unknown

398

Fifteen cents of every twenty-cent stamp goes for storage.

—Louis Rukeyser

399

The unique thing about Margaret Rutherford is that she can act with her chin alone. Among its many moods I especially cherish the chin commanding, the chin in doubt, and the chin at bay.

—*Kenneth Tynan*

400

Things are so bad on Broadway today an actor is lucky to be miscast.

—*George S. Kaufman (1889–1961)*

401

The race may not be to the swift nor the victory to the strong, but that's how you bet.

—*Damon Runyon (1844–1946)*

402

The Jewish position on abortion is that a foetus is a foetus until it gets out of medical school.

—*Unknown*

403

I'm impressed with people from Chicago. Hollywood is hype, New York is talk, Chicago is work.

—*Actor-producer Michael Douglas*

404

An empty taxi stopped, and Jack Warner got out.

—*Unknown*

405

A liberated woman is one who has sex before marriage and a job after.

—*Gloria Steinem*

406

If you haven't got anything nice to say about anybody, come sit next to me.

—*Alice Roosevelt Longworth (1884–1980)*

407

I'll try anything once.

—*Alice Roosevelt Longworth (1884–1980)*
on giving birth at age 41

408

Days off.

—Spencer Tracy (1900–1967) when asked what he looked for in a script

409

We are drawn to our television sets each April the way we are drawn to the scene of an accident.

—Vincent Canby on the Academy Awards

410

God sends meat and the devil sends cooks.

—Thomas Deloney (1543–1600)

411

Husbands are like fires. They go out if unattended.

—Zsa Zsa Gabor (Miss Hungary of 1936)

412

Go, and never darken my towels again.

—*Groucho Marx (1895–1977)*

413

California is the only state in the union where you can fall asleep under a rose bush in full bloom and freeze to death.

—*W. C. Fields (1880–1946)*

414

The difference between Los Angeles and yoghurt is that yoghurt has an active, living culture.

—*Unknown*

415

We can see California coming, and we're scared.

—*James Brady*

416

Many a man owes his success to his first wife and his second wife to his success.

—*Jim Backus (1913–1989)*

417

Nature has given us two ears but only one mouth.

—*Benjamin Disraeli (1804–1881)*

418

It is easier to stay out than get out.

—*Mark Twain (1835–1910)*

419

A fat paunch never breeds fine thoughts.

—*St. Jerome (340?–420)*

420

Absence makes the heart go yonder.

—*Robert Byrne*

421

Short, balding, Chinese gentleman seeks tall Negress with passion for leather and Brahms to attend openings.

—*Classified ad in the* Berkeley Barb

422

Yard sale—Recently married couple is combining households. All duplicates will be sold, except children.

—*Classified ad in the* San Jose Mercury News

423

It takes two to speak the truth—one to speak and another to hear.

—*Henry David Thoreau (1817–1862)*

424
Only sick music makes money today.
—*Friedrich Nietzsche (1844–1900) in 1888*

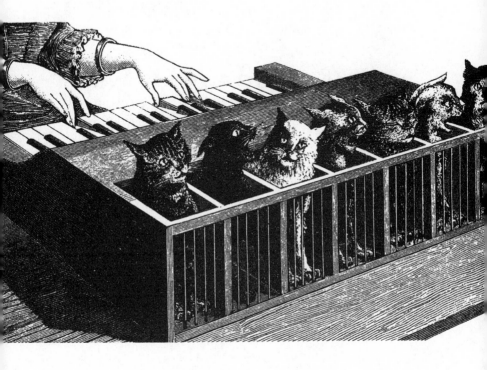

425
I never know how much of what I say is true.
—*Bette Midler*

426
I'm as pure as the driven slush.
—*Tallulah Bankhead (1903–1968)*

427

I went around the world last year and you want to know something? It hates each other.

—*Edward J. Mannix*

428

A great many people have come up to me and asked how I managed to get so much done and still look so dissipated.

—*Robert Benchley (1889–1945)*

429

I don't trust him. We're friends.

—*Bertolt Brecht (1898–1956)*

430

A man can't be too careful in the choice of his enemies.

—*Oscar Wilde (1854–1900)*

431

Anyone can win, unless there happens to be a second entry.

—*George Ade (1866–1944)*

432

We have long passed the Victorian era, when asterisks were followed after a certain interval by a baby.

—*Somerset Maugham (1874–1965)*

433

It was such a lovely day I thought it was a pity to get up.

—*Somerset Maugham (1874–1965)*

434

The biggest sin is sitting on your ass.

—*Florynce Kennedy*

435

Laugh and the world laughs with you, snore and you sleep alone.

—*Anthony Burgess (1917–1993)*

436

It was a blonde, a blonde to make a bishop kick a hole in a stained glass window.

—*Raymond Chandler (1888–1959)*

437

I go to the theater to be entertained . . . I don't want to see rape, sodomy, and drug addiction. I can get all that at home.

—*Roger Law cartoon caption*

438

The higher the buildings, the lower the morals.

—*Noël Coward (1899–1973)*

439
Nothing is illegal if a hundred businessmen decide to do it.
—*Andrew Young*

440
I wish Frank Sinatra would just shut up and sing.
—*Lauren Bacall*

441
England produces the best fat actors.
—*Jimmy Cannon (1910–1973)*

442

If it weren't for Philo T. Farnsworth, inventor of television, we'd still be eating frozen radio dinners.

—*Johnny Carson*

443

A luxury liner is just a bad play surrounded by water.

—*Clive James*

444

The future isn't what it used to be.

—*Variously ascribed*

445

Some of us are becoming the men we wanted to marry.

—*Gloria Steinem*

446

I haven't been wrong since 1961, when I thought I made a mistake.

—*Bob Hudson*

447

I may have my faults, but being wrong ain't one of them.

—*Jimmy Hoffa (1913–1975)*

448

He had a winning smile, but everything else was a loser.

—*George C. Scott at a Bob Hope roast*

449

He not only overflowed with learning, he stood in the slop.

—*Sydney Smith (1771–1845) on Macaulay*

450

Listening to the Fifth Symphony of Ralph Vaughan Williams is like staring at a cow for forty-five minutes.

—*Aaron Copland (1900–1990)*

451

Forgive your enemies, but never forget their names.

—*John F. Kennedy (1917–1963)*

452

There is no pleasure in having nothing to do; the fun is having lots to do and not doing it.

—*John W. Raper*

453

Hope is the feeling you have that the feeling you have isn't permanent.

—*Jean Kerr*

454
I was probably the only revolutionary ever referred to as "cute."

—*Abbie Hoffman (1936–1989)*

455
Success didn't spoil me; I've always been insufferable.

—*Fran Lebowitz*

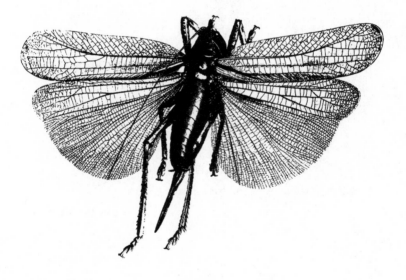

456
Men should stop fighting among themselves and start fighting insects.

—*Luther Burbank (1849–1926)*

457
They say you can't do it, but sometimes it doesn't always work.

—Casey Stengel (1891–1975)

458
Tumescence is the period between pubescence and senescence.

—Robert Byrne

459
If this is coffee, please bring me some tea; but if this is tea, please bring me some coffee.

—Abraham Lincoln (1809–1865)

460
Logic is in the eye of the logician.

—Gloria Steinem

461
Everything is in a state of flux, including the status quo.

—Robert Byrne

462

The only people with a right to complain about what I do for a living are vegetarian nudists.

—Ken Bates, one of California's
700 licensed fur trappers

463

I'm trying to arrange my life so that I don't even have to be present.

—Unknown

464

To travel is to discover that everyone is wrong about other countries.

—Aldous Huxley (1894–1963)

465

It can be great fun to have an affair with a bitch.

—Louis Auchincloss

466

Never accept a drink from a urologist.

—Erma Bombeck's father

467

In Rome I am weighed down by a lack of momentum, the inertia of a spent civilization. In New York I feel plugged into a strong alternating current of hope and despair.

—*Ted Morgan*

468

I'm six foot eleven. My birthday covers three days.

—*Darryl Dawkins*

469

He who hesitates is not only lost, but miles from the next exit.

—*Unknown*

470

You can't measure time in days the way you can money in dollars because every day is different.

—*Jorge Luis Borges (1899–1986)*

471

Time is nature's way of keeping everything from happening at once.

—*Unknown*

472

If Today Was a Fish, I'd Throw It Back In.

—*Song title*

473

From the Gutter to You Ain't Up.

—*Song title*

474

I look at ordinary people in their suits, them with no scars, and I'm different. I don't fit with them. I'm where everybody's got scar tissue on their eyes and got noses like saddles. I go to conventions of old fighters like me and I see the scar tissue and all them flat noses and it's beautiful. Galento, may he rest in peace. Giardello, LaMotta, Carmen Basilio. What a sweetheart Basilio is. They talk like me, like they got rocks in their throats. Beautiful!

—*Willie Pastrano (1935–1997)*

475

Reality is a crutch for people who can't cope with drugs.

—*Lily Tomlin*

476

A cap of good acid costs five dollars and for that you can hear the Universal Symphony with God singing solo and the Holy Ghost on drums.

—*Hunter S. Thompson as quoted by
William F. Buckley, Jr., who added: "Though
one should be prepared to vomit rather frequently
and disport with pink elephants and assorted
grotesqueries while trying, often unsuccessfully,
to make one's way to the toilet."*

477

The best way to lose weight is to get the flu and take a trip to Egypt.

—*Roz Lawrence*

478

Anyone who eats three meals a day should understand why cookbooks outsell sex books three to one.

—*L. M. Boyd*

479

We don't know a millionth of one percent about anything.

—*Thomas Alva Edison (1847–1931)*

480

Something ignoble, loathsome, undignified attends all associations between people and has been transferred to all objects, dwellings, tools, even the landscape itself.

—*Bertolt Brecht (1898–1956) on America*

481

If I had known I was going to live this long I would have taken better care of myself.

—*Unknown*

482

Is sloppiness in speech caused by ignorance or apathy?
I don't know and I don't care.

—*William Safire*

483

We had seen the light at the end of the tunnel, and it
was out.

—*John C. Clancy*

484

To err is human, to forgive supine.

—*S. J. Perelman (1904–1979)*

485

What is true is what I can't help believing.

—*Oliver Wendell Holmes, Jr. (1841–1935)*

486

I am the last of Britain's stately homos.

—*Quentin Crisp (1908–1999)*

487

I didn't want to be rich. I just wanted enough to get the
couch reupholstered.

—*Kate (Mrs. Zero) Mostel*

488

My father and he had one of those English friendships which begin by avoiding intimacies and eventually eliminate speech altogether.

—*Jorge Luis Borges (1899–1986)*

489

Shut up he explained.

—*Ring Lardner (1885–1933)*

490

She had two complexions, A.M. and P.M.

—*Ring Lardner (1885–1933)*

491

He writes so well he makes me feel like putting my quill back in my goose.

—*Fred Allen (1894–1956)*

492

If my film makes one more person miserable, I'll feel I've done my job.

—*Woody Allen*

493

The cloning of humans is on most of the lists of things to worry about from Science, along with behavior control, genetic engineering, transplanted heads, computer poetry and the unrestrained growth of plastic flowers.

—*Lewis Thomas (1913–1993)*

494

No one can earn a million dollars honestly.

—*William Jennings Bryan (1860–1925)*

495

There are very few Japanese Jews. As a result, there is no Japanese word for Alan King.

—*Johnny Carson*

496

From birth to age 18, a girl needs good parents; from 18 to 35 she needs good looks; from 35 to 55 she needs a good personality; and from 55 on she needs cash.

—*Sophie Tucker (1884–1966)*

497
Outer space is no place for a person of breeding.
—*Lady Violet Bonham Carter (1887–1969)*

498
Our national flower is the concrete cloverleaf.
—*Lewis Mumford (1895–1990)*

499
The only normal people are the ones you don't know very well.
—*Joe Ancis*

500

You sofa-crevice fondler!

—*Peter De Vries (1910–1993)*

501

Cats are like Baptists. They raise hell but you can't catch them at it.

—*Unknown*

502

So little time and so little to do.

—*Oscar Levant (1906–1972)*

503

It's a rare person who wants to hear what he doesn't want to hear.

—*Dick Cavett*

504

When I hear the word "culture" I reach for my gun.

—*Hans Johst (c. 1939)*

505

He washed his legs today and can't do a thing with them.

—*Sportscaster Lon Simmons on seeing a baseball player fall down twice in the first inning*

506

I like men to behave like men—strong and childish.

—Françoise Sagan

507

A kleptomaniac is a person who helps himself because he can't help himself.

—Henry Morgan

508

A hypocrite is a person who—but who isn't?

—Don Marquis (1878–1937)

509

Brain damage reading test:

People tell me one thing and out the other. I feel as much like I did yesterday as I did today. I never liked room temperature. My throat is closer than it seems. Likes and dislikes are among my favorites. No napkin is sanitary enough for me. I don't like any of my loved ones.

—Daniel M. Wegner

510

The two hardest things to handle in life are failure and success.

—Unknown

511

Progress might have been all right once but it has gone on too long.

—*Ogden Nash (1902–1971)*

512

I consider exercise vulgar. It makes people smell.

—*Alec Yuill Thornton*

513

There is no human problem which could not be solved if people would simply do as I advise.

—*Gore Vidal*

514

What's on your mind, if you will allow the overstatement?

—*Fred Allen (1894–1956)*

515

The young man who has not wept is a savage, and the old man who will not laugh is a fool.

—*George Santayana (1866–1952)*

516

Though I am not naturally honest, I am so sometimes by chance.

—*Shakespeare (1564–1616)*

517

Early to rise and early to bed makes a male healthy, wealthy and dead.

—*James Thurber (1894–1961)*

518

I have no relish for the country; it is a kind of healthy grave.

—*Sydney Smith (1771–1845)*

519

A farm is an irregular patch of nettles, bound by short term notes, containing a fool and his wife who didn't know enough to stay in the city.

—*S. J. Perelman (1904–1979)*

520

Everything has been figured out except how to live.

—*Jean-Paul Sartre (1905–1980)*

521

Howard Hughes was able to afford the luxury of madness, like a man who not only thinks he is Napoleon but hires an army to prove it.

—*Ted Morgan*

522

When it is not necessary to make a decision, it is necessary not to make a decision.

—*Lord Falkland (1610?–1643)*

523

This book fills a much-needed gap.

—*Moses Hadas (1900–1966) in a review*

524

Thank you for sending me a copy of your book. I'll waste no time reading it.

—*Moses Hadas (1900–1966) in a letter*

525

There are plenty of good five-cent cigars in the country. The trouble is they cost a quarter. What this country really needs is a good five-cent nickel.

—*Franklin P. Adams (1881–1960)*

526

Being perfectly well-dressed gives a feeling of tranquility
that religion is powerless to bestow.
—*Ralph Waldo Emerson (1803–1882),*
quoting a friend

527

We are here and it is now. Further than that all human knowledge is moonshine.

—*H. L. Mencken (1880–1956)*

528

There is no kind of dishonesty into which otherwise good people more easily and frequently fall than that of defrauding the government.

—*Benjamin Franklin (1706–1790)*

529

Don't get the idea that I'm knocking the American system.

—*Al Capone (1899–1947)*

530

It wasn't raining when Noah built the ark.

—*Howard Ruff*

531

The learned are seldom pretty fellows, and in many cases their appearance tends to discourage a love of study in the young.

—*H. L. Mencken (1880–1956)*

532

There is something going on now in Mexico that I happen to think is cruelty to animals. What I'm taking about, of course, is cat juggling.

—*Steve Martin*

533

Truth is beautiful, without doubt; but so are lies.

—*Ralph Waldo Emerson (1803–1882)*

534

We will march forward to a better tomorrow so long as separate groups like the blacks, the Negroes, and the coloreds can come together to work out their differences.

—*Steve Allen at a Redd Foxx roast*

535

Ninety-eight percent of the adults in this country are decent, hard-working, honest Americans. It's the other lousy two percent that get all the publicity. But then—we elected them.

—*Lily Tomlin*

536

There are more of them than us.

—*Herb Caen*

537

Suppose you were an idiot and suppose you were a member of Congress. But I repeat myself.

—*Mark Twain (1835–1910)*

538

Never go to bed mad. Stay up and fight.

—*Phyllis Diller*

539

When I go to the beauty parlor, I always use the emergency entrance. Sometimes I just go for an estimate.

—*Phyllis Diller*

540

Orthodox medicine has not found an answer to your complaint. However, luckily for you, I happen to be a quack.

—*Richter cartoon caption*

541

One of a hostess's duties is to act as a procuress.

—*Marcel Proust (1871–1922)*

542

Here is a supplementary bulletin from the Office of Fluctuation Control, Bureau of Edible Condiments, Soluble and Indigestible Fats and Glutinous Derivatives, Washington, D.C. Correction of Directive 943456201, issued a while back, concerning the fixed price of groundhog meat. In the directive above named, the quotation on groundhog meat should read ground hogmeat.

—*Bob and Ray*

543

I've known what it is to be hungry, but I always went right to a restaurant.

—*Ring Lardner (1885–1933)*

544

What dreadful hot weather we have! It keeps me in a continual state of inelegance.

—*Jane Austen (1775–1817)*

545

A single sentence will suffice for modern man: He fornicated and read the papers.

—*Albert Camus (1913–1960)*

546

The rich are the scum of the earth in every country.

—*G. K. Chesterton (1874–1936)*

547

One should never know too precisely whom one has married.

—*Friedrich Nietzsche (1844–1900) on Lohengrin*

548

I never lecture, not because I am shy or a bad speaker, but simply because I detest the sort of people who go to lectures and don't want to meet them.

—*H. L. Mencken (1880–1956)*

549

Bed is the poor man's opera.

—*Italian proverb*

550

I'd rather be black than gay because when you're black you don't have to tell your mother.

—*Charles Pierce*

551

Roses are red, violets are blue,
I'm a schizophrenic, and so am I.

—*Frank Crow*

552

Lie Down and Roll Over and 159 Other Ways To Say I Love You.

—*1981 book title*

553

I improve on misquotation.

—*Cary Grant (1904–1986)*

554

Partying is such sweet sorrow.

—*Robert Byrne*

555

Honest criticism is hard to take, particularly from a relative, a friend, an acquaintance, or a stranger.

—*Franklin P. Jones*

556

If any cleric or monk speaks jocular words, such as provoke laughter, let him be anathema.

—*Ordinance, Second Council of Constance (1418)*

557

Better that a girl has beauty than brains because boys see better than they think.

—*Unknown*

558

I talk to myself because I like dealing with a better class of people.

—*Jackie Mason*

559

It is better to have a permanent income than to be fascinating.

—*Oscar Wilde (1854–1900)*

560

I did not sleep. I never do when I am over-happy, over-unhappy, or in bed with a strange man.

—*Edna O'Brien*

561

Dostoyevsky was one of those neurotics who recover their health and even their serenity when disaster at last occurs.

—*V. S. Pritchett (1900–1997)*

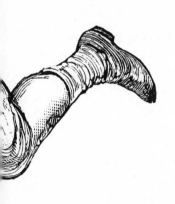

562

Exit, pursued by a bear.

—*Stage direction in Shakespeare's*
The Winter's Tale *(1611)*

563

¿Cómo frijoles? (Spanish for How have you bean?)

—*Unknown*

564

I don't make jokes. I just watch the government and report the facts.

—*Will Rogers (1879–1935)*

565

Even in civilized mankind faint traces of monogamous instinct can be perceived.

—*Bertrand Russell (1872–1970)*

566

Things to do in Burbank:
1. Go to the Safeway parking lot for the roller skating festival called Holiday on Tar.

—*Johnny Carson*

567

I would rather be a coward than brave because people hurt you when you are brave.

—*E. M. Forster (1879–1970) as a small child*

568

One day there will be only five kings left, hearts, spades, diamonds, clubs, and England.

—*King Farouk (1920–1965)*
after his overthrow by Gamal Abdel Nasser

569

When ideas fail, words come in very handy.

—*Johann Wolfgang von Goethe (1749–1832)*

570

Music with dinner is an insult both to the cook and the violinist.

—*G. K. Chesterton (1874–1936)*

571

The place of the father in the modern suburban family is a very small one, particularly if he plays golf.

—*Bertrand Russell (1872–1970)*

572

Avarice is the sphincter of the heart.

—*Matthew Green (c. 1737)*

573
It is easier to be gigantic than to be beautiful.
—*Friedrich Nietzsche (1844–1900)*

574
By the time we've made it, we've had it.
—*Malcolm Forbes (1919–1990)*

575
I only like two kinds of men: domestic and foreign.
—*Mae West (1893–1980)*

576
Where but in Kenya can a man whose grandfather was a cannibal watch a really good game of polo?
—*Marina Sulzberger (1920–1976)*

577
France was a long despotism tempered by epigrams.
—*Thomas Carlyle (1759–1881)*

578
Never trust anyone over-dirty.

—*Robert Byrne*

579

There are more pleasant things to do than beat up people.

—Muhammad Ali on the occasion
of one of his retirements

580

Mirrors and copulation are abominable because they increase the numbers of men.

—Jorge Luis Borges (1899–1986)

581

I don't worry about getting old. I'm old already. Only young people worry about getting old. When I was 65 I had cupid's eczema. I don't believe in dying. It's been done. I'm working on a new exit. Besides, I can't die now—I'm booked.

—George Burns (1896–1996)

582

Men who never get carried away should be.

—Malcolm Forbes (1919–1990)

583

If you aren't fired with enthusiasm, you will be fired with enthusiasm.

—Vince Lombardi (1913–1970)

584

When I was kidnapped, my parents snapped into action.
They rented out my room.

—*Woody Allen*

585

The best cure for hypochondria is to forget about your
body and get interested in somebody else's.

—*Goodman Ace (1899–1982)*

586

New invention: Snap-on acne for people who want to
look younger.

—*Johnny Carson*

587

Love teaches even asses to dance.

—*French proverb*

588

Ammonia is beautiful.

—*Bumper sticker*

589

FECK OPUC.

—*Bumper sticker*

590

There is one fault that I must find
    With the twentieth century,
And I'll put it in a couple of words:
    Too adventury.
What I'd like would be some nice dull monotony
    If anyone's gotony.

—*Ogden Nash (1902–1971)*

591

If called by a panther
Don't anther.

—*Ogden Nash (1902–1971)*

592

First secure an independent income, then practice virtue.

—Greek saying

593

What we call real estate—the solid ground to build a house on—is the broad foundation on which nearly all of the guilt of the world rests.

—Nathaniel Hawthorne (1804–1864)

594

I have never liked working. To me a job is an invasion of privacy.

—Danny McGoorty (1901–1970)

595

Boy, the things I do for England.

*—Prince Charles
on sampling snake meat*

596

Victory goes to the player who makes the next-to-last mistake.

—*Savielly Grigorievitch Tartakower (1887–1956)*

597

Of all noises, I think music is the least disagreeable.

—*Samuel Johnson (1709–1784)*

598

One, two, three,
Buckle my shoe.

—*Robert Benchley (1889–1945)*

599

It is rather to be chosen than great riches, unless I have omitted something from the quotation.

—*Robert Benchley (1889–1945) in*
Maxims From the Chinese

600

There must be 500,000 rats in the United States; of course, I am only speaking from memory.

—*Bill Nye (1850–1896)*

601

Newspapermen learn to call a murderer "an alleged murderer" and the King of England "the alleged King of England" to avoid libel suits.

—*Stephen Leacock (1869–1944)*

602

Lord Ronald said nothing; he flung himself from the room, flung himself upon his horse and rode madly off in all directions.

—*Stephen Leacock (1869–1944)*

603

I do not take a single newspaper, nor read one a month, and I feel myself infinitely the happier for it.

—*Thomas Jefferson (1743–1826)*

604

Show me a hero and I will write you a tragedy.

—*F. Scott Fitzgerald (1896–1940)*

605

We can't all be heroes because somebody has to sit on the curb and clap as they go by.

—*Will Rogers (1879–1935)*

606

Some things have to be believed to be seen.

—*Ralph Hodgson on ESP*

607

One of the most astounding cases of clairvoyance is that of the noted Greek psychic Achilles Loudos. Loudos realized that he had unusual powers by the age of ten, when he could lie in bed and, by concentrating, make his father's false teeth jump out of his mouth.

—*Woody Allen*

608

A cucumber should be well-sliced, dressed with pepper and vinegar, and then thrown out.

—*Samuel Johnson (1709–1784)*

609

Middle age is when you've met so many people that every new person you meet reminds you of someone else.

—*Ogden Nash (1902–1971)*

610

Wagner's music is better than it sounds.

—*Bill Nye (1850–1896)*

611

With those delicate features of his he would have made a pretty woman, and he probably never has.

—*Josefa Heifetz*

612

I don't want any yes-men around me. I want everybody to tell me the truth even if it costs them their jobs.

—*Samuel Goldwyn (1882–1974)*

613

The advantage of the emotions is that they lead us astray.

—*Oscar Wilde (1854–1900)*

614

In the first place, God made idiots. That was for practice. Then he made school boards.

—*Mark Twain (1835–1910)*

615

She wears her clothes as if they were thrown on with a pitchfork.

—*Jonathan Swift (1667–1745)*

616

A man is known by the company he avoids.

—*Unknown*

617

Underneath this flabby exterior is an enormous lack of character.

—*Oscar Levant (1906–1972)*

618

Nobody roots for Goliath.

—*Wilt Chamberlain (1936–1999)*

619

He went to Europe as a boy, where in Geneva his father arranged for a prostitute. He was so terrified by the experience that he didn't marry until he was 67 years old.

—*John Leonard on Borges*

620

Keep breathing.

—*Sophie Tucker (1884?–1966)*

621

If people don't want to come out to the ball park, nobody's going to stop them.

—*Yogi Berra*

622

Tradition is what you resort to when you don't have the time or the money to do it right.

—*Kurt Herbert Adler*

623

It is impossible to imagine Goethe or Beethoven being good at billiards or golf.

—*H. L. Mencken (1880–1956)*

624

All truths are half-truths.

—*Alfred North Whitehead (1861–1947)*

625

To generalize is to be an idiot.

—*William Blake (1757–1827)*

626

If you look like your passport photo, you're too ill to travel.

—*Will Kommen*

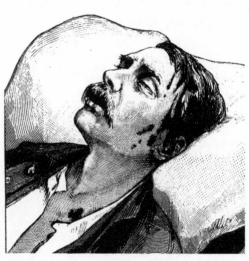

627

How can one conceive of a one-party system in a country that has over 200 varieties of cheese?

—Charles de Gaulle (1890–1970)

628

When you have got an elephant by the hind legs and he is trying to run away, it is best to let him run.

—Abraham Lincoln (1809–1865)

629

After three days, fish and guests stink.

—John Lyly (1554?–1606)

630

I was born in Australia because my mother wanted me to be near her.

—Unknown

631

I will always cherish the initial misconceptions I had about you.

—Unknown

632

The majority of those who put together collections of verses or epigrams resemble those who eat cherries or oysters; they begin by choosing the best and end by eating everything.

—Chamfort (1741–1794)

633

If you were a member of Jesse James's band and people asked you what you were, you wouldn't say, "Well, I'm a desperado." You'd say something like, "I work in banks," or "I've done some railroad work." It took me a long time just to say "I'm a writer." It's really embarrassing.

—Roy Blount, Jr.

634

It takes about ten years to get used to how old you are.

—Unknown

635

After all is said and done, more is said than done.

—Unknown

636

In the end, everything is a gag.

—Charlie Chaplin (1889–1977)

637

Science has not yet found a cure for the pun.

—*Robert Byrne*

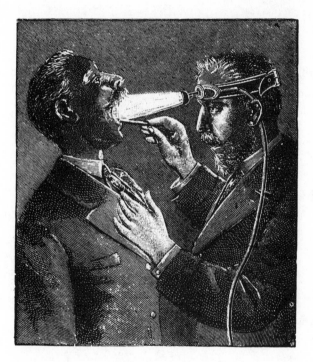

638

My theology, briefly, is that the universe was dictated but not signed.

—*Christopher Morley (1890–1957)*

639

God made everything out of nothing, but the nothingness shows through.

—*Paul Valéry (1871–1945)*

640

God was satisfied with his own work, and that is fatal.
—*Samuel Butler (1835–1902)*

641

God is not dead but alive and well and working on a much less ambitious project.

—*Graffito*

642

Why attack God? He may be as miserable as we are.
—*Erik Satie (1866–1925)*

643

Every day people are straying away from the church and going back to God.

—*Lenny Bruce (1925–1966)*

644

Religion is what keeps the poor from murdering the rich.
—*Napoleon (1769–1821)*

645

What if there had been room at the inn?
—*Linda Festa on the origins of Christianity*

646

Christ died for our sins. Dare we make his martyrdom meaningless by not committing them?

—*Jules Feiffer*

647

Catholicism has changed tremendously in recent years. Now when Communion is served there is also a salad bar.

—*Bill Marr*

648

Faith is believing what you know ain't so.

—*"A schoolboy" quoted by Mark Twain (1835–1910)*

649

Faith is under the left nipple.

—*Martin Luther (1483–1546)*

650

Because I'm Jewish, a lot of people ask why I killed Christ. What can I say? It was an accident. It was one of those parties that got out of hand. I killed him because he wouldn't become a doctor.

—*Lenny Bruce (1925–1966)*

651

Your chances of getting hit by lightning go up if you stand under a tree, shake your fist at the sky, and say, "Storms suck!"

—*Johnny Carson*

652

Trust in Allah, but tie your camel.

—*Arabian proverb*

653

The last time I saw him he was walking down Lover's Lane holding his own hand.

—*Fred Allen (1894–1956)*

654

The nice thing about egotists is that they don't talk about other people.

—*Lucille S. Harper*

655

It is far more impressive when others discover your good qualities without your help.

—*Miss Manners (Judith Martin)*

656

In an age when the fashion is to be in love with yourself, confessing to be in love with somebody else is an admission of unfaithfulness to one's beloved.

—*Russell Baker*

657

If only it was as easy to banish hunger by rubbing the belly as it is to masturbate.

—*Diogenes the Cynic (412?–323 B.C.)*

658

Self-abuse is the most certain road to the grave.

—*Dr. George M. Calhoun in 1855*

659

Many mothers are wholly ignorant of the almost universal prevalence of secret vice, or self-abuse, among the young. Why hesitate to say firmly and without quibble that personal abuse lies at the root of much of the feebleness, paleness, nervousness, and good-for-nothingness of the entire community?

—Dr. J. H. Kellogg (1852–1943)

660

Masturbation! The amazing availability of it!

—James Joyce (1882–1941)

661

Philosophy is to the real world as masturbation is to sex.

—Karl Marx (1818–1883)

662

I was the best I ever had.

—Woody Allen

663

The good thing about masturbation is that you don't have to dress up for it.

—Truman Capote (1924–1984)

664

My brain is my second favorite organ.

—*Woody Allen*

665

Love is not the dying moan of a distant violin—it's the triumphant twang of a bedspring.

—*S. J. Perelman (1904–1979)*

666

Love is what you've been through with somebody.

—*James Thurber (1894–1961)*

667

Love is the delusion that one woman differs from another.

—*H. L. Mencken (1880–1956)*

668

Love is being stupid together.

—*Paul Valéry (1871–1945)*

669

Love is an obsessive delusion that is cured by marriage.

—*Dr. Karl Bowman (1888–1973)*

670

Love is the only game that is not called on account of darkness.

—M. Hirschfield

671

The greatest love is a mother's, then a dog's, then a sweetheart's.

—Polish proverb

672

If I love you, what business is it of yours?

—Johann Wolfgang von Goethe (1749–1832)

673

A man in love mistakes a pimple for a dimple.

—Japanese proverb

674

A lover without indiscretion is no lover at all.

—Thomas Hardy (1840–1928)

675

The most important thing in a relationship between a man and a woman is that one of them be good at taking orders.

—Linda Festa

676

In a great romance, each person basically plays a part that the other really likes.

—*Elizabeth Ashley*

677

I love Mickey Mouse more than any woman I've ever known.

—*Walt Disney (1901–1966)*

678

I like young girls. Their stories are shorter.

—*Tom McGuane*

679

The most romantic thing any woman ever said to me in bed was "Are you sure you're not a cop?"

—*Larry Brown*

680

Someday we'll look back on this moment and plow into a parked car.

—*Evan Davis*

681

Sex is dirty only when it's done right.

—*Woody Allen*

682

For flavor, instant sex will never supersede the stuff you have to peel and cook.

—*Quentin Crisp (1908–1999)*

683

Why won't you let me kiss you goodnight? Is it something I said?

—*Tom Ryan*

684

Give a man a free hand and he'll run it all over you.

—*Mae West (1892–1980)*

685

I've been in more laps than a napkin.

—*Mae West (1892–1980)*

686

I used to be Snow White, but I drifted.

—*Mae West (1892–1980)*

687

He who hesitates is a damned fool.

—*Mae West (1892–1980)*

688

I wasn't kissing her, I was whispering in her mouth.

—*Chico Marx (1891–1961)*

689

Contraceptives should be used on every conceivable occasion.

—*From* The Last Goon Show of All

690

Bisexuality immediately doubles your chances for a date
on Saturday night.

—*Woody Allen*

691

What do hookers do on their nights off, type?

—*Elayne Boosler*

692

I have perfumed my bed with myrrh, aloes, and cinna-
mon. Come, let us take our fill of love until the morning.

—*Proverbs 7: 17–18*

693

All the men on my staff can type.

—*Bella Abzug (1920–1998)*

694

A is for Apple.

—*Hester Prynne*

695

The perfect lover is one who turns into a pizza at 1:00 A.M.

—*Charles Pierce*

696

If God had meant us to have group sex, he'd have given us more organs.

—*Malcolm Bradbury*

697

It's been so long since I made love I can't even remember who gets tied up.

—*Joan Rivers*

698

Ouch! That felt good!

—*Karen Elizabeth Gordon*

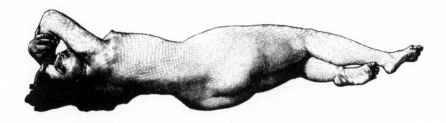

699

I never expected to see the day when girls would get sun-
burned in the places they do today.

—*Will Rogers (1879–1935)*

700

The first time we slept together she drove a recreational
vehicle into the bedroom.

—*Richard Lewis*

701

A man can sleep around, no questions asked, but if a
woman makes nineteen or twenty mistakes she's a tramp.

—*Joan Rivers*

702

What do you give a man who has everything? Penicillin.

—*Jerry Lester*

703

Some men are so macho they'll get you pregnant just to kill a rabbit.

—*Maureen Murphy*

704

Chaste makes waste.

—*Unknown*

705

The trouble with incest is that it gets you involved with relatives.

—*George S. Kaufman (1889–1961)*

706

After we made love he took a piece of chalk and made an outline of my body.

—*Joan Rivers*

707

It's easy to make a friend. What's hard is to make a stranger.

—*Unknown*

708

The reason people sweat is so they won't catch fire when making love.

—*Don Rose*

709

He's such a hick he doesn't even have a trapeze in his bedroom.

—*Unknown*

710

The trouble with group sex is that you never know where to put your elbows.

—*Martin Cruz Smith*

711

If you want to read about love and marriage you've got to buy two separate books.

—*Alan King*

712

'Tis more blessed to give than receive; for example, wedding presents.

—*H. L. Mencken (1880–1956)*

713

Men have a much better time of it than women; for one thing they marry later; for another thing they die earlier.

—*H. L. Mencken (1880–1956)*

714

Monogamy is the Western custom of one wife and hardly any mistresses.

—*H. H. Munro (Saki) (1870–1916)*

715

Marriage is based on the theory that when a man discovers a brand of beer exactly to his taste he should at once throw up his job and go to work in the brewery.

—*George Jean Nathan (1882–1958)*

716

A wife lasts only for the length of the marriage, but an ex-wife is there *for the rest of your life.*

—*Jim Samuels*

717

A man in love is incomplete until he is married. Then he is finished.

—*Zsa Zsa Gabor*

718

A husband is what is left of the lover after the nerve has been extracted.

—*Helen Rowland (1876–1950)*

719

When a girl marries she exchanges the attentions of many men for the inattention of one.

—*Helen Rowland (1876–1950)*

720

One man's folly is another man's wife.

—*Helen Rowland (1876–1950)*

721

The most happy marriage I can imagine to myself would be the union of a deaf man to a blind woman.

—*Samuel Taylor Coleridge (1772–1834)*

722

The trouble with some women is that they get all excited about nothing—and then marry him.

—*Cher*

723

Trust your husband, adore your husband, and get as much as you can in your own name.

—Advice to Joan Rivers from her mother

724

Honesty has ruined more marriages than infidelity.

—Charles McCabe (1915–1983)

725

Bachelors should be heavily taxed. It is not fair that some men should be happier than others.

—Oscar Wilde (1854–1900)

726

I believe in the institution of marriage and I intend to keep trying until I get it right.

—Richard Pryor

727
I was a fifty-four-year-old virgin, but I'm all right now.
—*Unknown*

728

Eighty percent of married men cheat in America. The rest cheat in Europe.

—*Jackie Mason*

729

A man can have two, maybe three love affairs while he's married. After that it's cheating.

—*Yves Montand (1921–1991)*

730

Marriage has driven more than one man to sex.

—*Peter De Vries (1910–1993)*

731

It destroys one's nerves to be amiable every day to the same human being.

—*Benjamin Disraeli (1804–1881)*

732

If you are looking for a kindly, well-to-do older gentleman who is no longer interested in sex, take out an ad in *The Wall Street Journal*.

—*Abigail Van Buren*

733

Divorce is a game played by lawyers.

—*Cary Grant (1904–1986)*

734

She cried, and the judge wiped her tears with my check-book.

—*Tommy Manville (1894–1967)*

735

I can't mate in captivity.

—*Gloria Steinem on why she had never married*

736

It wasn't exactly a divorce—I was traded.

—*Tim Conway*

737

You don't know anything about a woman until you meet her in court.

—*Norman Mailer*

738

I'm very old-fashioned. I believe that people should marry for life, like pigeons and Catholics.

—*Woody Allen*

739

Marriage is like a bank account. You put it in, you take it out, you lose interest.

—*Professor Irwin Corey*

740

I hate babies. They're so human.

—*H. H. Munro (Saki) (1870–1916)*

741

The baby was so ugly they had to hang a pork chop around its neck to get the dog to play with it.

—*Unknown*

742

My mother didn't breast-feed me. She said she liked me as a friend.

—*Rodney Dangerfield*

743

It is no wonder that people are so horrible when they start life as children.

—*Sir Kingsley Amis (1922–1995)*

744
I was toilet-trained at gunpoint.

—Billy Braver

745
Life does not begin at the moment of conception or the moment of birth. It begins when the kids leave home and the dog dies.

—Unknown

746
One father is more than a hundred schoolmasters.
—George Herbert (1593–1633)

747

An ounce of mother is worth a ton of priest.

—*Spanish proverb*

748

Happy is the child whose father died rich.

—*Proverb*

749

Reinhart was never his mother's favorite—and he was an only child.

—*Thomas Berger*

750

Nature makes boys and girls lovely to look upon so they can be tolerated until they acquire some sense.

—*William Lyon Phelps (1865–1943)*

751

The first half of our lives is ruined by our parents and the second half by our children.

—*Clarence Darrow (1857–1938)*

752

Literature is mostly about having sex and not much about having children. Life is the other way around.

—*David Lodge*

753

If you have never been hated by your child, you have never been a parent.

—*Bette Davis (1908–1989)*

754

How to Raise Your I.Q. by Eating Gifted Children
     —*Book title by Lewis B. Frumkes (1983)*

755

Never raise your hand to your children—it leaves your midsection unprotected.

—*Robert Orben*

756

Blessed are the young, for they shall inherit the national debt.

—*Herbert Hoover (1874–1964)*

757

The denunciation of the young is a necessary part of the hygiene of older people, and greatly assists in the circulation of the blood.

—*Logan Pearsall Smith (1865–1946)*

758

One of the disadvantages of having children is that they eventually get old enough to give you presents they make at school.

—*Robert Byrne*

759

Never have children, only grandchildren.

—*Gore Vidal*

760

No matter how old a mother is, she watches her middle-aged children for signs of improvement.

—*Florida Scott-Maxwell*

761

Youth is such a wonderful thing. What a crime to waste it on children.

—*George Bernard Shaw (1856–1950)*

762

Having children is like having a bowling alley installed in your brain.

—*Martin Mull*

763

If you think education is expensive, try ignorance.

—*Derek Bok*

764

I'm for bringing back the birch, but only for consenting adults.

—*Gore Vidal*

765

Education is the process of casting false pearls before real swine.

—*Irwin Edman (1896–1954)*

766

Good teaching is one-fourth preparation and three-fourths theatre.

—*Gail Godwin*

767

University politics are vicious precisely because the takes are so small.

—*Henry Kissinger*

768

Political history is far too criminal a subject to be a fit thing to teach children.

—*W. H. Auden (1907–1973)*

769

I think the world is run by C students.

—*Al McGuire*

770

Smartness runs in my family. When I went to school I was so smart my teacher was in my class for five years.

—*George Burns (1896–1996)*

771

I was thrown out of college for cheating on the meta-physics exam; I looked into the soul of the boy next to me.

—*Woody Allen*

772

You can't expect a boy to be vicious till he's been to a good school.

—*H. H. Munro (Saki) (1870–1916)*

773

Beware of the man who does not drink.

—*Proverb*

774

Water, taken in moderation, cannot hurt anybody.

—*Mark Twain (1835–1910)*

775

A productive drunk is the bane of moralists.

—*Unknown*

776

Come quickly, I am tasting stars!

—*Dom Pérignon (1638–1715) at the moment
of his discovery of champagne*

777

The worst thing about some men is that when they are not drunk they are sober.

—*William Butler Yeats (1865–1939)*

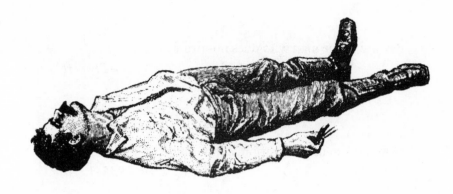

778
An Irishman is not drunk as long as he still has a blade of
grass to hang onto.

—*Unknown*

779
Alcohol is the anesthesia by which we endure the operation of life.

—*George Bernard Shaw (1856–1950)*

780

To drink is a Christian diversion, unknown to the Turk or
the Persian.

—*William Congreve (1670–1729)*

781

To one large turkey add one gallon of vermouth and a demijohn of Angostura bitters. Shake.

—*Recipe for turkey cocktail from F. Scott Fitzgerald (1896–1940)*

782

An alcoholic is someone you don't like who drinks as much as you do.

—*Dylan Thomas (1914–1953)*

783

I can't die until the government finds a safe place to bury my liver.

—*Phil Harris*

784

My uncle was the town drunk—and we lived in Chicago.

—*George Gobel (1919–1991)*

785

I've never been drunk, but often I've been overserved.

—*George Gobel (1919–1991)*

786

Somebody left the cork out of my lunch.

—*W. C. Fields (1880–1946)*

787

I have to think hard to name an interesting man who does not drink.

—Richard Burton (1925–1984)

788

I always wake up at the crack of ice.

—Joe E. Lewis (1902–1971)

789

The graveyards are full of indispensable men.

—Charles de Gaulle (1890–1970)

790

There are more dead people than living, and their numbers are increasing.

—*Eugène Ionesco*

791

Defeat is worse than death because you have to live with defeat.

—*Bill Musselman*

792

The executioner is, I hear, very expert, and my neck is very slender.

—*Anne Boleyn (1507?–1536)*

793

I didn't know he was dead; I thought he was British.

—*Unknown*

794

I believe in sex and death—two experiences that come once in a lifetime.

—*Woody Allen*

795

There are worse things in life than death. Have you ever spent an evening with an insurance salesman?

—*Woody Allen*

796

Go away. I'm all right.

—*Last words of H. G. Wells (1886–1946)*

797

You can pretend to be serious; you can't pretend to be witty.

—*Sacha Guitry (1885–1957)*

798

Everybody likes a kidder, but nobody lends him money.

—*Arthur Miller*

799

One doesn't have a sense of humor. It has you.

—*Larry Gelbart*

800

The aim of a joke is not to degrade the human being but to remind him that he is already degraded.

—*George Orwell (1903–1950)*

801

If you don't count some of Jehovah's injunctions, there are no humorists in the Bible.

—*Mordecai Richler (1931–2001)*

802

Dying is easy. Comedy is difficult.
—*Actor Edmond Gwenn (1875–1959)*
on his deathbed

803

Humorists always sit at the children's table.
—*Woody Allen*

804

I don't care where I sit as long as I get fed.
—*Calvin Trillin*

805

What is comedy? Comedy is the art of making people laugh without making them puke.
—*Steve Martin*

806

Until Eve arrived, this was a man's world.
—*Richard Armour*

807

Whatever women do they must do twice as well as men to be thought half as good. Luckily, this is not difficult.

—*Charlotte Whitton (1896–1975)*

808

Don't accept rides from strange men, and remember that all men are strange.

—*Robin Morgan*

809

There are only two kinds of men—the dead and the deadly.

—*Helen Rowland (1876–1950)*

810

Men are creatures with two legs and eight hands.

—*Jayne Mansfield (1932–1967)*

811

I refuse to consign the whole male sex to the nursery. I insist on believing that some men are my equals.

—*Brigid Brophy (1929–1995)*

812

Being a woman is a terribly difficult trade, since it consists principally of dealing with men.

—*Joseph Conrad (1857–1924)*

813

Being a woman is of special interest only to aspiring male transsexuals. To actual women it is simply a good excuse not to play football.

—*Fran Lebowitz*

814

My advice to the women's clubs of America is raise more hell and fewer dahlias.

—William Allen White (1868–1944)

815

A lady is one who never shows her underwear unintentionally.

—Lillian Day

816

Anyone who says he can see through women is missing a lot.

—Groucho Marx (1895–1977)

817

The most popular labor-saving device today is still a husband with money.

—Joey Adams

818

A gentleman never strikes a lady with his hat on.

—Fred Allen (1894–1956)

819

I've never struck a woman in my life, not even my own mother.
                    —W. C. Fields (1880–1946)

820

If you become a star, *you* don't change, everyone else does.
                    —Kirk Douglas

821

I'm not a real movie star—I've still got the same wife I started out with twenty-eight years ago.
                    —Will Rogers (1879–1935)

822

Fame lost its appeal for me when I went into a public restroom and an autograph seeker handed me a pen and paper under the stall door.
                    —Marlo Thomas

823

If I had done everything I'm credited with, I'd be speaking to you from a laboratory jar at Harvard.
                    —Frank Sinatra (1915–1998)

824

AS USUAL, YOUR INFORMATION STINKS.
—Telegram to Time *magazine from Frank Sinatra*

825

As an anti-American, I thank you for your rotten article devoted to my person.
—Letter to Time *magazine from Prince Sihanouk*

826

I am a deeply superficial person.
—Andy Warhol (1928?–1987)

827

I have bursts of being a lady, but it doesn't last long.
—Shelley Winters

828

Working with Julie Andrews is like getting hit over the head with a valentine.
—Christopher Plummer

829

I should have been a country-western singer. After all, I'm older than most western countries.
—George Burns (1896–1996)

830

Never face facts; if you do you'll never get up in the morning.

—*Marlo Thomas*

831

Nothing succeeds like the appearance of success.

—*Christopher Lasch*

832

She's the kind of girl who climbed the ladder of success wrong by wrong.

—*Mae West (1892–1980)*

833

Nothing fails like success.

—*Gerald Nachman*

834

Anyone seen on a bus after the age of thirty has been a failure in life.

—*Loelia, Duchess of Westminster*

835
To err is human
And stupid.

—*Robert Byrne*

836
You may already be a loser.

—*Form letter received by Rodney Dangerfield*

837
How should they answer?

—*Abigail Van Buren in reply to the
question "Why do Jews always
answer a question with a question?"*

838
If you live in New York, even if you're Catholic, you're
Jewish.

—*Lenny Bruce (1925–1966)*

839
Jews always know two things: suffering and where to find
great Chinese food.

—*From the movie* My Favorite Year, *1982*

840

The goys have proven the following theorem. . . .
—*Physicist John von Neumann (1903–1957)*
at the start of a classroom lecture

841

I want to be the white man's brother, not his brother-in-law.
—*Martin Luther King, Jr. (1929–1968)*

842

I have just enough white in me to make my honesty questionable.
—*Will Rogers (1879–1935)*

843

I never believed in Santa Claus because I knew no white dude would come into my neighborhood after dark.
—*Dick Gregory*

844

Work is of two kinds: first, altering the position of matter at or near the earth's surface relative to other matter; second, telling other people to do so.
—*Bertrand Russell (1872–1970)*

845
All jobs should be open to everybody, unless they actually require a penis or a vagina.

—*Florynce Kennedy*

846
It is impossible to enjoy idling unless there is plenty of work to do.

—*Jerome K. Jerome (1859–1927)*

847

Anybody who works is a fool. I don't work, I merely inflict myself on the public.

—*Robert Morley (1908–1992)*

848

Hard work never killed anybody, but why take a chance?

—*Charlie McCarthy (Edgar Bergen, 1903–1978)*

849

If you have a job without aggravations, you don't have a job.

—*Malcolm Forbes (1919–1990)*

850

People who work sitting down get paid more than people who work standing up.

—*Ogden Nash (1902–1971)*

851

Work is much more fun than fun.

—*Noël Coward (1899–1973)*

852

The trouble with the rat race is that even if you win you're still a rat.

—*Lily Tomlin*

853

Money is good for bribing yourself through the inconveniences of life.

—*Gottfried Reinhardt*

854

A billion here, a billion there—pretty soon it adds up to real money.

—*Senator Everett Dirksen (1896–1969)*

855

I have enough money to last me the rest of my life, unless I buy something.

—*Jackie Mason*

856

The rich have a passion for bargains as lively as it is pointless.

—*Françoise Sagan*

857

Whoever said money can't buy happiness didn't know where to shop.

—*Unknown*

858

Behind every great fortune there is a crime.

—*Honoré de Balzac (1799–1850)*

859

The richer your friends, the more they will cost you.

—*Elisabeth Marbury (1856–1933)*

860

Money is always there, but the pockets change.

—*Gertrude Stein (1874–1946)*

861

There must be more to life than having everything.

—*Maurice Sendak*

862

If women didn't exist, all the money in the world would have no meaning.

—*Aristotle Onassis (1906–1975)*

863

Better to be nouveau than never to have been riche at all.

—*Unknown*

864

Save a little money each month and at the end of the year you'll be surprised at how little you have.

—*Ernest Haskins*

865

My problem lies in reconciling my gross habits with my net income.

—*Errol Flynn (1909–1959)*

866

Any man who has $10,000 left when he dies is a failure.

—*Errol Flynn (1909–1959)*

867

The wages of sin are unreported.

—*Unknown*

868

I'm living so far beyond my income that we may almost be said to be living apart.

—*e. e. cummings (1894–1962)*

869

To get back on your feet, miss two car payments.

—*Unknown*

870

When I first arrived in this country I had only fifteen cents in my pocket and a willingness to compromise.

—*Weber cartoon caption*

871

Fashion is a form of ugliness so intolerable that we have to alter it every six months.

—*Oscar Wilde (1856–1900)*

872

Every generation laughs at the old fashions but religiously follows the new.

—*Henry David Thoreau (1817–1862)*

873

If you look good and dress well, you don't need a purpose
in life.

—*Fashion consultant Robert Pante*

874

I base my fashion taste on what doesn't itch.

—*Gilda Radner (1946–1989)*

875

War is a series of catastrophes that results in a victory.

—*Georges Clemenceau (1841–1929)*

876

You can no more win a war than you can win an earth-quake.

—*Jeannette Rankin (1880–1973)*

877

I'd like to see the government get out of war altogether and leave the whole field to private industry.

—*Joseph Heller (1923–1999)*

878

The object of war is not to die for your country but to make the other bastard die for his.

—*General George Patton (1885–1945)*

879

Name me an emperor who was ever struck by a cannonball.

—*Charles V (1500–1558)*

880

While you're saving your face you're losing your ass.

—*President Lyndon Johnson (1908–1973)*

881

You can't say civilization don't advance . . . in every war
they kill you a new way.

—*Will Rogers (1879–1935)*

882

I have already given two cousins to the war and I stand
ready to sacrifice my wife's brother.

—*Artemus Ward (1834–1867)*

883

Join the army, see the world, meet interesting people, and kill them.

—*Unknown*

884

Being in the army is like being in the Boy Scouts, except that the Boy Scouts have adult supervision.

—*Blake Clark*

885

The Israelis are the Doberman pinschers of the Middle East. They treat the Arabs like postmen.

—*Franklyn Ajaye*

886

Start slow and taper off.

—*Walt Stack*

887

Never get into fights with ugly people because they have nothing to lose.

—*Unknown*

888

Never miss a good chance to shut up.

—*Scott Beach's grandfather*

889

The best way to keep one's word is not to give it.

—*Napoleon (1769–1821)*

890

It's all right letting yourself go as long as you can let yourself back.

—*Mick Jagger*

891

Sometimes a scream is better than a thesis.

—*Ralph Waldo Emerson (1803–1882)*

892

Aaeeeyaaayaaayaayaa . . .

—*Johnny Weissmuller (1904–1984)*

893

When walking through a melon patch, don't adjust your sandals.

—*Chinese proverb*

894
Sometimes a fool makes a good suggestion.
—*Nicolas Boileau (1636–1711)*

895
Good advice is one of those insults that ought to be forgiven.
—*Unknown*

896
It's no longer a question of staying healthy. It's a question of finding a sickness you like.
—*Jackie Mason*

897
I've just learned about his illness. Let's hope it's nothing trivial.
—*Variously ascribed*

898
I don't deserve this award, but I have arthritis and I don't deserve that either.
—*Jack Benny (1894–1974)*

899

As for me, except for an occasional heart attack, I feel as young as I ever did.

—*Robert Benchley (1889–1945)*

900

I get my exercise acting as a pallbearer to my friends who exercise.

—*Chauncey Depew (1834–1928)*

901

Avoid running at all times.

—*Satchel Paige (1906?–1982)*

902

It is more profitable for your congressman to support the tobacco industry than your life.

—*Jackie Mason*

903

Smoking is one of the leading causes of statistics.

—*Fletcher Knebel*

904

Quit worrying about your health. It'll go away.

—*Robert Orben*

905

Health nuts are going to feel stupid someday, lying in hospitals dying of nothing.

—*Redd Foxx (1922–1991)*

906

To eat is human
To digest divine.

—*Mark Twain (1835–1910)*

907

There is no sincerer love than the love of food.

—*George Bernard Shaw (1856–1950)*

908

The most dangerous food is wedding cake.

—*American proverb*

909

Roumanian-Yiddish cooking has killed more Jews than Hitler.

—*Zero Mostel (1915–1977)*

910

I believe that eating pork makes people stupid.

—*David Steinberg*

911

Eat, drink, and be merry, for tomorrow we may diet.

—*Unknown*

912

When men reach their sixties and retire, they go to pieces. Women go right on cooking.

—*Gail Sheehy*

913

I've been on a diet for two weeks and all I've lost is two weeks.

—*Totie Fields (1931–1978)*

914

I'm on a seafood diet. I see food and I eat it.

—*Variously ascribed*

915

Eat as much as you like—just don't swallow it.

—*Harry Secombe's diet*

916

Recipe for chili from Allan Shivers, former governor of Texas:

Put a pot of chili on the stove to simmer.

Let it simmer. Meanwhile, broil a good steak.

Eat the steak. Let the chili simmer. Ignore it.

917

The two biggest sellers in any bookstore are the cookbooks and the diet books. The cookbooks tell you how to prepare the food and the diet books tell you how not to eat any of it.

—*Andy Rooney*

918

It's so beautifully arranged on the plate—you know someone's fingers have been all over it.

—*Julia Child on nouvelle cuisine*

919

A gourmet who thinks of calories is like a tart who looks
at her watch.

—*James Beard (1903–1985)*

920

Where do you go to get anorexia?

—*Shelley Winters*

921

Nachman's Rule: When it comes to foreign food, the less
authentic the better.

—*Gerald Nachman*

922

I eat merely to put food out of my mind.

—*N. F. Simpson*

923

Isn't there any other part of the matzo you can eat?

—*Marilyn Monroe (1926–1962) on being
served matzo ball soup three meals in a row*

924

A gourmet restaurant in Cincinnati is one where you leave
the tray on the table after you eat.

—*Unknown*

925

When compelled to cook, I produce a meal that would make a sword swallower gag.

—*Russell Baker*

926

Poets have been mysteriously silent on the subject of cheese.

—*G. K. Chesterton (1874–1936)*

927

I don't even butter my bread. I consider that cooking.

—*Katherine Cebrian*

928

Life is too short to stuff a mushroom.

—*Storm Jameson (1891–1986)*

929

The most remarkable thing about my mother is that for thirty years she served the family nothing but leftovers. The original meal has never been found.

—*Calvin Trillin*

930

I'm in favor of liberalized immigration because of the effect it would have on restaurants. I'd let just about everybody in except the English.

—*Calvin Trillin*

931

No man is lonely while eating spaghetti.

—*Robert Morley (1908–1992)*

932

I prefer my oysters fried;
That way I know my oysters died.

—*Roy Blount, Jr.*

933
The trouble with life in the fast lane is that you get to the other end in an awful hurry.

—*John Jensen*

934
It is not true that life is one damn thing after another—it is one damn thing over and over.

—*Edna St. Vincent Millay (1892–1950)*

935

Life is thirst.

—*Leonard Michaels*

936

The less things change, the more they remain the same.

—*Sicilian proverb*

937

There are days when it takes all you've got just to keep up with the losers.

—*Robert Orben*

938

If you can see the light at the end of the tunnel you are looking the wrong way.

—*Barry Commoner*

939

I have found little that is good about human beings. In my experience most of them are trash.

—*Sigmund Freud (1856–1939)*

940

The brotherhood of man is not a mere poet's dream; it is a most depressing and humiliating reality.

—*Oscar Wilde (1854–1900)*

941

We're all in this alone.

—*Lily Tomlin*

942

Our ignorance of history makes us libel our own times. People have always been like this.

—*Gustave Flaubert (1821–1880)*

943

The British tourist is always happy abroad so long as the natives are waiters.

—*Robert Morley (1908–1992)*

944

You can't judge Egypt by *Aïda.*

—*Ronald Firbank (1886–1926)*

945

France is a country where the money falls apart and you can't tear the toilet paper.

—*Billy Wilder (1906–2002)*

946

In Marseilles they make half the toilet soap we consume in America, but the Marseillaise only have a vague theoretical idea of its use, which they have obtained from books of travel.

—*Mark Twain (1835–1910)*

947

Gaiety is the most outstanding feature of the Soviet Union.

—*Joseph Stalin (1879–1953)*

948

In Italy, for thirty years under the Borgias, they had warfare, terror, murder, and bloodshed, but they produced Michelangelo, Leonardo da Vinci, and the Renaissance. In Switzerland, they had brotherly love, they had five hundred years of democracy and peace—and what did they produce? The cuckoo clock.

—*From the movie* The Third Man, *1949*

949

Canada is so square even the female impersonators are women.

—*From the movie* Outrageous, *1983*

950

Most Texans think Hanukkah is some sort of duck call.

—*Richard Lewis*

951

Historians have now definitely established that Juan Cabrillo, discoverer of California, was not looking for Kansas, thus setting a precedent that continues to this day.

—*Wayne Shannon*

952

The big cities of America are becoming Third World countries.

—*Nora Ephron*

953

New York now leads the world's great cities in the number of people around whom you shouldn't make a sudden move.

—*David Letterman*

954

It isn't necessary to have relatives in Kansas City in order to be unhappy.

—*Groucho Marx (1895–1977)*

955

Isn't it nice that people who prefer Los Angeles to San Francisco live there?

—*Herb Caen*

956

San Francisco is like granola: Take away the fruits and the nuts, and all you have are the flakes.

—*Unknown*

957

In San Francisco, Halloween is redundant.

—*Will Durst*

958

Detroit is Cleveland without the glitter.

—*Unknown*

959

When I saw a sign on the freeway that said, "Los Angeles 445 miles," I said to myself, "I've got to get out of this lane."

—*Franklyn Ajaye*

960
Traffic signals in New York are just rough guidelines.

—*David Letterman*

961

I have an existential map. It has "You are here" written all over it.

—*Steven Wright*

962

I hate small towns because once you've seen the cannon in the park there's nothing else to do.

—*Lenny Bruce (1925–1966)*

963

Schizophrenia beats dining alone.

—*Unknown*

964

When we talk to God, we're praying. When God talks to us, we're schizophrenic.

—*Lily Tomlin*

965

When dealing with the insane, the best method is to pretend to be sane.

—*Hermann Hesse (1877–1962)*

966

I don't really trust a sane person.

—*Pro football lineman Lyle Alzado*

967

Sometimes when you look in his eyes you get the feeling that someone else is driving.

—*David Letterman*

968

I'm going to give my psychoanalyst one more year, then I'm going to Lourdes.

—*Woody Allen*

969

When a book and a head collide and there is a hollow sound, is it always from the book?

—*Georg Christoph Lichtenberg (1742–1799)*

970

I've given up reading books. I find it takes my mind off myself.

—*Oscar Levant (1906–1972)*

971

Where do I find the time for not reading so many books?

—*Karl Kraus (1874–1936)*

972

A person who publishes a book appears willfully in public with his pants down.

—Edna St. Vincent Millay (1892–1950)

973

The reason why so few good books are written is that so few people who can write know anything.

—Walter Bagehot (1826–1877)

974

The newspaper is the natural enemy of the book, as the whore is of the decent woman.

—The Goncourt Brothers, 1858

975

Manuscript: Something submitted in haste and returned at leisure.

—Oliver Herford (1863–1935)

976

Your manuscript is both good and original, but the part that is good is not original and the part that is original is not good.

—Samuel Johnson (1709–1784)

977

Autobiography is an unrivaled vehicle for telling the truth about other people.

—*Philip Guedalla (1889–1944)*

978

A well-written life is almost as rare as a well-spent one.

—*Thomas Carlyle (1795–1881)*

979

I have read your book and much like it.

—*Moses Hadas (1900–1966)*

980

A novel is a piece of prose of a certain length with something wrong with it.

—*Unknown*

981

There are two kinds of books: those that no one reads and those that no one ought to read.

—*H. L. Mencken (1880–1956)*

982

The covers of this book are too far apart.

—*Ambrose Bierce (1842–1914?)*

983

[He] took me into his library and showed me his books, of which he had a complete set.

—*Ring Lardner (1885–1933)*

984

The man who reads nothing at all is better educated than the man who reads nothing but newspapers.

—*Thomas Jefferson (1743–1826)*

985

Journalism largely consists in saying "Lord Jones is dead" to people who never knew Lord Jones was alive.

—*G. K. Chesterton (1874–1936)*

986

There is so much to be said in favor of modern journalism. By giving us the opinions of the uneducated it keeps us in touch with ignorance of the community.

—*Oscar Wilde (1854–1900)*

987

Small Earthquake in Chile;
Not Many Killed

—*Headline suggested for* The Times
of London by Claud Cockburn

988

Writers have two main problems. One is writer's block, when the words won't come at all, and the other is logorrhea, when the words come so fast that they can hardly get to the wastebasket in time.

—*Cecilia Bartholomew*

989

All of us learn to write in the second grade. Most of us go on to greater things.

—*Basketball coach Bobby Knight*

990

When writers refer to themselves as "we" and to the reader as "you," it's two against one.

—*Judith Rascoe*

991

Most writers regard the truth as their most valuable possession, and therefore are most economical in its use.

—*Mark Twain (1835–1910)*

992

Writing is turning one's worst moments into money.

—*J. P. Donleavy*

993
Writing is the only profession in which one can make no
money without being ridiculous.
—*Jules Renard (1864–1910)*

994
Writers should be read, but neither seen nor heard.
—*Daphne du Maurier (1907–1989)*

995
If you can't annoy somebody, there is little point in writing.
—*Kingsley Amis*

996
Unprovided with original learning, unformed in the habits
of thinking, unskilled in the arts of composition, I re-
solved to write a book.
—*Edward Gibbon (1737–1794)*

997
Everywhere I go I'm asked if I think the university stifles
writers. My opinion is that they don't stifle enough of
them. There's many a bestseller that could have been pre-
vented by a good teacher.
—*Flannery O'Connor (1925–1964)*

998

Great Moments in Literature: In 1936, Ernest Hemingway, while trout fishing, caught a carp and decided not to write about it.

—*Guindon cartoon caption*

999

All writing is garbage.

—*French playwright Antonin Artaud (1896–1948)*

1,000

Novelists who go to psychiatrists are paying for what they should be paid for.

—*Unknown*

1,001

Every author, however modest, keeps a most outrageous vanity chained like a madman in the padded cell of his breast.

—*Logan Pearsall Smith (1865–1946)*

1,002

The trouble with our younger writers is that they are all in their sixties.

—*W. Somerset Maugham (1874–1965)*

1,003
Authors are easy to get on with—if you like children.
—*Michael Joseph (1897–1958)*

1,004
I write fiction because it's a way of making statements I can disown, and I write plays because dialogue is the most respectable way of contradicting myself.
—*Tom Stoppard*

1,005

An essayist is a lucky person who has found a way to discourse without being interrupted.

—*Charles Poore*

1,006

Writers aren't exactly people . . . they're a whole lot of people trying to be one person.

—*F. Scott Fitzgerald (1896–1940)*

1,007

An author's first duty is to let down his country.

—*Brendan Behan (1923–1964)*

1,008

Asking a working writer what he thinks about critics is like asking a lamp-post how it feels about dogs.

—*Christopher Hampton*

1,009

I can't read ten pages of Steinbeck without throwing up.

—*James Gould Cozzens (1903–1978)*

1,010

A poem is never finished, only abandoned.

—*Paul Valéry (1871–1945)*

1,011

Immature poets imitate; mature poets steal.

—*T. S. Eliot (1888–1965)*

1,012

Good swiping is an art in itself.

—*Jules Feiffer*

1,013

Finishing a book is just like you took a child out in the back yard and shot it.

—*Truman Capote (1924–1984)*

1,014

Dear Contributor: Thank you for not sending us anything lately. It suits our present needs.

—*Note from publisher received by Snoopy in comic strip "Peanuts" (Charles Schulz, 1922–2000)*

1,015

You call this a script? Give me a couple of 5,000-dollar-a-week writers and I'll write it myself.

—*Movie producer Joe Pasternak*

1,016

I do most of my writing sitting down. That's where I shine.

—*Robert Benchley (1889–1945)*

1,017

When in doubt, have two guys come through the door
with guns.

—*Raymond Chandler (1888–1959)*

1,018

Too many pieces of music finish too long after the end.

—*Igor Stravinsky (1882–1971)*

1,019

My music is best understood by children and animals.

—*Igor Stravinsky (1882–1971)*

1,020

You want something by Bach? Which one, Johann Sebastian or Jacques Offen?

—*Victor Borge (1909–2000)*

1,021

Even Bach comes down to the basic suck, blow, suck, suck, blow.

—*Mouth organist Larry Adler*

1,022

Classical music is the kind we keep thinking will turn into a tune.

—*Kin Hubbard (1868–1930)*

1,023

Opera in English is, in the main, just about as sensible as baseball in Italian.

—*H. L. Mencken (1880–1956)*

1,024

I tried to resist his overtures, but he plied me with symphonies, quartettes, chamber music, and cantatas.

—*S. J. Perelman (1904–1979)*

1,025

Anything that is too stupid to be spoken is sung.

—*Voltaire (1694–1778)*

1,026
Massenet
Never wrote a Mass in A.
It'd have been just too bad
If he had.

—Anthony Butts

1,027
No statue has ever been put up to a critic.

—Jean Sibelius (1865–1957)

1,028
Music played at weddings always reminds me of the music
played for soldiers before they go into battle.

—Heinrich Heine (1797–1856)

1,029
I don't know anything about music. In my line you don't
have to.

—Elvis Presley (1935–1977)

1,030

Hell is full of musical amateurs.

—*George Bernard Shaw (1856–1950)*

1,031
No sane man will dance.

—*Cicero (106–43 B.C.)*

1,032
Rock and roll is the hamburger that ate the world.

—*Peter York*

1,033
Use an accordion, go to jail! That's the law!
—*Bumper sticker*

1,034
You can make a killing as a playwright in America, but you can't make a living.
—*Sherwood Anderson (1876–1941)*

1,035

All playwrights should be dead for three hundred years.

—*Joseph L. Mankiewicz (1909–1992)*

1,036

Actresses will happen in the best regulated families.

—*Oliver Herford (1863–1935)*

1,037

My tears stuck in their little ducts, refusing to be jerked.

—*Peter Stack in a movie review*

1,038

His performance is so wooden you want to spray him with Liquid Pledge.

—*John Stark in a movie review*

1,039

Working in the theater has a lot in common with unemployment.

—*Arthur Gingold*

1,040

Only in show business could a guy with a C-minus average be considered an intellectual.

—*Mort Sahl on himself*

1,041

I don't want to see the uncut version of anything.

—*Jean Kerr*

1,042

It's always easier to see a show you don't like the second time because you know it ends.

—*Walter Slezak (1902–1983)*

1,043

Hell is a half-filled auditorium.

—*Robert Frost (1874–1963)*

1,044

A critic is a man who knows the way but can't drive the car.

—*Kenneth Tynan (1927–1980)*

1,045

Hollywood is a place where they place you under contract instead of under observation.

—*Walter Winchell (1897–1972)*

1,046

The Hollywood tradition I like best is called "sucking up to the stars."

—*Johnny Carson*

1,047

"Hello," he lied.

—*Don Carpenter quoting a Hollywood agent*

1,048

An associate producer is the only guy in Hollywood who will associate with a producer.

—*Fred Allen (1894–1956)*

1,049

The dead actor requested in his will that his body be cremated and ten percent of his ashes thrown in his agent's face.

—*Unknown*

1,050

It was like passing the scene of a highway accident and being relieved to learn that nobody had been seriously injured.

—*Martin Cruz Smith on being asked how he liked the movie version of his novel* Gorky Park

1,051

If you want to make it in show business, get the hell out of Oregon.

—*Advice from Sophie Tucker (1884–1966)*
to a young Johnnie Ray

1,052

Television has proved that people will look at anything rather than each other.

—*Ann Landers (1918–2002)*

1,053

Television is more interesting than people. If it were not, we would have people standing in the corners of our rooms.

—*Alan Corenk*

1,054

Television is a medium because anything well done is rare.

—*Either Fred Allen (1894–1956)*
or Ernie Kovacs (1919–1962)

1,055

Your picture tube is okay, but your cabinet has Dutch elm disease.

—*TV repairman in a Ziggy cartoon*

1,056

I'm So Miserable Without You
It's Almost Like Having You Here
—*Stephen Bishop song title*

1,057

She Got the Gold Mine, I Got the Shaft
—*Jerry Reed song title*

1,058

When My Love Comes Back from the Ladies Room
Will I Be Too Old to Care?
—*Lewis Grizzard song title*

1,059

I Don't Know Whether to Kill Myself or Go Bowling
—*Song title by Unknown*

1,060

Why won't you lemme feelya, Cecilia?
I got two winnin' hands I wanna dealya.
—*Lyrics by Robert Byrne*

1,061

They Tore Out My Heart and Stomped That Sucker Flat
—*Book title by Lewis Grizzard*

1,062

[Americans] are a race of convicts and ought to be thankful for anything we allow them short of hanging.

—*Samuel Johnson (1709–1784)*

1,063

America is a large friendly dog in a small room. Every time it wags its tail it knocks over a chair.

—*Arnold Toynbee (1889–1975)*

1,064

The United States is like the guy at the party who gives cocaine to everybody and still nobody likes him.

—*Jim Samuels*

1,065

On Thanksgiving Day all over America, families sit down to dinner at the same moment—halftime.

—*Unknown*

1,066

In America there are two classes of travel—first and with children.

—*Robert Benchley (1889–1945)*

1,067

Animals have these advantages over man: they never hear the clock strike, they die without any idea of death, they have no theologians to instruct them, their last moments are not disturbed by unwelcome and unpleasant ceremonies, their funerals cost them nothing, and no one starts lawsuits over their wills.

—*Voltaire (1694–1778)*

1,068

A boy can learn a lot from a dog: obedience, loyalty, and the importance of turning around three times before lying down.

—*Robert Benchley (1889–1945)*

1,069

Man is the only animal that can remain on friendly terms with the victims he intends to eat until he eats them.

—*Samuel Butler (1835–1902)*

1,070

Fox hunting is the unspeakable in pursuit of the inedible.

—*Oscar Wilde (1856–1900)*

1,071

If you are a police dog, where's your badge?

—*The question James Thurber (1894–1961)*
used to drive his German shepherd crazy

1,072

I loathe people who keep dogs. They are cowards who haven't got the guts to bite people themselves.

—*August Strindberg (1849–1912)*

1,073

We tolerate shapes in human beings that would horrify us if we saw them in a horse.

—*W. R. Inge (1860–1954)*

1,074

People on horses look better than they are, people in cars look worse.

—*Marya Mannes*

1,075

You're a good example of why some animals eat their young.

—*Jim Samuels to a heckler*

1,076

Cats are intended to teach us that not everything in nature has a function.

—*Garrison Keillor*

1,077

Groundhog Day has been observed only once in Los Angeles because when the groundhog came out of its hole, it was killed by a mud slide.

—*Johnny Carson*

1,078

Is that a beard, or are you eating a muskrat?

—*Dr. Gonzo*

1,079

To err is human
To purr feline.

—*Robert Byrne*

1,080

It isn't easy being green.

—*Kermit the Frog*

1,081

Never go to a doctor whose office plants have died.
—*Erma Bombeck (1927–1996)*

1,082

Three out of four doctors recommend another doctor.
—*Graffito*

1,083

I suppose one has a greater sense of intellectual degradation after an interview with a doctor than from any human experience.
—*Alice James (1848–1892)*

1,084

A young doctor means a new graveyard.
—*German proverb*

1,085

I'm going to Boston to see my doctor. He's a very sick man.
—*Fred Allen (1894–1956)*

1,086

People who take cold baths never have rheumatism, but they have cold baths.
—*Unknown*

1,087

His ideas of first-aid stopped short of squirting soda water.

—*P. G. Wodehouse (1881–1975)*

1,088

Before undergoing a surgical operation, arrange your temporal affairs. You may live.

—*Ambrose Bierce (1842–1914?)*

1,089

Psychoanalysis is that mental illness for which it regards itself a therapy.

—*Karl Kraus (1874–1936)*

1,090

Show me a sane man and I will cure him for you.

—*C. G. Jung (1875–1961)*

1,091

Psychiatry is the care of the id by the odd.

—*Unknown*

1,092

After twelve years of therapy my psychiatrist said something that brought tears to my eyes. He said, "*No hablo inglés.*"

—*Ronnie Shakes*

1,093

Doctors and lawyers must go to school for years and years, often with little sleep and with great sacrifice to their first wives.

—*Roy Blount, Jr.*

1,094

I never did give anybody hell. I just told the truth and they thought it was hell.

—*Harry S Truman (1884–1972)*

1,095

I can think of nothing more boring for the American people than to have to sit in their living rooms for a whole half hour looking at my face on their television screens.

—*Dwight David Eisenhower (1890–1969)*

1,096

Do you realize the responsibility I carry? I'm the only person standing between Nixon and the White House.

—*John F. Kennedy (1917–1963), in 1960*

1,097

I'm not sure I've even got the brains to be President.

—*Barry Goldwater in 1964*

1,098

I would not like to be a political leader in Russia. They never know when they're being taped.

—*Richard Nixon (1913–1994)*

1,099

I love America. You always hurt the one you love.

—*David Frye impersonating Nixon*

1,100

The thought of being President frightens me and I do not think I want the job.

—*Ronald Reagan in 1973*

1,101

God! The country that produced George Washington has got this collection of crumb-bums!

—*Barbara Tuchman on the
1980 presidential candidates*

1,102

Reagan won because he ran against Jimmy Carter. Had he run unopposed he would have lost.

—*Mort Sahl*

1,103

Ronald Reagan is a triumph of the embalmer's art.

—*Gore Vidal*

1,104

Ronald Reagan's platform seems to be: Hey, I'm a big good-looking guy and I need a lot of sleep.

—*Roy Blount, Jr.*

1,105

Walter Mondale has all the charisma of a speed bump.

—*Will Durst*

1,106

You've got to be careful quoting Ronald Reagan, because when you quote him accurately it's called mudslinging.

—*Walter Mondale*

1,107

Women are being considered as candidates for Vice President of the United States because it is the worst job in America. It's amazing that men will take it. A job with real power is First Lady. I'd be willing to run for that. As far as the men who are running for President are concerned, they aren't even people I would date.

—*Nora Ephron*

1,108

The man with the best job in the country is the Vice President. All he has to do is get up every morning and say, "How's the President?"

—*Will Rogers (1879–1935)*

1,109

The vice-presidency ain't worth a pitcher of warm spit.
—*Vice President John Nance Garner*
(1868–1967)

1,110

If it were not for the government, we would have nothing to laugh at in France.
—*Sébastian Chamfort (1740–1794)*

1,111

Every decent man is ashamed of the government he lives under.
—*H. L. Mencken (1880–1956)*

1,112

It has been said that democracy is the worst form of government except all the others that have been tried.
—*Winston Churchill (1874–1965)*

1,113

You can't beat City Hall, but you can drive by and egg it.
—*John Wagner*

1,114

Get all the fools on your side and you can be elected to anything.

—*Frank Dane*

1,115

If voting changed anything, they'd make it illegal.

—*Unknown*

1,116

Vote early and vote often.

—*Al Capone (1899–1947)*

1,117

Ninety percent of the politicians give the other ten percent a bad reputation.

—*Henry Kissinger*

1,118

Politics is applesauce.

—*Will Rogers (1879–1935)*

1,119

I might have gone to West Point, but I was too proud to speak to a congressman.

—*Will Rogers (1879–1935)*

1,120

An ambassador is an honest man sent abroad to lie for his country.

—*Sir Henry Wotton (1568–1639)*

1,121

A statesman is a politician who has been dead ten or fifteen years.

—*Harry S Truman (1884–1972)*

1,122

Right in the middle of Prague, Wenceslaus Square, there's this guy throwing up. And this other guy comes along, takes a look at him, shakes his head, and says, "I know just what you mean."

—*Milan Kundera*

1,123

When you go into court you are putting your fate into the hands of twelve people who weren't smart enough to get out of jury duty.

—*Norm Crosby*

1,124

Getting kicked out of the American Bar Association is like getting kicked out of the Book-of-the-Month Club.

—*Melvin Belli on the occasion of his getting kicked out of the American Bar Association*

1,125

Laws are like sausages. It's better not to see them being made.

—*Otto von Bismarck (1815–1898)*

1,126

I always turn to the sports pages first, which record people's accomplishments. The front page has nothing but man's failures.

—*Chief Justice Earl Warren (1891–1974)*

1,127

I was not successful as a ballplayer, as it was a game of skill.

—*Casey Stengel (1891–1975)*

1,128

It matters not whether you win or lose; what matters is whether *I* win or lose.

—*Darrin Weinberg*

1,129

I'm glad we don't have to play in the shade.

—*Golfer Bobby Jones (1902–1971) on being told that it was 105 degrees in the shade*

1,130

Very few blacks will take up golf until the requirement for plaid pants is dropped.

—*Franklyn Ajaye*

1,131

San Francisco has always been my favorite booing city. I don't mean the people boo louder or longer, but there is a very special intimacy. When they boo you, you know they mean *you*. Music, that's what it is to me. One time in Kezar Stadium they gave me a standing boo.

—*Pro football coach George Halas (1895–1983)*

1,132

Most weightlifters are biceptual.

—*John Rostoni*

1,133

I never met a man I didn't want to fight.

—*Pro football lineman Lyle Alzado*

1,134

If politicians and scientists were lazier, how much happier we should all be.

—*Evelyn Waugh (1903–1966)*

1,135
If we see the light at the end of the tunnel
It's the light of an oncoming train.
—*Robert Lowell (1917–1977)*

1,136
Ninety percent of everything is crap.
—*Theodore Sturgeon*

1,137
You've always made the mistake of being yourself.
—*Eugène Ionesco (1912–1994)*

1,138
There is such a build-up of crud in my oven there is only
room to bake a single cupcake.
—*Phyllis Diller*

1,139
Cleaning your house while your kids are still growing is
like shoveling the walk before it stops snowing.
—*Phyllis Diller*

1,140

There is no need to do any housework at all. After the first four years the dirt doesn't get any worse.

—*Quentin Crisp (1908–1999)*

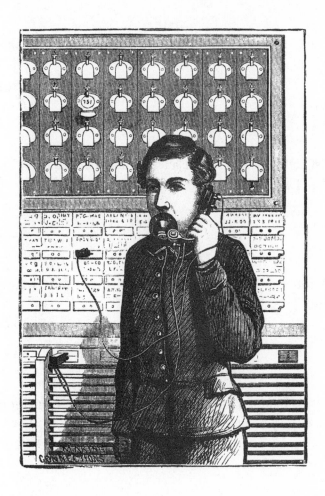

1,141

All phone calls are obscene.

—*Karen Elizabeth Gordon*

1,142

Coincidences are spiritual puns.

—*G. K. Chesterton (1874–1936)*

1,143

If I had to live my life again, I'd make the same mistakes, only sooner.

—*Tallulah Bankhead (1903–1968)*

1,144

Last night I dreamed I ate a ten-pound marshmallow, and when I woke up the pillow was gone.

—*Tommy Cooper*

1,145

It's better to be wanted for murder than not to be wanted at all.

—*Marty Winch*

1,146

I have a hundred times wished that one could resign life as an officer resigns a commission.

—*Robert Burns (1759–1796)*

1,147

If you tell the truth you don't have to remember anything.

—*Mark Twain (1835–1910)*

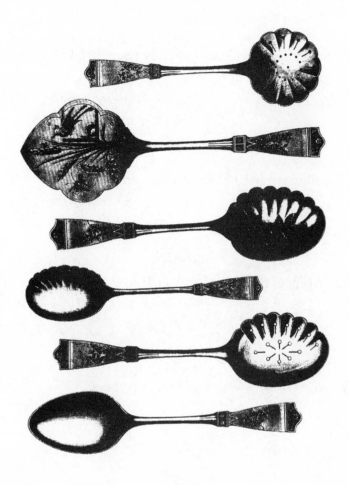

1,148

The more he talked of his honor the faster we counted our spoons.

—*Ralph Waldo Emerson (1803–1882)*

1,149

The truth is the safest lie.

—*Anonymous*

1,150

No one can have a higher opinion of him than I have, and
I think he's a dirty little beast.

—*W. S. Gilbert (1836–1911)*

1,151

The future is much like the present, only longer.

—*Dan Quisenberry*

1,152

Advertising is the rattling of a stick inside a swill bucket.

—*George Orwell (1903–1950)*

1,153

Winter is nature's way of saying, "Up yours."

—*Robert Byrne*

1,154

I like winter because I can stay indoors without feeling
guilty.

—*Teressa Skelton*

1,155

Weather forecast for tonight: dark.

—*George Carlin*

1,156

If I were two-faced, would I be wearing this one?
—*Abraham Lincoln (1809–1865)*

1,157

A person can take only so much comforting.
—*Calvin Trillin*

1,158

I have a rock garden. Last week three of them died.
—*Richard Diran*

1,159

Nice guys finish last, but we get to sleep in.
—*Evan Davis*

1,160

Illegal aliens have always been a problem in the United States. Ask any Indian.
—*Robert Orben*

1,161

Few things are harder to put up with than a good example.
—*Mark Twain (1835–1910)*

1,162

I just got wonderful news from my real estate agent in Florida. They found land on my property.

—*Milton Berle (1908–2002)*

1,163

Immigration is the sincerest form of flattery.

—*Jack Paar*

1,164

The art of living is more like wrestling than dancing.

—*Marcus Aurelius (121–180)*

1,165

We must believe in luck. For how else can we explain the success of those we don't like?

—*Jean Cocteau (1889–1963)*

1,166

Hell is other people.

—*Jean-Paul Sartre (1905–1980)*

1,167

Some people are always late, like the late King George V.

—*Spike Milligan (1918–2002)*

1,168

It is easier to get forgiveness than permission.

—*Stewart's Law of Retroaction in*
Murphy's Law, Book Two

1,169

The popularity of a bad man is as treacherous as he is himself.

—*Pliny the Younger (c. 62–c. 113)*

1,170

The hatred of relatives is the most violent.

—*Tacitus (c. 55–c. 117)*

1,171

Every man sees in his relatives a series of grotesque caricatures of himself.

—*H. L. Mencken (1880–1956)*

1,172

The first Rotarian was the first man to call John the Baptist "Jack."

—*H. L. Mencken (1880–1956)*

1,173

H. L. Mencken suffers from the hallucination that he is H. L. Mencken. There is no cure for a disease of that magnitude.

—*Maxwell Bodenheim (1893–1954)*

1,174

Even if you're on the right track, you'll get run over if you just sit there.

—*Will Rogers (1879–1935)*

1,175

I prefer rogues to imbeciles because they sometimes take a rest.

—*Alexandre Dumas the Younger (1824–1895)*

1,176

A wedding cake left out in the rain.

—*Stephen Spender commenting on the face of*
W. H. Auden (1907–1973)

1,177

Is this the party to whom I am speaking?

—*Lily Tomlin as Ernestine the operator*

1,178

Let others praise ancient times; I am glad I was born in these.

—*Ovid (43 B.C.–A.D. 18)*

1,179

Happiness is good health and a bad memory.

—*Ingrid Bergman (1917–1982)*

1,180

Never keep up with the Joneses. Drag them down to your level.

—*Quentin Crisp (1908–1999)*

1,181

People who think they know everything are very irritating to those of us who do.

—*Unknown*

1,182

I want a house that has got over all its troubles; I don't want to spend the rest of my life bringing up a young and inexperienced house.

—*Jerome K. Jerome (1859–1927)*

1,183

There is something about a closet that makes a skeleton restless.

—*Unknown*

1,184

By dint of railing at idiots you run the risk of becoming idiotic yourself.

—*Gustave Flaubert (1821–1880)*

1,185

There is no gravity. The earth sucks.

—*Graffito*

1,186

When the going gets tough, the smart get lost.

—*Robert Byrne*

1,187

Miss Erickson looked more peculiar than ever this morning. Is her spiritualism getting worse?

—*Noël Coward (1889–1973)*

1,188

I shot an arrow into the air, and it stuck.

—*Graffito in Los Angeles*

1,189

There's so much pollution in the air now that if it weren't for our lungs there'd be no place to put it all.

—*Robert Orben*

1,190

I don't know how old I am because the goat ate the Bible that had my birth certificate in it. The goat lived to be twenty-seven.

—*Satchel Paige (1906?–1982)*

1,191

Nothing ever goes away.

—*Barry Commoner*

1,192

There's nothing wrong with you that reincarnation won't cure.

—*Jack E. Leonard (1911–1973)*
to Ed Sullivan (1902–1974)

1,193

A lie is an abomination unto the Lord and a very present help in time of trouble.

—*Adlai Stevenson (1900–1965)*

1,194

During a carnival men put masks over their masks.

—*Xavier Forneret, 1838*

1,195

One hundred thousand lemmings can't be wrong.

—*Graffito*

1,196

He was the world's only armless sculptor. He put the chisel in his mouth and his wife hit him on the back of the head with a mallet.

—*Fred Allen (1894–1956)*

1,197

Modern art is what happens when painters stop looking at girls and persuade themselves that they have a better idea.

—*John Ciardi (1916–1986)*

1,198

Either this wallpaper goes or I do.

—*Almost certainly not the last words of Oscar Wilde (1856–1900)*

1,199

A life spent making mistakes is not only more honorable but more useful than a life spent doing nothing.

—*George Bernard Shaw (1856–1950)*

1,200

Friends may come and go, but enemies accumulate.

—*Thomas Jones*

1,201

When down in the mouth, remember Jonah. He came out all right.

—*Thomas Edison (1847–1931)*

1,202

Retirement at sixty-five is ridiculous. When I was sixty-five I still had pimples.

—*George Burns (1896–1996)*

1,203

Old age is the only disease you don't look forward to being cured of.

—*From the movie* Citizen Kane, *1941*

1,204

Start every day off with a smile and get it over with.
—*W. C. Fields (1880–1946)*

1,205

I took a course in speed reading and was able to read *War and Peace* in twenty minutes. It's about Russia.
—*Woody Allen*

1,206

When your IQ rises to 28, sell.
—*Professor Irwin Corey to a heckler*

1,207

Some people are like popular songs that you only sing for a short time.
—*La Rochefoucauld (1613–1680)*

1,208

George the Third
Ought never to have occurred.
One can only wonder
At so grotesque a blunder.
—*Edmund Clerihew (1875–1956)*

1,209

There are two kinds of pedestrians . . . the quick and the dead.

—*Lord Thomas Robert Dewar (1864–1930)*

1,210

I used to work in a fire hydrant factory. You couldn't park anywhere near the place.

—*Steven Wright*

1,211

I don't have any trouble parking. I drive a forklift.

—*Jim Samuels*

1,212

God help those who do not help themselves.

—*Wilson Mizner (1876–1933)*

1,213

There is only one good substitute for the endearments of a sister, and that is the endearments of some other fellow's sister.

—*Josh Billings (1818–1885)*

1,214

When smashing monuments, save the pedestals—they always come in handy.

—*Stanislaw Lem*

1,215

Great men are not always idiots.

—*Karen Elizabeth Gordon*

1,216

Few great men could pass Personnel.

—*Paul Goodman (1911–1972)*

1,217

Fanaticism consists of redoubling your effort when you have forgotten your aim.

—*George Santayana (1863–1952)*

1,218

Mountains appear more lofty the nearer they are approached, but great men resemble them not in this particular.

—*Lady Marguerite Blessington (1789–1849)*

1,219

There's a great woman behind every idiot.

—*John Lennon (1940–1980) on Yoko Ono*

1,220

Nothing is more conducive to peace of mind than not having any opinions at all.

—*Georg Christoph Lichtenberg (1742–1799)*

1,221

The mome rath isn't born that could outgrabe me.

—*Nicol Williamson*

1,222

If you live to the age of a hundred you have it made because very few people die past the age of a hundred.

—*George Burns (1896–1996)*

1,223

Never accept an invitation from a stranger unless he gives you candy.

—*Linda Festa*

1,224

You can choose your friends, but you only have one mother.

—*Max Shulman*

1,225

One is not superior merely because one sees the world as odious.

—*Chateaubriand (1768–1848)*

1,226

If it weren't for the last minute, nothing would get done.

—*Unknown*

1,227

If I were a grave-digger or even a hangman, there are some people I could work for with a great deal of enjoyment.

—*Douglas Jerrold (1803–1857)*

1,228

It is easier to forgive an enemy than to forgive a friend.

—*William Blake (1757–1827)*

1,229

You are no bigger than the things that annoy you.

—*Jerry Bundsen*

1,230

It is unpleasant to go alone, even to be drowned.

—*Russian proverb*

1,231

Stay with me; I want to be alone.

—*Joey Adams*

1,232

They made love only during total eclipses of the sun because they wouldn't take off their clothes unless it was dark in the entire world.

—*Unknown*

1,233

We are what we pretend to be.

—*Kurt Vonnegut, Jr.*

1,234

Thank you, but I have other plans.

—*Response to "Have a nice day"*
suggested by Paul Fussell

1,235

WARNING TO ALL PERSONNEL

Firings will continue until morale improves.

—*Unknown*

1,236

Do we really deserve top billing?

—*Fred Allen (1894–1956) to Henry Morgan*
at a meeting of the National Conference
of Christians and Jews

1,237

Psychics will lead dogs to your body.

—*Alleged fortune cookie message*

1,238

I don't worry about crime in the streets; it's the sidewalks
I stay off of.

—*Johnson Letellier*

1,239

Carney's Law: There's at least a 50-50 chance that someone will print the name Craney incorrectly.

—*Jim Canrey*

1,240

Bad spellers of the world, untie!

—*Graffito*

1,241

Complete this sentence:
I never met a man I didn't like
a. to cheat.
b. at first.
c. to avoid.
d. better than you.

—*Robert Byrne*

1,242

Fix this sentence:
He put the horse before the cart.

—*Stephen Price*

1,243

I am firm. You are obstinate. He is a pig-headed fool.
—*Katharine Whitehorn*

1,244

Dr. Livingstone I Presume
Full name of Dr. Presume

—*Unknown*

1,245

A language is a dialect with an army and navy.

—*Max Weinreich (1894–1969)*

1,246

I can't seem to bring myself to say, "Well, I guess I'll be toddling along." It isn't that I can't toddle. It's that I can't guess I'll toddle.

—*Robert Benchley (1889–1945)*

1,247

Hamlet as performed at the Brooklyn Shakespeare Festival:

"To be, or what?"

—*Steven Pearl*

1,248

Smoking is, as far as I'm concerned, the entire point of being an adult.

—*Fran Lebowitz*

1,249

There is only one word for aid that is genuinely without strings, and that word is blackmail.

—*Colm Brogan*

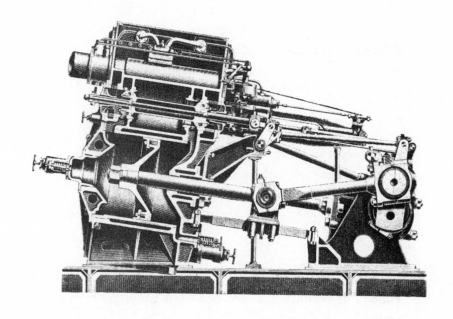

1,250

A steam engine has always got character. It's the most human of all man-made machines.

—*Reverend William Vere Awdrey*

1,251

Al didn't smile for forty years. You've got to admire a man like that.

—*From the television series*
Mary Hartman, Mary Hartman

1,252

All professions are conspiracies against the laity.

—*George Bernard Shaw (1856–1950)*

1,253

Very few people do anything creative after the age of thirty-five. The reason is that very few people do anything creative before the age of thirty-five.

—*Joel Hildebrand (1881–1983)*

1,254

There is no they, only us.

—*Bumper sticker*

1,255

I was in a beauty contest once. I not only came in last, I was hit in the mouth by Miss Congeniality.

—*Phyllis Diller*

1,256

You can get more with a kind word and a gun than you can with a kind word alone.

—*Johnny Carson*

1,257

I think it would be a good idea.

—*Mahatma Gandhi (1869–1948) when asked what he thought of Western civilization*

1,258

Remember that a kick in the ass is a step forward.

—*Unknown*

1,259

What is algebra, exactly? Is it those three-cornered things.

—*J. M. Barrie (1860–1937)*

1,260

Computers are useless. They can only give you answers.

—*Pablo Picasso (1881–1973)*

1,261

Peace, n. In international affairs, a period of cheating between two periods of fighting.

—*Ambrose Bierce (1842–1914?)*

1,262

Let thy maid servant be faithful, strong, and homely.

—*Benjamin Franklin (1706–1790)*

1,263

At twenty-six, Kate, though not promiscuous, had slept with most of the decent men in public life.

—*Renata Adler*

1,264

The egg cream is psychologically the opposite of circumcision—it *pleasurably* reaffirms your Jewishness.

—*Mel Brooks*

1,265

His absence is good company.

—*Scottish saying*

1,266

The happiest liaisons are based on mutual misunder-
standing.

—*La Rochefoucauld (1613–1680)*

1,267

So many beautiful women and so little time.

—*John Barrymore (1882–1942)*

1,268

The art of *not* reading is extremely important. It consists
in our not taking up whatever happens to occupy the
larger public.

—*Arthur Schopenhauer (1788–1860)*

1,269

Nowadays the illiterates can read and write.

—*Alberto Moravia (1907–1990)*

1,270

A good man is always a beginner.

—*Martial (c. 40–c. 104)*

1,271

I knew a very interesting Italian woman last winter, but
now she's married.

—*Percy Bysshe Shelley (1792–1822)*

1,272

How much money did you make last year? Mail it in.

—*Simplified tax form
suggested by Stanton Delaplane*

1,273

Gray hair is God's graffiti.

—*Bill Cosby*

1,274

The gods too are fond of a joke.

—*Aristotle (384–322 B.C.)*

1,275

The only thing that stops God from sending another flood
is that the first one was useless.

—*Nicolas Chamfort (1741–1794)*

1,276

The world is proof that God is a committee.

—*Bob Stokes*

1,277

God is dead, but fifty thousand social workers have risen
to take his place.

—*J. D. McCoughey*

1,278

Which is it, is man one of God's blunders or is God one of man's?

—*Friedrich Nietzsche (1844–1900)*

1,279

Nietzsche was stupid and abnormal.

—*Leo Tolstoy (1828–1910)*

1,280

Millions long for immortality who don't know what to do on a rainy Sunday afternoon.

—*Susan Ertz*

1,281

A pious man is one who would be an atheist if the king were.

—*Jean de La Bruyère (1645–1696)*

1,282

I detest converts almost as much as I do missionaries.

—*H. L. Mencken (1880–1956)*

1,283

Most of my friends are not Christians, but I have some who are Anglicans or Roman Catholics.

—*Dame Rose Macaulay (1881–1958)*

1,284

Promise me that if you become a Christian you'll become a Presbyterian.

—*Lord Beaverbrook (1879–1964)*
to Josef Stalin in 1941

1,285

The history of saints is mainly the history of insane people.

—*Benito Mussolini (1883–1945)*

1,286

In Burbank there's a drive-in church called Jack-in-the-Pew. You shout your sins into the face of a plastic priest.

—*Johnny Carson*

1,287

When I was a kid in the ghetto, a gang started going around harassing people, so some of the toughest kids formed a gang called The Sharks to stop them. The other gang was called The Jehovah's Witnesses.

—*Charles Kosar*

1,288

Jesus was a Jew, yes, but only on his mother's side.

—*Archie Bunker*

1,289

Unless you hate your father and mother and wife and brothers and sisters and, yes, even your own life, you can't be my disciple.

—*Jesus Christ (0?–32?), if*
St. Luke is to be believed
(see Luke 14:26)

1,290

Jesus was a crackpot.

—*Bhagwan Shree Rajneesh*

1,291

Let Bhagwans be Bhagwans.

—*Headline considered by*
The Washington Post

1,292

Jesus died too soon. If he had lived to my age he would have repudiated his doctrine.

—*Friedrich Nietzsche (1844–1900)*

Nietzsche was stupid and abnormal.

—*Leo Tolstoy (1828–1910)*

1,293

I'm not going to climb into the ring with Tolstoy.

—*Ernest Hemingway (1898–1961)*

1,294

Hemingway was a jerk.

—*Harold Robbins (1916–1997)*

1,295

The purpose of life is a life of purpose.

—*Robert Byrne*

1,296

I like life. It's something to do.

—*Ronnie Shakes*

1,297

Life is divided into the horrible and the miserable.

—*Woody Allen*

1,298

Life is just a bowl of pits.

—*Rodney Dangerfield*

1,299
Life being what it is, one dreams of revenge.
—*Paul Gauguin (1848–1903)*

1,300
If I had my life to live over, I'd live over a delicatessen.
—*Unknown*

1,301

Man is more an ape than many of the apes.
—*Friedrich Nietzsche (1844–1900)*

Nietzsche was stupid and abnormal.
—*Leo Tolstoy (1828–1910)*

1,302

He who looketh upon a woman loseth a fender.
—*Sign in auto repair shop*

1,303

Mahatma Gandhi was what wives wish their husbands were: thin, tan, and moral.

—*Unknown*

1,304

The only time a woman really succeeds in changing a man is when he's a baby.
—*Natalie Wood (1938–1981)*

1,305

I'm a disgrace to my sex. I should work in an Arabian palace as a eunuch.

—*Woody Allen*

1,306

Girls are always running through my mind. They don't dare walk.

—*Andy Gibb (1958–1988)*

1,307

One good thing about being a man is that men don't have to talk to each other.

—*Peter Cocotas*

1,308

Of all the wild beasts of land or sea, the wildest is woman.

—*Menander (342?–291? B.C.)*

1,309

A woman is always buying something.

—*Ovid (43 B.C.–A.D. 18)*

1,310

Nothing is more intolerable than a wealthy woman.

—*Juvenal (60?–140?)*

1,311

A woman talks to one man, looks at a second, and thinks of a third.

—*Bhartrihari, c. 625*

1,312

Woman was God's second mistake.

—*Friedrich Nietzsche (1844–1900)*

Nietzsche was stupid and abnormal.

—*Leo Tolstoy (1828–1910)*

1,313

Women speak two languages, one of which is verbal.

—*Steve Rubenstein*

1,314

Women who seek to be equal with men lack ambition.

—*Timothy Leary*

1,315

Women are like elephants to me. I like to look at them but I wouldn't want to own one.

—*W. C. Fields (1880–1946)*

1,316

Phyllis Schlafly speaks for all American women who oppose equal rights for themselves.

—*Andy Rooney*

1,317

Housework can kill you if done right.

—*Erma Bombeck (1927–1996)*

1,318

What do women want? Shoes.

—*Mimi Pond*

1,319

Shopping tip: You can get shoes for 85 cents at bowling alleys.

—*Al Clethen*

1,320

Can you imagine a world without men? No crime and lots of happy fat women.

—*Sylvia (Nicole Hollander)*

1,321

Veni, vidi, Visa. (*We came, we saw, we went shopping.*)

—*Jan Barrett*

1,322

Any girl can be glamorous; all you have to do is stand still and look stupid.

—*Hedy Lamarr (1913–2000)*

1,323

If they could put one man on the moon, why can't they put them all?

—*Unknown*

1,324

Good breeding consists of concealing how much we think of ourselves and how little we think of the other person.

—*Mark Twain (1835–1910)*

1,325

Charm is a way of getting the answer yes without asking a clear question.

—*Albert Camus (1913–1960)*

1,326

Good taste is the worst vice ever invented.

—*Dame Edith Sitwell (1887–1964)*

1,327

We are all born charming, fresh, and spontaneous and must be civilized before we are fit to participate in society.

—*Miss Manners (Judith Martin)*

1,328

Cats are smarter than dogs. You can't get eight cats to pull a sled through snow.

—*Jeff Valdez*

1,329

Dogs come when they're called; cats take a message and
get back to you.

—*Missy Dizick*

1,330

If a cat spoke, it would say things like "Hey, I don't see the
problem here."

—*Roy Blount, Jr.*

1,331

A man who was loved by 300 women singled me out to
live with him. Why? I was the only one without a cat.

—*Elayne Boosler*

1,332

I take my pet lion to church every Sunday. He has to eat.

—*Marty Pollio*

1,333

Cute rots the intellect.

—*Garfield (Jim Davis)*

1,334

Distrust any enterprise that requires new clothes.

—*Henry David Thoreau (1817–1862)*

1,335

Fashions are induced epidemics.

—*George Bernard Shaw (1856–1950)*

1,336

You'd be surprised how much it costs to look this cheap.

—*Dolly Parton*

1,337

There is a new awareness of style in the Soviet Union. The premier's wife recently appeared on the cover of *House and Tractor.*

—*Johnny Carson*

1,338

I should warn you that underneath these clothes I'm wearing boxer shorts and I know how to use them.

—*Robert Orben*

1,339

What you have when everyone wears the same playclothes for all occasions, is addressed by nickname, expected to participate in Show and Tell, and bullied out of any desire for privacy, is not democracy; it is kindergarten.

—*Miss Manners (Judith Martin)*

1,340

Being named as one of the world's best-dressed men
doesn't necessarily mean that I am a bad person.
—*Anthony R. Cucci, Mayor of Jersey City*

1,341

In love there are two evils: war and peace.

—*Horace (65–8 B.C.)*

1,342

Love is the crocodile on the river of desire.

—*Bhartrihari (c. 625)*

1,343

Love is what happens to men and women who don't know each other.

—*W. Somerset Maugham (1874–1965)*

1,344

Love is blond.

—*Herbert Gold's mother*

1,345

The trouble with loving is that pets don't last long enough and people last too long.

—*Unknown*

1,346

A man always remembers his first love with special tenderness, but after that he begins to bunch them.

—*H. L. Mencken (1880–1956)*

1,347

When you are in love with someone you want to be near him all the time, except when you are out buying things and charging them to him.

—*Miss Piggy, according to Henry Beard,*
Miss Piggy's Guide to Life, *1981*

1,348

Better to have loved and lost a short person than never to have loved a tall.

—*David Chambless*

1,349

One of the advantages of living alone is that you don't have to wake up in the arms of a loved one.

—*Marion Smith*

1,350

Dear Sweetheart:
    Last night I thought of you.
    At least I think it was you.
—*Love letter by Snoopy (Charles Schulz, 1922–2000)*

1,351

In the race for love, I was scratched.

—*Joan Davis (1912–1961)*

1,352

Outside every thin woman is a fat man trying to get in.

—*Katherine Whitehorn*

1,353

Sex is natural, but not if it's done right.

—*Unknown*

1,354

Sex is good, but not as good as fresh sweet corn.

—*Garrison Keillor*

1,355

There is hardly anyone whose sexual life, if it were broadcast, would not fill the world at large with surprise and horror.

—*W. Somerset Maugham (1874–1965)*

1,356

There is nothing a young man can get by wenching but duels, the clap, and bastards.

—*Kathleen Winsor*

1,357

It is more fun contemplating somebody else's navel than your own.

—*Arthur Hoppe*

1,358

Of all the sexual aberrations, perhaps the most peculiar is chastity.

—*Remy de Gourmont (1858–1915)*

1,359

We may eventually come to realize that chastity is no more a virtue than malnutrition.

—*Alex Comfort (1920–2000)*

1,360

I used to be a virgin, but I gave it up because there was no money in it.

—*Marsha Warfield*

1,361

A terrible thing happened again last night—nothing.

—*Phyllis Diller*

1,362

Celibacy is not hereditary.

—*Guy Goden*

1,363

Kissing is a means of getting two people so close together
that they can't see anything wrong with each other.

—*René Yasenek*

1,364

Oh, what lies there are in kisses!

—Heinrich Heine (1797–1856)

1,365

Whenever I'm caught between two evils, I take the one I've never tried.

—Mae West (1892–1980)

1,366

It is better to copulate than never.

—Robert Heinlein (1907–1988)

1,367

Vasectomy means never having to say you're sorry.

—Unknown

1,368

Last night I discovered a new form of oral contraceptive. I asked a girl to go to bed with me and she said no.

—Woody Allen

1,369

I told my girl friend that unless she expressed her feelings and told me what she liked I wouldn't be able to please her, so she said, "Get off me."

—Garry Shandling

1,370

She was so wild that when she made French toast she got her tongue caught in the toaster.

—*Rodney Dangerfield*

1,371

I'm too shy to express my sexual needs except over the phone to people I don't know.

—*Garry Shandling*

1,372

Sex Appeal—Give Generously

—*Bumper sticker*

1,373

How did sex come to be thought of as dirty in the first place? God must have been a Republican.

—*Will Durst*

1,374

Before we make love, my husband takes a pain killer.

—*Joan Rivers*

1,375

My wife was in labor with our first child for thirty-two hours and I was faithful to her the whole time.

—*Jonathan Katz*

1,376

My wife has cut our lovemaking down to once a month, but I know two guys she's cut out entirely.

—*Rodney Dangerfield*

1,377

Chains required, whips optional.

—*California highway sign*

1,378

The fantasy of every Australian man is to have two women—one cleaning and the other dusting.

—*Maureen Murphy*

1,379
Ouch! You're on My Hair!

—*Sex manual title suggested by Richard Lewis*

1,380
The difference between pornography and erotica is lighting.

—*Gloria Leonard*

1,381
If homosexuality were normal, God would have created Adam and Bruce.

—*Anita Bryant*

1,382
Rub-a-dub-dub
Three men in a tub
And that's on a slow night.

—*Sign in a San Francisco bath house*

1,383
Never play leapfrog with a unicorn.

—*Unknown*

1,384

Get in good physical condition before submitting to
bondage. You should be fit to be tied.

—*Robert Byrne*

1,385

I caused my husband's heart attack. In the middle of love-making I took the paper bag off my head. He dropped the Polaroid and keeled over and so did the hooker. It would have taken me half an hour to untie myself and call the paramedics, but fortunately the Great Dane could dial.

—*Joan Rivers*

1,386

A British mother's advice to her daughter on how to survive the wedding night: "Close your eyes and think of England."

—*Pierre Daninos*

1,387

I have so little sex appeal that my gynecologist calls me "sir."

—*Joan Rivers*

1,388

What men call gallantry and gods adultery
Is much more common where the climate's sultry.

—*Lord Byron (1788–1824)*

1,389

Of all the tame beasts, I hate sluts.

—*John Ray (1627?–1705)*

1,390

I'd like to have a girl, and I'm saving my money so I can get a good one.

—*Bob Nickman*

1,391

A relationship is what happens between two people who are waiting for something better to come along.

—*Unknown*

1,392

I have such poor vision I can date anybody.

—*Garry Shandling*

1,393

It's relaxing to go out with my ex-wife because she already knows I'm an idiot.

—*Warren Thomas*

1,394

I used to go out exclusively with actresses and other female impersonators.

—*Mort Sahl*

1,395

The trouble with living in sin is the shortage of closet space.

—*Missy Dizick*

1,396

The fickleness of the women I love is only equalled by the infernal constancy of the women who love me.

—*George Bernard Shaw (1856–1950)*

1,397

Burt Reynolds once asked me out. I was in his room.

—*Phyllis Diller*

1,398

He's the kind of man a woman would have to marry to get rid of.

—*Mae West (1892–1980)*

1,399

Brains are an asset, if you hide them.

—*Mae West (1892–1980)*

1,400

He promised me earrings, but he only pierced my ears.

—*Arabian saying*

1,401

Marriage is a necessary evil.

—*Menander (342?–291? B.C.)*

1,402

Marriage is the only war in which you sleep with the enemy.

—*Unknown*

1,403

Nothing anybody tells you about marriage helps.

—*Max Siegel*

1,404

There is so little difference between husbands you might as well keep the first.

—*Adela Rogers St. Johns (1894–1988)*

1,405

Marriage is really tough because you have to deal with feelings and lawyers.

—*Richard Pryor*

1,406

Marriage could catch on again because living together is not quite living and not quite together. Premarital sex slowly evolves into premarital sox.

—*Gerald Nachman*

1,407

Marriage is part of a sort of 50's revival package that's back in vogue along with neckties and naked ambition.

—*Calvin Trillin*

1,408

I'll have to marry a virgin. I can't stand criticism.

—*From the movie* Out of Africa, *1985*

1,409

If you are living with a man, you don't have to worry about whether you should sleep with him after dinner.

—*Stephanie Brush*

1,410

I'd like to get married because I like the idea of a man being required by law to sleep with me every night.

—*Carrie Snow*

1,411

Alimony is like buying oats for a dead horse.

—*Arthur Baer (1896–1975)*

1,412

I hated my marriage, but I always had a great place to park.

—*Gerald Nachman*

1,413

Where I come from, when a Catholic marries a Lutheran it is considered the first step on the road to Minneapolis.

—*Garrison Keillor*

1,414

I was married by a judge. I should have asked for a jury.

—*George Burns (1896–1996)*

1,415

I wouldn't trust my husband with a young woman for five minutes, and he's been dead for 25 years.

—*Brendan Behan's mother*

1,416

I want a girl just like the girl that married dear old Dad.

—*Lyrics by Oedipus Rex*

1,417

Adultery is a meanness and a stealing, a taking away from someone what should be theirs, a great selfishness, and surrounded and guarded by lies lest it should be found out. And out of the meanness and selfishness and lying flow love and joy and peace beyond anything that can be imagined.

—*Dame Rose Macaulay (1881–1958)*

1,418

I am a marvelous housekeeper. Every time I leave a man I keep his house.

—*Zsa Zsa Gabor*

1,419

The happiest time in any man's life is just after the first divorce.

—*John Kenneth Galbraith*

1,420

One reason people get divorced is that they run out of gift ideas.

—*Robert Byrne*

1,421

I've married a few people I shouldn't have, but haven't we all?

—*Mamie Van Doren*

1,422

What I like about masturbation is that you don't have to talk afterwards.

—*Milos Forman*

1,423

If sex is so personal, why do we have to share it with someone?

—*Unknown*

1,424

Enjoy yourself. If you can't enjoy yourself, enjoy somebody else.

—*Jack Schaefer*

1,425

The only reason I feel guilty about masturbation is that I do it so badly.

—*David Steinberg*

1,426

Philip Roth is a good writer, but I wouldn't want to shake hands with him.

—*Jacqueline Susann (1921–1974)*
after reading Portnoy's Complaint

1,427

I can't believe I forgot to have children.

—*Unknown*

1,428

If God wanted sex to be fun, He wouldn't have included children as punishment.

—*Ed Bluestone*

1,429

I am determined my children shall be brought up in their father's religion, if they can find out what it is.

—*Charles Lamb (1775–1834)*

1,430

I could now afford all the things I never had as a kid, if I didn't have kids.

—*Robert Orben*

1,431

My mother had a great deal of trouble with me, but I think she enjoyed it.

—*Mark Twain (1835–1910)*

1,432

I'll probably never have children because I don't believe in touching people for any reason.

—*Paula Poundstone*

1,433

I take my children everywhere, but they always find their way back home.

—*Robert Orben*

1,434

My parents put a live teddy bear in my crib.

—*Woody Allen*

1,435

I phoned my dad to tell him I had stopped smoking. He called me a quitter.

—*Steven Pearl*

1,436

Never lend your car to anyone to whom you have given birth.

—*Erma Bombeck (1927–1996)*

1,437

The best revenge is to live long enough to be a problem to your children.

—*Unknown*

1,438

Children today are tyrants. They contradict their parents, gobble their food, and tyrannize their teachers.

—*Socrates (470–399 B.C.)*

1,439

An ugly baby is a very nasty object, and the prettiest is frightful when undressed.

—*Queen Victoria (1819–1901)*

1,440

What is more enchanting than the voices of young people when you can't hear what they say?

—*Logan Pearsall Smith (1865–1946)*

1,441

At my lemonade stand I used to give the first glass away free and charge five dollars for the second glass. The refill contained the antidote.

—*Emo Philips*

1,442

When you are eight years old, nothing is any of your business.

—*Lenny Bruce (1925–1966)*

1,443

What is youth except a man or woman before it is fit to be seen?

—*Evelyn Waugh (1903–1966)*

1,444

My eleven-year-old daughter mopes around the house all day waiting for her breasts to grow.

—*Bill Cosby*

1,445

If you're not beguiling by age twelve, forget it.

—*Lucy (Charles Schulz, 1922–2000)*

1,446

I was so naive as a kid I used to sneak behind the barn and do nothing.

—*Johnny Carson*

1,447

My schoolmates would make love to anything that moved, but I never saw any reason to limit myself.

—*Emo Philips*

1,448

I almost got a girl pregnant in high school. It's costing me a fortune to keep the rabbit on a life-support system.

—*Will Shriner*

1,449

The trouble with the 1980's as compared with the 1970's is that teenagers no longer rebel and leave home.

—*Marion Smith*

1,450

Learning to dislike children at an early age saves a lot of expense and aggravation later in life.

—*Robert Byrne*

1,451

Adolescence is the stage between infancy and adultery.

—*Unknown*

1,452

I like work; it fascinates me. I can sit and look at it for hours.

—*Jerome K. Jerome (1859–1927)*

1,453

Work is for cowards.

—*Pool hustler U. J. Puckett*
in 1984 at age 76

1,454

Always be smarter than the people who hire you.

—*Lena Horne*

1,455

The trouble with unemployment is that the minute you wake up in the morning you're on the job.

—*Slappy White*

1,456

The volume of paper expands to fill the available brief-cases.

—*Jerry Brown*

1,457

Any new venture goes through the following stages: enthusiasm, complication, disillusionment, search for the guilty, punishment of the innocent, and decoration of those who did nothing.

—*Unknown*

1,458

When I realized that what I had turned out to be was a lousy, two-bit pool hustler and drunk, I wasn't depressed at all. I was glad to have a profession.

—*Danny McGoorty (1901–1970)*

1,459

The reason American cities are prosperous is that there is no place to sit down.

—*Alfred J. Talley*

1,460

Gardner's Law: Eighty-seven percent of all people in all professions are incompetent.

—*John Gardner*

1,461

It is time I stepped aside for a less experienced and less able man.

—*Professor Scott Elledge on his retirement from Cornell*

1,462

The only way to succeed is to make people hate you.

—*Josef von Sternberg (1894–1969)*

1,463

A man can't get rich if he takes proper care of his family.

—*Navajo saying*

1,464

I believe that the power to make money is a gift from God.

—*John D. Rockefeller (1839–1937)*

1,465

It is the wretchedness of being rich that you have to live with rich people.

—*Logan Pearsall Smith (1865–1946)*

1,466

Never invest in anything that eats or needs repairing.

—*Billy Rose (1899–1966)*

1,467

Every morning I get up and look through the Forbes list of the richest people in America. If I'm not there, I go to work.

—*Robert Orben*

1,468

I enjoy being a highly overpaid actor.

—*Roger Moore*

1,469

Buy old masters. They bring better prices than young mistresses.

—*Lord Beaverbrook (1879–1964)*

1,470

The income tax has made liars out of more Americans than golf.

—*Will Rogers (1879–1935)*

1,471

Why is there so much month left at the end of the money?

—*Unknown*

1,472

Today you can go to a gas station and find the cash register open and the toilets locked. They must think toilet paper is worth more than money.

—*Joey Bishop*

1,473

Enjoy money while you have it. Shrouds don't have pockets.

—*Virginia Esberg's grandmother*

1,474

It is no disgrace to be poor, but it might as well be.

—*Jim Grue*

1,475

So he's short . . . he can stand on his wallet.

—*Jewish mother*

1,476

Business is a good game—lots of competition and a minimum of rules. You keep score with money.

—*Atari founder Nolan Bushnell*

1,477

Economists are people who work with numbers but who don't have the personality to be accountants.

—*Unknown*

1,478

An economist's guess is liable to be as good as anybody else's.

—*Will Rogers (1879–1935)*

1,479

Mathematics has given economics rigor, but alas, also mortis.

—*Robert Heilbroner*

1,480

Organized crime in America takes in over forty billion dollars a year and spends very little on office supplies.

—*Woody Allen*

1,481

Getting caught is the mother of invention.

—*Robert Byrne*

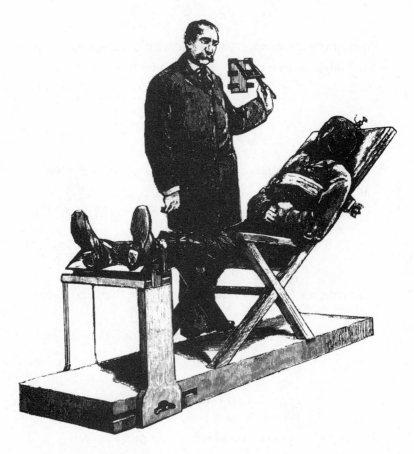

1,482

Capital punishment is either an affront to humanity or a
potential parking place.

—*Larry Brown*

1,483

I believe that people would be alive today if there were a
death penalty.

—*Nancy Reagan*

1,484

There is never enough time, unless you're serving it.

—Malcolm Forbes (1919–1990)

1,485

At age fifty, every man has the face he deserves.

—George Orwell (1903–1950)

1,486

The secret of staying young is to live honestly, eat slowly, and lie about your age.

—Lucille Ball (1911–1989)

1,487

I am in the prime of senility.

—Joel Chandler Harris (1848–1908)
at age 58

1,488

I am not young enough to know everything.

—Oscar Wilde (1854–1900)

1,489

The closing years of life are like the end of a masquerade party, when the masks are dropped.

—Arthur Schopenhauer (1788–1860)

1,490

Old age is not for sissies.

—*Variously ascribed*

1,491

Old age is when the liver spots show through your gloves.

—*Phyllis Diller*

1,492

Old age is like a plane flying through a storm. Once you are aboard there is nothing you can do.

—*Golda Meir (1898–1978)*

1,493

When I was young there was no respect for the young, and now that I am old there is no respect for the old. I missed out coming and going.

—*J. B. Priestley (1894–1984)*

1,494

Middle age begins with the first mortgage and ends when you drop dead.

—*Herb Caen*

1,495

You know you're old when you notice how young the derelicts are getting.

—*Jeanne Phillips*

1,496

My grandfather used to make home movies and edit out the joy.

—*Richard Lewis*

1,497

I smoke cigars because at my age if I don't have something to hang onto I might fall down.

—*George Burns (1896–1996)*

1,498

The hardest years in life are those between ten and seventy.

—*Helen Hayes at age 83*

1,499

After age seventy it's patch, patch, patch.

—*Jimmy Stewart (1908–1997)*

1,500

You have to be an antique to appreciate them.

—*Fay Madigan Lange*

1,501

Death is just a distant rumor to the young.

—*Andy Rooney*

1,502

They say such nice things about people at their funerals that it makes me sad to realize that I'm going to miss mine by just a few days.

—*Garrison Keillor*

1,503

Big deal! I'm used to dust.

—*Gravestone epitaph requested by Erma Bombeck*
(1927–1996)

1,504

There is no reason for me to die. I already died in Altoona.

—*George Burns (1896–1996)*

1,505

I know a man who gave up smoking, drinking, sex, and rich food. He was healthy right up to the time he killed himself.

—*Johnny Carson*

1,506

The only thing wrong with immortality is that it tends to go on forever.

—*Herb Caen*

1,507

There will be sex after death; we just won't be able to feel it.

—*Lily Tomlin*

1,508

Dying ought to be done in black and white. It is simply not a colorful activity.

—*Russell Baker*

1,509

What Einstein was to physics, what Babe Ruth was to home runs, what Emily Post was to table manners . . . that's what Edward G. Robinson was to dying like a dirty rat.

—*Russell Baker*

1,510

Idealism is what precedes experience; cynicism is what follows.

—*David T. Wolf*

1,511

The cynics are right nine times out of ten.

—*H. L. Mencken (1880–1956)*

1,512

No matter how cynical you get, it is impossible to keep up.

—*Lily Tomlin*

1,513

When there are two conflicting versions of a story, the wise course is to believe the one in which people appear at their worst.

—*H. Allen Smith (1906–1976)*

1,514

Half the people in America are faking it.

—*Robert Mitchum (1917–1997)*

1,515

Ignorance is the mother of admiration.

—*George Chapman (1599?–1634)*

1,516

I was going to buy a copy of *The Power of Positive Thinking,* and then I thought: What the hell good would that do?

—*Ronnie Shakes*

1,517

Nothing matters very much, and few things matter all.

—*Arthur Balfour (1848–1930)*

1,518

Doing a thing well is often a waste of time.

—*Robert Byrne*

1,519

Happiness is a Chinese meal; sorrow is a nourishment forever.

—*Carolyn Kizer*

1,520

There is no happiness; there are only moments of happiness.

—*Spanish proverb*

1,521

I am a kind of paranoiac in reverse. I suspect people of plotting to make me happy.

—*J. D. Salinger*

1,522

Happiness is having a large, loving, caring, close-knit family in another city.

—*George Burns (1896–1996)*

1,523

O Lord, help me to be pure, but not yet.

—*St. Augustine (354–430)*

1,524

An evil mind is a constant solace.

—*Unknown*

1,525

A thing worth having is a thing worth cheating for.

—*W. C. Fields (1880–1946)*

1,526

He without benefit of scruples
His fun and money soon quadruples.

—*Ogden Nash (1902–1971)*

1,527

Living with a conscience is like driving a car with the brakes on.

—*Budd Schulberg*

1,528

In order to preserve your self-respect, it is sometimes necessary to lie and cheat.

—*Robert Byrne*

1,529

It has been my experience that folks who have no vices have very few virtues.

—*Abraham Lincoln (1809–1865)*

1,530

The price of purity is purists.

—*Calvin Trillin*

1,531

A bore is someone who, when you ask him how he is, tells you.

—*Variously ascribed*

1,532

Some people stay longer in an hour than others do in a month.

—*William Dean Howells (1837–1920)*

1,533

There are very few people who don't become more interesting when they stop talking.

—*Mary Lowry*

1,534

The opposite of talking isn't listening. The opposite of talking is waiting.

—*Fran Lebowitz*

1,535

When the Emperor Constantine turned Christian, he banned the eating of sausage, which of course immediately created a whole army of sausage bootleggers and may explain why Al Capone always looked like a sausage.

—*Donald E. Westlake*

1,536

A louse in the cabbage is better than no meat at all.

—*Pennsylvania Dutch proverb*

1,537

The food in Yugoslavia is fine if you like pork tartare.

—*Ed Begley, Jr.*

1,538

Eating an artichoke is like getting to know someone really well.

—*Willi Hastings*

1,539

I will not eat oysters. I want my food dead—not sick, not wounded—dead.

—*Woody Allen*

1,540

Only Irish coffee provides in a single glass all four essential food groups: alcohol, caffeine, sugar, and fat.

—*Alex Levine*

1,541

Cogito ergo dim sum. (*Therefore I think these are pork buns.*)

—*Robert Byrne*

1,542

Anybody who doesn't think that the best hamburger place in the world is in his home town is a sissy.

—*Calvin Trillin*

1,543

You can find your way across the country using burger joints the way a navigator uses stars.

—*Charles Kuralt (1934–1997)*

1,544

Part of the secret of success in life is to eat what you like and let the food fight it out inside.

—*Mark Twain (1835–1910)*

1,545

We didn't starve, but we didn't eat chicken unless we were sick, or the chicken was.

—*Bernard Malamud (1914–1986)*

1,546

In Mexico we have a word for sushi: bait.

—*José Simon*

1,547

Everything you see I owe to spaghetti.

—*Sophia Loren*

1,548

Blow in its ear.

—*Johnny Carson on the best way
to thaw a frozen turkey*

1,549

If you want to look young and thin, hang around old fat
people.

—*Jim Eason*

1,550

The cherry tomato is a marvelous invention, producing as
it does a satisfactorily explosive squish when bitten.

—*Miss Manners (Judith Martin)*

1,551

I prefer Hostess fruit pies to pop-up toaster tarts because
they don't require so much cooking.

—*Carrie Snow*

1,552

You are where you eat.

—*Unknown*

1,553

No diet will remove all the fat from your body because the brain is entirely fat. Without a brain you might look good, but all you could do is run for public office.

—*Covert Bailey*

1,554

I can get along with anybody . . . provided they're fat.

—*Susan Richman*

1,555

Anybody who believes that the way to a man's heart is through his stomach flunked geography.

—*Robert Byrne*

1,556

The waist is a terrible thing to mind.

—*Ziggy (Tom Wilson)*

1,557

I have learned to spell hors d'oeuvres,
Which grates on many people's nerves.

—*Unknown*

1,558

The trouble with eating Italian food is that five or six days later you're hungry again.

—*George Miller*

1,559

I don't eat salmon because I identify too much with spawning, thrashing around, and death.

—*Michael Feldman*

1,560

Statistics show that of those who contract the habit of eating, very few survive.

—*Wallace Irwin (1875–1959)*

1,561

Marriage is not merely sharing the fettucini, but sharing the burden of finding the fettucini restaurant in the first place.

—*Calvin Trillin*

1,562

My wife and I tried to breakfast together, but we had to stop or our marriage would have been wrecked.

—*Winston Churchill (1874–1965)*

1,563

My doctor gave me two weeks to live. I hope they're in August.

—*Ronnie Shakes*

1,564

The trouble with heart disease is that the first symptom is often hard to deal with: sudden death.

—*Michael Phelps, M.D.*

1,565

One of my problems is that I internalize everything. I can't express anger; I grow a tumor instead.

—*Woody Allen*

1,566

A male gynecologist is like an auto mechanic who has never owned a car.

—*Carrie Snow*

1,567

After a year in therapy, my psychiatrist said to me, "Maybe life isn't for everyone."

—*Larry Brown*

1,568

Half of analysis is anal.

—*Marty Indik*

1,569

Why should I tolerate a perfect stranger at the bedside of my mind?

—*Vladimir Nabokov (1899–1977)*
on psychoanalysis

1,570

People who say you're just as old as you feel are all wrong, fortunately.

—*Russell Baker*

1,571

To reduce stress, avoid excitement. Spend more time with your spouse.

—*Robert Orben*

1,572

Nancy Reagan has agreed to be the first artificial heart donor.

—*Andrea C. Michaels*

1,573
Be true to your teeth or your teeth will be false to you.
—*Dental proverb*

1,574
You're ugly. Not only that, you need a root canal.
—*James J. Garrett, D.D.S.*

1,575

Attention to health is life's greatest hindrance.

—Plato (427?–348? B.C.)

Plato was a bore.

—Friedrich Nietzsche (1844–1900)

Nietzsche was stupid and abnormal.

—Leo Tolstoy (1828–1910)

1,576

Never give a party if you will be the most interesting person there.

—Mickey Friedman

1,577

Support wildlife. Throw a party.

—Unknown

1,578

Cockroaches and socialites are the only things that can stay up all night and eat anything.

—Herb Caen

1,579

Never mistake endurance for hospitality.

—Unknown

1,580

Nothing spoils a good party like a genius.

—*Elsa Maxwell (1883–1963)*

1,581

For a single woman, preparing for company means wiping the lipstick off the milk carton.

—*Elayne Boosler*

1,582

In America, you can always find a party. In Russia, the party always finds you.

—*Yakov Smirnoff*

1,583

The best thing about a cocktail party is being asked to it.

—*Gerald Nachman*

1,584

There is nothing for a case of nerves like a case of beer.

—*Joan Goldstein*

1,585

Reminds me of my safari in Africa. Somebody forgot the corkscrew and for several days we had to live on nothing but food and water.

—*W. C. Fields (1880–1946)*

1,586

Sometimes too much to drink is barely enough.

—*Mark Twain (1835–1910)*

1,587

Like a camel, I can go without a drink for seven days—
and have on several horrible occasions.

—*Herb Caen*

1,588

My grandmother is over eighty and still doesn't need
glasses. Drinks right out of the bottle.

—*Henny Youngman (1906–1998)*

1,589

There is no law against composing music when one has no ideas whatsoever. The music of Wagner, therefore, is perfectly legal.

—*The* National, *Paris, 1850*

1,590

The prelude to *Tristan and Isolde* sounded as if a bomb had fallen into a large music factory and had thrown all the notes into confusion.

—*The* Tribune, *Berlin, 1871*

1,591

The prelude to *Tristan and Isolde* reminds me of the Italian painting of the martyr whose intestines are slowly being unwound from his body on a reel.

—*Eduard Hanslick (1825–1904), 1868*

1,592

Wagner drives the nail into your head with swinging hammer blows.

—*P. A. Fiorentino (1806–1864), Paris, 1867*

1,593

9W.

    Answer to the question: Do you spell your name with a V, Mr. Vagner?

—*Steve Allen (1921–2000)*

1,594

A gentleman is a man who can play the accordion but doesn't.

—Unknown

1,595

There are some experiences in life which should not be demanded twice from any man, and one of them is listening to the Brahms Requiem.

—George Bernard Shaw (1856–1950)

1,596

Classical music is music written by famous dead foreigners.

—*Arlene Heath*

1,597

The main thing the public demands of a composer is that he be dead.

—*Arthur Honegger (1892–1955)*

1,598

Do it big or stay in bed.

—*Opera producer Larry Kelly*

1,599

Assassins!

—*Arturo Toscanini (1867–1957) to his orchestra*

1,600

I only know two pieces—one is *Clair de Lune* and the other one isn't.

—*Victor Borge (1909–2000)*

1,601

Elvis Presley had nothing to do with excellence, just myth.

—*Marlon Brando*

1,602

Anybody who has listened to certain kinds of music, or read certain kinds of poetry, or heard certain kinds of performances on the concertina, will admit that even suicide has its brighter aspects.

—*Stephen Leacock (1869–1944)*

1,603

MTV is the lava lamp of the 1980's.

—*Doug Ferrari*

1,604

When I was young we didn't have MTV; we had to take drugs and go to concerts.

—*Steven Pearl*

1,605

Music is essentially useless, as life is.

—*George Santayana (1863–1952)*

1,606

Show me a good loser and I'll show you a loser.

—*Unknown*

1,607

Show me a good loser and I'll show you an idiot.

—*Leo Durocher (1905–1991)*

1,608

Try to hate your opponent. Even if you are playing your grandmother, try to beat her fifty to nothing. If she already has three, try to beat her fifty to three.

—*Danny McGoorty (1901–1969), billiard player*

1,609

I probably couldn't play for me. I wouldn't like my attitude.

—*John Thompson,*
Georgetown basketball coach

1,610

A team should be an extension of the coach's personality. My teams were arrogant and obnoxious.

—*Al McGuire, former basketball coach*

1,611

My toughest fight was with my first wife.

—*Muhammad Ali*

1,612

Hurting people is my business.

—*Sugar Ray Robinson (1921–1989)*

1,613

Football players, like prostitutes, are in the business of ruining their bodies for the pleasure of strangers.

—*Merle Kessler*

1,614

I'm no different from anybody else with two arms, two
legs, and forty-two hundred hits.

—*Pete Rose*

1,615

Any pitcher who throws at a batter and deliberately tries to hit him is a communist.

—*Alvin Dark, former baseball coach*

1,616

The highlight of my baseball career came in Philadelphia's Connie Mack Stadium when I saw a fan fall out of the upper deck. When he got up and walked away the crowd booed.

—Bob Uecker

1,617

One night we play like King Kong, the next night like Fay Wray.

—Terry Kennedy, catcher for the San Diego Padres

1,618

If I ever needed a brain transplant, I'd choose a sports-writer because I'd want a brain that had never been used.

—Norm Van Brocklin (1926–1983)

1,619

Stuffed deer heads on walls are bad enough, but it's worse when they are wearing dark glasses and have streamers and ornaments in their antlers because then you know they were enjoying themselves at a party when they were shot.

—Ellen DeGeneres

1,620

Golf is a game with the soul of a 1956 Rotarian.

—*Bill Mandel*

1,621

Golf is the most fun you can have without taking your clothes off.

—*Chi Chi Rodriguez*

1,622

If Borg's parents hadn't liked the name, he might never have been Bjorn.

—Marty Indik

1,623

The Rose Bowl is the only bowl I've ever seen that I didn't have to clean.

—Erma Bombeck (1927–1996)

1,624

How could I lose to such an idiot?

—A shout from chess grandmaster
Aaron Nimzovich (1886–1935)

1,625

I hate all sports as rabidly as a person who likes sports hates common sense.

—H. L. Mencken (1880–1956)

1,626

Running is an unnatural act, except from enemies and to the bathroom.

—Unknown

1,627

I believe that professional wrestling is clean and everything else in the world is fixed.

—Frank Deford

1,628

Art, like morality, consists of drawing the line somewhere.
—G. K. Chesterton (1874–1936)

1,629

These is not art to me, all these squares and things. Real art has, you know, like a madonna in it.

—*Unknown (from the guest book at an exhibition of modern art)*

1,630

I'm glad the old masters are all dead, and I only wish they had died sooner.

—*Mark Twain (1835–1910)*

1,631

Give me a museum and I'll fill it.

—*Pablo Picasso (1881–1973)*

1,632

Agree, for the law is costly.

—*William Camden (1551–1623)*

1,633

It is better to be a mouse in a cat's mouth than a man in a lawyer's hands.

—*Spanish proverb*

1,634

Two farmers each claimed to own a certain cow. While one pulled on its head and the other pulled on its tail, the cow was milked by a lawyer.

—*Jewish parable*

1,635

Whatever their other contributions to our society, lawyers could be an important source of protein.

—*Guindon cartoon caption*

1,636

Law school is the opposite of sex. Even when it's good it's lousy.

—*Unknown*

1,637

How to win a case in court: If the law is on your side, pound on the law; if the facts are on your side, pound on the facts; if neither is on your side, pound on the table.

—*Unknown*

1,638

Injustice is relatively easy to bear; what stings is justice.

—*H. L. Mencken (1880–1956)*

1,639

Nobody wants justice.

> —*Alan Dershowitz*

1,640

I'm not an ambulance chaser. I'm usually there before the ambulance.

> —*Melvin Belli (1907–1996)*

1,641

I never travel without my diary. One should always have something sensational to read.

> —*Oscar Wilde (1854–1900)*

1,642

The Irish are a fair people—they never speak well of one another.

> —*Samuel Johnson (1709–1784)*

1,643

There are still parts of Wales where the only concession to gaiety is a striped shroud.

> —*Gwyn Thomas*

1,644

I don't have any idea what I'm doing here. I didn't even know Alaska Airlines had a flight to Leningrad.

—*Bob and Ray*

1,645
In Italy a woman can have a face like a train wreck if she's blonde.

—*Unknown*

1,646
If you are going to America, bring food.

—*Fran Lebowitz*

1,647
California is a great place to live if you're an orange.

—*Fred Allen (1894–1956)*

1,648
In California you lose a point off your IQ every year.

—*Truman Capote (1924–1984)*

1,649
Nothing is wrong with Southern California that a rise in the ocean level wouldn't cure.

—*Ross MacDonald (1915–1983)*

1,650

There are two million interesting people in New York and only seventy-eight in Los Angeles.

—*Neil Simon*

1,651

It is true that I was born in Iowa, but I can't speak for my twin sister.

—*Abigail Van Buren (Dear Abby)*

1,652

Parts of Texas look like Kansas with a goiter.

—*Unknown*

1,653

I have just returned from Boston. It is the only thing to do if you find yourself there.

—*Fred Allen (1894–1956)*

1,654
Thanks to the Interstate Highway System, it is now possible to travel from coast to coast without seeing anything.
—*Charles Kuralt (1934–1997)*

1,655

One of the first things schoolchildren in Texas learn is how to compose a simple declarative sentence without the word *shit* in it.

—*Unknown*

1,656

The town was so dull that when the tide went out it refused to come back.

—*Fred Allen (1894–1956)*

1,657

If you don't miss a few planes during the year you are spending too much time at airports.

—*Paul C. Martin*

1,658

It is now possible for a flight attendant to get a pilot pregnant.

—*Richard J. Ferris,*
president, United Airlines

1,659

Avoid airlines that have anyone's first name in their titles, like Bob's International or Air Fred.

—*Miss Piggy (Henry Beard)*

1,660

If God had intended us to fly, He would never have given us railways.

—*Michael Flanders*

1,661

There are two kinds of air travel in the United States, first class and third world.

—*Bobby Slayton*

1,662

Thank God men cannot as yet fly and lay waste the sky as well as the earth!

—*Henry David Thoreau (1817–1862)*

1,663

Art is I; science is we.

—*Claude Bernard (1813–1878)*

1,664

Life is extinct on other planets because their scientists were more advanced than ours.

—*Unknown*

1,665

A stitch in time would have confused Einstein.

—*Unknown*

1,666

Great moments in science: Einstein discovers that time is actually money.

—*Gary Larson cartoon caption*

1,667

Technological progress is like an axe in the hands of a pathological criminal.

—*Albert Einstein (1879–1955)*

1,668

Technology is a way of organizing the universe so that man doesn't have to experience it.

—*Max Frisch (1911–1991)*

1,669

Horsepower was a wonderful thing when only horses had it.

—*Unknown*

1,670

Men have become the tools of their tools.

—*Henry David Thoreau (1817–1862)*

1,671

The computer is down. I hope it's something serious.

—*Stanton Delaplane*

1,672

Rivers in the United States are so polluted that acid rain makes them cleaner.

—*Andrew Malcolm*

1,673

A two-pound turkey and a fifty-pound cranberry—that's Thanksgiving dinner at Three-Mile Island.

—*Johnny Carson*

1,674

The scientific theory I like best is that the rings of Saturn
are composed entirely of lost airline luggage.

—*Mark Russell*

1,675

Energy experts have announced the development of a new
fuel made from human brain tissue. It's called assohol.

—*George Carlin*

1,676

What a beautiful fix we are in now; peace has been de-
clared.

—*Napoleon Bonaparte (1769–1821)*
after the Treaty of Amiens, 1802

1,677

I thoroughly disapprove of duels. If a man should chal-
lenge me, I would take him kindly and forgivingly by the
hand and lead him to a quiet place and kill him.

—*Mark Twain (1835–1910)*

1,678

There is nothing more exhilarating than to be shot at
without result.

—*Winston Churchill (1874–1965)*

1,679

Nobody ever forgets where he buried the hatchet.

—*Kin Hubbard (1868–1930)*

1,680

Will the last person out of the tunnel turn out the light?

—*Graffito in Saigon, 1973*

1,681

We are what we are.

—Motto of Lake Wobegone,
according to Garrison Keillor

1,682

You gotta live somewhere.

—Motto for Cleveland
suggested by Jimmy Brogan

1,683

It's a living.

—Motto for the U.S. Army
suggested by Mort Sahl

1,684

What died?

—Motto for New Jersey
suggested by Steven Pearl

1,685

What the hell are you looking at?

—License plate slogan for New York
suggested by Steven Pearl

1,686

Eat cheese or die.

—Motto for Wisconsin
suggested by Joel McNally

1,687

Not you.

—Bumper sticker in the state where
the license plate slogan is You've
Got a Friend in Pennsylvania

1,688

You appeal to a small, select group of confused people.

—Message in fortune cookie

1,689

Ignore previous cookie.

—Message in fortune cookie

1,690

You make God sick.

—Message in fortune cookie
received by Rick Reynolds

1,691

There is nothing wrong with Hollywood that six first-class funerals wouldn't solve.

—Unknown

1,692

The length of a film should be directly related to the endurance of the human bladder.

—Alfred Hitchcock (1899–1980)

1,693

A team effort is a lot of people doing what I say.

—Michael Winner, British film director

1,694

You just gotta save Christianity, Richard! You gotta!

*—Loretta Young to Richard the Lionhearted
in the movie* The Crusades, *1935*

1,695

Yer beautiful in yer wrath! I shall keep you, and in responding to my passions, yer hatred will kindle into love.

*—John Wayne as Genghis Khan to Susan Hayward
in the movie* The Conqueror, *1956*

1,696

I've met a lot of hard-boiled eggs in my time, but you—
you're twenty minutes!

—*From the movie* Ace in the Hole, *1951*

1,697

When Elizabeth Taylor meets a man she takes him and
squeezes the life out of him and then throws away the
pulp.

—*Eddie Fisher's mother*

1,698

Elsa Lanchester looks as though butter wouldn't melt in
her mouth, or anywhere else.

—*Maureen O'Hara*

1,699

They used to photograph Shirley Temple through gauze.
They should photograph me through linoleum.

—*Tallulah Bankhead (1903–1968)*

1,700

Clark Gable's ears make him look like a taxicab with the
doors open.

—*Howard Hughes (1905–1976)*

1,701

I saw the sequel to the movie *Clones,* and you know what?
It was the same movie!

—*Jim Samuels*

1,702

If you get to be a really big headliner, you have to be prepared for people throwing bottles at you in the night.

—*Mick Jagger*

1,703

You have to have a talent for having talent.

—*Ruth Gordon (1897–1985)*

1,704

Now that I'm over sixty I'm veering toward respectability.

—*Shelley Winters*

1,705

A starlet is any woman under thirty not actively employed
in a brothel.

—*Unknown*

1,706

The human race is faced with a cruel choice: work or day-
time television.

—*Unknown*

1,707

Television is democracy at its ugliest.

—*Paddy Chayevsky (1923–1982)*

1,708

Television enables you to be entertained in your home by people you wouldn't have in your home.

—*David Frost*

1,709

Imitation is the sincerest form of television.

—*Fred Allen (1894–1956)*

1,710

Never miss a chance to have sex or appear on television.

—*Gore Vidal*

1,711

The cable TV sex channels don't expand our horizons, don't make us better people, and don't come in clearly enough.

—*Bill Maher*

1,712

Babies on television never spit up on the Ultrasuede.

—*Erma Bombeck (1927–1996)*

1,713

Men and nations behave wisely once they have exhausted all the other alternatives.

—*Abba Eban*

1,714

What luck for rulers that men do not think.

—*Adolf Hitler (1889–1945)*

1,715

Every government is run by liars and nothing they say should be believed.

—*I. F. Stone (1907–1989)*

1,716

It is dangerous to be right when the government is wrong.

—*Voltaire (1694–1778)*

1,717

Patriotism is the veneration of real estate above principles.

—*George Jean Nathan (1882–1958)*

1,718

Patriotism is a pernicious, psychopathic form of idiocy.

—*George Bernard Shaw (1856–1950)*

1,719

There is but one way for a newspaperman to look at a politician and that is down.

—*Frank H. Simonds (1878–1936)*

1,720

Don't burn the flag; wash it.

—*Norman Thomas (1884–1968)*

1,721

The reason there are so few female politicians is that it is too much trouble to put makeup on two faces.

—*Maureen Murphy*

1,722

Democracy is being allowed to vote for the candidate you dislike least.

—*Robert Byrne*

1,723

Diplomacy is the art of saying "Nice doggie" until you can find a rock.

—*Will Rogers (1879–1935)*

1,724

An honest politician is one who when he is bought will stay bought.

—*Simon Cameron (1799–1889)*

1,725

A communist is a person who publicly airs his dirty Lenin.

—*Jack Pomeroy*

1,726

A conservative is a man who wants the rules changed so that no one can make a pile the way he did.

—*Gregory Nunn*

1,727

Liberals feel unworthy of their possessions. Conservatives feel they deserve everything they've stolen.

—*Mort Sahl*

1,728

A conservative doesn't want anything to happen for the first time; a liberal feels it should happen, but not now.

—*Mort Sahl*

1,729

Conservatives are satisfied with present evils; liberals want to replace them with new ones.

—*Unknown*

1,730

They dug up an ancient Chinese emperor a while back who was encased in jade. I prefer gold.

—*Ed Koch, Mayor of New York City*

1,731

Too bad the only people who know how to run the country are busy driving cabs and cutting hair.

—*George Burns (1896–1996)*

1,732

Those who are too smart to engage in politics are punished by being governed by those who are dumber.

—*Plato (427?–348? B.C.)*

Plato was a bore.

—*Friedrich Nietzsche (1844–1900)*

Nietzsche was stupid and abnormal.

—*Leo Tolstoy (1828–1910)*

1,733

If the Republicans will stop telling lies about the Democrats, we will stop telling the truth about them.

—*Adlai Stevenson (1900–1965)*

1,734

In America, anyone can become president. That's one of the risks you take.

—*Adlai Stevenson (1900–1965)*

1,735

Calvin Coolidge didn't say much, and when he did he didn't say much.

—*Will Rogers (1879–1935)*

1,736

I think the American public wants a solemn ass as president. And I think I'll go along with them.

—*Calvin Coolidge (1872–1933)*

1,737

He's alive but unconscious, just like Gerald Ford.

—*From the movie* Airplane, *1980*

1,738

Your public servants serve you right.

—*Adlai Stevenson (1900–1965)*

1,739

It's the responsibility of the media to look at the president with a microscope, but they go too far when they use a proctoscope.

—*Richard M. Nixon (1913–1994)*

1,740

When we got into office, the thing that surprised me the most was that things were as bad as we'd been saying they were.

—*John F. Kennedy (1917–1963)*

1,741

It's our fault. We should have given him better parts.

—*Jack Warner on hearing that Ronald Reagan had been elected governor of California*

1,742

I have left orders to be awakened at any time in case of national emergency, even if I'm in a cabinet meeting.

—*Ronald Reagan*

1,743

Ronald Reagan is the first president to be accompanied by a Silly Statement Repair Team.

—*Mark Russell*

1,744

I'm glad Reagan is president. Of course, I'm a professional comedian.

—*Will Durst*

1,745

Reagan is proof that there is life after death.

—*Mort Sahl*

1,746

There is no distinctly American criminal class—except Congress.

—*Mark Twain (1835–1910)*

1,747

They should stop calling Reagan and Gorbachev the two most powerful men in the world. Between the two of them they couldn't bench press a hundred pounds.

—*Al Ordover*

1,748

Gary Hart is just Jerry Brown without the fruit flies.

—*Robert Strauss*

1,749

Author's Prayer:
    Our Father, which art in heaven,
    And has also written a book . . .

—*Unknown*

1,750

The only reason for being a professional writer is that you can't help it.

—*Leo Rosten*

1,751

In Hollywood, writers are considered only the first drafts of human beings.

—*Frank Deford*

1,752

What an author likes to write most is his signature on the back of a check.

—*Brendan Francis*

1,753

Very few things happen at the right time and the rest do not happen at all. The conscientious historian will correct these defects.

—*Herodotus (484–425 B.C.)*

1,754

History will be kind to me for I intend to write it.

—*Winston Churchill (1874–1965)*

1,755

It is a mean thief or a successful author that plunders the dead.

—*Austin O'Malley (1858–1932)*

1,756

The best part of the fiction in many novels is the notice that the characters are purely imaginary.

—*Franklin P. Adams (1881–1960)*

1,757

A detective digs around in the garbage of people's lives. A novelist invents people and then digs around in their garbage.

—*Joe Gores*

1,758
Fiction is obliged to stick to possibilities. Truth isn't.
—*Mark Twain (1835–1910)*

1,759
Truth is shorter than fiction.

—*Irving Cohen*

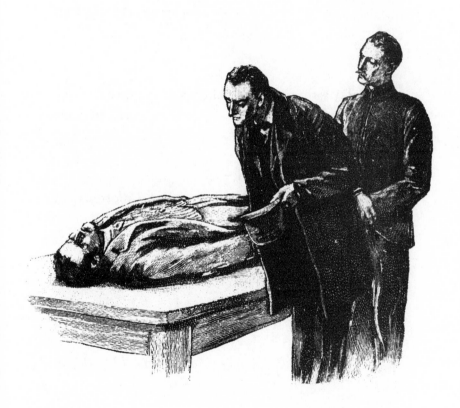

1,760
The only good author is a dead author.
—*Book editor Patrick O'Connor*

1,761

In six pages I can't even say "hello."

—*James Michener (1907–1997)*

1,762

Copy from one, it's plagiarism; copy from two, it's research.

—*Wilson Mizner (1876–1933)*

1,763

Originality is the art of concealing your sources.

—*Unknown*

1,764

There are three rules for writing a novel. Unfortunately, no one knows what they are.

—*W. Somerset Maugham (1874–1965)*

1,765

Get your facts first, then you can distort them as you please.

—*Mark Twain (1835–1910)*

1,766

Why don't you write books people can read?
　　　　　—*Nora Joyce to her husband, James (1882–1941)*

1,767

A Treasury of Filthy Religious Art Masterpieces.
　　　　　—*Book once proposed to Simon & Schuster*

1,768

Changing literary agents is like changing deck chairs on
the *Titanic*.

　　　　　　　　　　—*Unknown*

1,769

You can always tell book people. They are well dressed
and their hair is really clean.
　　　　　—*Overheard by Constance Casey*
　　　　　　at a booksellers' convention

1,770

Teaching has ruined more American novelists than drink.
　　　　　　　　—*Gore Vidal*

1,771

I felt like poisoning a monk.

—*Umberto Eco on why he wrote the novel*
The Name of the Rose

1,772

With the single exception of Homer, there is no eminent writer, not even Sir Walter Scott, whom I despise so entirely as I despise Shakespeare.

—*George Bernard Shaw (1856–1950)*

1,773

I feel very old sometimes . . . I carry on and would not like to die before having emptied a few more buckets of shit on the heads of my fellow men.

—*Gustave Flaubert (1821–1880)*

1,774

To read your own poetry in public is a kind of mental incest.

—*Brendan Behan's father*

1,775

Nobody ever committed suicide while reading a good book, but many have while trying to write one.

—*Robert Byrne*

1,776

All newspaper editorial writers ever do is come down from the hills after the battle is over and shoot the wounded.

—Unknown

1,777

The difference between literature and journalism is that journalism is unreadable and literature is not read.

—Oscar Wilde (1854–1900)

1,778

Advertisements contain the only truths to be relied on in a newspaper.

—Thomas Jefferson (1743–1826)

1,779

Never argue with people who buy ink by the gallon.

—Tommy Lasorda

1,780

Some editors are failed writers, but so are most writers.

—T. S. Eliot (1888–1965)

1,781

Every great man has his disciples, and it is always Judas who writes the biography.

—*Oscar Wilde (1854–1900)*

1,782

Biography lends to death a new terror.

—*Oscar Wilde (1854–1900)*

1,783

Autobiography is now as common as adultery and hardly less reprehensible.

—*Lord Altrincham*

1,784

Autobiography is the last refuse of scoundrels.

—*Henry Gray*

1,785

It's not a bad idea to get in the habit of writing down one's thoughts. It saves one having to bother anyone else with them.

—*Isabel Colegate*

1,786
Book reviewers are little old ladies of both sexes.
—*John O'Hara (1905–1970)*

1,787
Any reviewer who expresses rage and loathing for a novel
is preposterous. He or she is like a person who has put on
full armor and attacked a hot fudge sundae.
—*Kurt Vonnegut*

1,788
People who like this sort of thing will find this the sort of
thing they like.
—*Book review by Abraham Lincoln
(1809–1865)*

1,789
A bad review is like baking a cake with all the best ingre-
dients and having someone sit on it.
—*Danielle Steel*

1,790
Criticism is prejudice made plausible.
—*H. L. Mencken (1880–1956)*

1,791

Praise and criticism are both frauds.

—*Unknown*

1,792

I am sitting in the smallest room in the house. I have your review in front of me. Soon it will be behind me.

—*Max Reger (1873–1916)*

1,793

Quotations are a columnist's bullpen. Stealing someone else's words frequently spares the embarrassment of eating your own.

—*Peter Anderson*

1,794

It is better to be quotable than to be honest.

—*Tom Stoppard*

1,795

This isn't much of a quote book if I'm in it.

—*Richard Dowd, quoted here*
for the first time anywhere

1,796

There will be a rain dance Friday night, weather permitting.

—*George Carlin*

1,797

Gifts are like hooks.

—*Martial (40?–102?)*

1,798

Every time a friend succeeds, I die a little.

—*Gore Vidal*

1,799

The goal of all inanimate objects is to resist man and ultimately defeat him.

—*Russell Baker*

1,800

Cleaning anything involves making something else dirty, but anything can get dirty without something else getting clean.

—*Lawrence J. Peter*

1,801

You know it's not a good wax museum when there are wicks coming out of people's heads.

—*Rick Reynolds*

1,802

Everything changes but the avant garde.

—*Paul Valéry (1871–1945)*

1,803

If you can't laugh at yourself, make fun of other people.

—*Bobby Slayton*

1,804

The world is divided into two classes—invalids and nurses.

—*James McNeill Whistler (1834–1903)*

1,805

Never mistake motion for action.

—*Ernest Hemingway (1889–1961)*

Hemingway was a jerk.

—*Harold Robbins (1916–1997)*

1,806

I wish everybody would go back into the closet.

—*Josefa Heifetz*

1,807

Some luck lies in not getting what you thought you wanted but getting what you have, which once you have got it you may be smart enough to see is what you would have wanted had you known.

—*Garrison Keillor*

1,808

All God's children are not beautiful. Most of God's children are, in fact, barely presentable.

—*Fran Lebowitz*

1,809

Providence protects children and idiots. I know because I have tested it.

—*Mark Twain (1835–1910)*

1,810

The easiest kind of relationship for me is with ten thousand people. The hardest is with one.

—*Joan Baez*

1,811

Five Kids Who Make Your Kids Look Sick
—*Magazine article suggested*
by Garrison Keillor

1,812

I'll not listen to reason. Reason always means what someone else has to say.
—*Elizabeth Cleghorn Gaskell (1810–1865)*

1,813

Suggested magazines:

Crotch: The International Sex Weekly
—*Thomas Berger*

Cocker Spaniel Annual Manual
—*Luther Vrettos*

Gimme! The Magazine of Money
—*Robert Byrne*

The Shining (Formerly Bald World)
—*Robert Byrne*

Beautiful Spot: A Magazine of Parking
—*Calvin Trillin*

Poor Housekeeping (ten times the circulation of
Good Housekeeping)
—*Robert Byrne*

1,814

Nothing is impossible for the man who doesn't have to do it himself.

—*A. H. Weiler*

1,815

A censor is a man who knows more than he thinks you ought to.

—*Granville Hicks (1901–1982)*

1,816

A committee is a cul-de-sac down which ideas are lured and then quietly strangled.

—*Sir Barnett Cocks (c. 1907)*

1,817

As scarce as truth is, the supply has always been in excess of the demand.

—*Josh Billings (1818–1885)*

1,818
I never forget a face, but in your case I'll be glad to make an exception.

—*Groucho Marx (1895–1977)*

1,819
I can mend the break of day, heal a broken heart, and provide temporary relief to nymphomaniacs.

—*Larry Lee*

1,820

Hell is paved with Good Samaritans.

—*William M. Holden*

1,821

Enough.

Definition of "Once."

—*Ambrose Bierce (1842–1914?)*

1,822

Anybody who thinks of going to bed before 12 o'clock is a scoundrel.

—*Samuel Johnson (1709–1784)*

1,823

A fanatic is a man who does what he thinks the Lord would do if He knew the facts of the case.

—*Finley Peter Dunne (1867–1936)*

1,824

All movements go too far.

—*Bertrand Russell (1872–1970)*

1,825

Never engage in a battle of wits with an unarmed person.

—*Unknown*

1,826

Flies spread disease—keep yours zipped.

—*Unknown*

1,827

Ya gotta do what ya gotta do.

—*Sylvester Stallone in the movie* Rocky IV, *1985*

1,828

There is one thing to be said for country clubs; they drain off a lot of people you wouldn't want to associate with anyway.

—*Joseph Prescott*

1,829

I do not want people to be agreeable, as it saves me the trouble of liking them.

—*Jane Austen (1775–1817)*

1,830

A friend in need is a friend to dodge.

—*Unknown*

1,831

Analyzing humor is like dissecting a frog. Few people are interested and the frog dies of it.

—*E. B. White (1899–1985)*

1,832

A lot of people like snow. I find it to be an unnecessary freezing of water.

—*Carl Reiner*

1,833

I've only met four perfect people in my life and I didn't like
any of them.

—*Unknown*

1,834

I dote on his very absence.

—*William Shakespeare (1564–1616)*

Shakespeare is crude, immoral, vulgar, and senseless.

—*Leo Tolstoy (1828–1910)*

1,835

Often it does seem a pity that Noah and his party did not
miss the boat.

—*Mark Twain (1835–1910)*

1,836

You can't depend on your eyes when your imagination is
out of focus.

—*Mark Twain (1835–1910)*

1,837

Only dead fish swim with the stream.

—*Unknown*

1,838

I wish people wouldn't say, "Excuse me," when I *want* them to step on my feet.

—*Karen Elizabeth Gordon*

1,839

Either I've been missing something or nothing has been going on.

—*Karen Elizabeth Gordon*

1,840

There are 350 varieties of shark, not counting loan and pool.

—*L. M. Boyd*

1,841

When in doubt, duck.

—*Malcolm Forbes (1919–1990)*

1,842

American college students are like American colleges— each has half-dulled faculties.

—*James Thurber (1894–1961)*

1,843

It took me twenty years of studied self-restraint, aided by the natural decay of my faculties, to make myself dull enough to be accepted as a serious person by the British public.

—*George Bernard Shaw (1856–1950)*

1,844

The longer I live the more I see that I am never wrong about anything, and that all the pains I have so humbly taken to verify my notions have only wasted my time.

—*George Bernard Shaw (1856–1950)*

1,845

I don't care what you ♥.

—*Bumper sticker*

1,846

I ♠ my pets.

—*Bumper sticker*

1,847

Love your enemies in case your friends turn out to be a bunch of bastards.

—*R. A. Dickson*

1,848

One should forgive one's enemies, but not before they are hanged.

—*Heinrich Heine (1797–1856)*

1,849

Experience teaches you to recognize a mistake when you've made it again.

—*Unknown*

1,850

Good judgment comes from experience, and experience comes from bad judgment.

—*Barry LePatner*

1,851

The trouble with using experience as a guide is that the final exam often comes first and then the lesson.

—*Unknown*

1,852

It's not what we don't know that hurts, it's what we know that ain't so.

—*Will Rogers (1879–1935)*

1,853

The world is a madhouse, so it's only right that it is patrolled by armed idiots.

—*Brendan Behan*

1,854

Consistency requires you to be as ignorant today as you were a year ago.

—*Bernard Berenson (1865–1959)*

1,855

Correct me if I'm wrong, but hasn't the fine line between sanity and madness gotten finer?

—*George Price*

1,856

The reason lightning doesn't strike twice in the same place is that the same place isn't there the second time.

—*Willie Tyler*

1,857

The nail that sticks up gets hammered down.

—*Japanese proverb*

1,858

You can lead a horse to water, but you can't make him float.

—*Unknown*

1,859

If you want a place in the sun, prepare to put up with a few blisters.

—*Abigail Van Buren (Dear Abby)*

1,860

I don't know, I've never been kippled.

Answer to the question: Do you like Kipling?

—*Unknown*

1,861

Ford used to have a better idea; now they don't have a clue.

—*Steve Kravitz*

1,862

I can't believe that out of 100,000 sperm, you were the quickest.

—*Steven Pearl*

1,863

Honesty is the best image.

—*Ziggy (Tom Wilson)*

1,864

Silence is argument carried on by other means.

—*Ernesto "Che" Guevara (1928–1967)*

1,865

Soderquist's Paradox:
 There are more horse's asses than horses.
  —*From* 1,001 Logical Laws, *compiled by John Peers*

1,866

Do Not Disturb signs should be written in the language of
the hotel maids.

—*Tim Bedore*

1,867

What ought to be done to the man who invented the cele-
brating of anniversaries? Mere killing would be too light.
  —*Mark Twain (1835–1910)*

1,868

Status quo. Latin for the mess we're in.

—*Jeve Moorman*

1,869

Never put off until tomorrow what you can do the day
after tomorrow.

—*Mark Twain (1835–1910)*

1,870

Nobody can make you feel inferior without your consent.

—*Eleanor Roosevelt (1884–1962)*

1,871

An intellectual is a person whose mind watches itself.

—*Albert Camus (1913–1960)*

1,872

The average person thinks he isn't.

—*Father Larry Lorenzoni*

1,873

Sleep is an eight-hour peep show of infantile erotica.

—*J. G. Ballard*

1,874

No man can think clearly when his fists are clenched.

—*George Jean Nathan (1882–1958)*

1,875

Propaganda is the art of persuading others of what you don't believe yourself.

—*Abba Eban*

1,876

Never believe anything until it has been officially denied.

—*Claud Cockburn (1904–1981)*

1,877

There are only two ways of telling the complete truth—anonymously and posthumously.

—*Thomas Sowell*

1,878

There is only one thing about which I am certain, and that is that there is very little about which one can be certain.

—*W. Somerset Maugham (1874–1965)*

1,879

Before they made S. J. Perelman they broke the mold.

—*Unknown*

1,880

Here's to our wives and sweethearts—may they never meet.

—*John Bunny (1866–1939)*

1,881

Man Robs, Then Kills Himself.

—*Headline in* Vancouver Province, *June 21, 1978*

1,882

Don't jump on a man unless he's down.
—*Finley Peter Dunne (1867–1936)*

1,883

Just because your voice reaches halfway around the world doesn't mean you are wiser than when it reached only to the end of the bar.
—*Edward R. Murrow (1908–1965)*

1,884

Glory is fleeting, but obscurity is forever.
—*Napoleon Bonaparte (1769–1821)*

1,885

It is fun being in the same decade with you.
—*Franklin Delano Roosevelt (1882–1945)*
in a letter to Churchill, 1942

1,886

Although prepared for martyrdom, I preferred that it be postponed.
—*Winston Churchill (1874–1965)*

1,887

The higher a monkey climbs, the more you see of its behind.

—*General Joseph "Vinegar Joe" Stilwell (1883–1946)*

1,888

Marie Osmond makes Mother Teresa look like a slut.

—*Joan Rivers*

1,889

What a strange illusion it is to suppose that beauty is goodness.

—*Leo Tolstoy (1828–1910)*

I'm not going to climb into the ring with Tolstoy.

—*Ernest Hemingway (1889–1961)*

Hemingway was a jerk.

—*Harold Robbins (1916–1997)*

1,890

As Miss America, my goal is to bring peace to the entire world and then to get my own apartment.

—*Jay Leno*

1,891

I hate the outdoors. To me the outdoors is where the car is.

—*Will Durst*

1,892

The other day a dog peed on me. A bad sign.

—*H. L. Mencken (1880–1956)*

1,893

He grounds the warship he walks on.

—*John Bracken on Captain Barney Kelly,*
who ran the USS Enterprise *into the mud*
of San Francisco Bay in May of 1983

1,894
These are the souls that time men's tries.
　　—Sports Illustrated *on official timers at track meets*

1,895
Astrology is Taurus.
　　　　　　　　　　　—*F. W. Dedering*

1,896
Nobody outside of a baby carriage or a judge's chamber
believes in an unprejudiced point of view.
　　　　　—*Lillian Hellman (1907–1984)*

1,897
If I don't get a part for my artificial heart
I'm gonna stop caring for you.
　　　　　—*Lyrics by Bernie Sheehan*

1,898
I Can't Give You Anything But Love and a Baby
　　　　　—*Song title by Willie Tyler*

1,899
If the Phone Doesn't Ring, It's Me
　　　　　—*Song title by Jimmy Buffett*

1,900

It isn't that gentlemen really prefer blondes, it's just that we look dumber.

—*Anita Loos (1893–1981)*

1,901

She was what we used to call a suicide blonde—dyed by her own hand.

—*Saul Bellow*

1,902

For people who like peace and quiet: a phoneless cord.

—*Unknown*

1,903

The best audience is intelligent, well-educated, and a little drunk.

—*Alben W. Barkley (1877–1956)*

1,904

What is this, an audience or an oil painting?

—*Milton Berle (1908–2002)*

1,905

Civilization exists by geological consent, subject to change without notice.

—*Will Durant (1885–1981)*

1,906

In Biblical times, a man could have as many wives as he could afford. Just like today.

—*Abigail Van Buren (Dear Abby)*

1,907

The first human being who hurled an insult instead of a stone was the founder of civilization.

—*Attributed to Sigmund Freud (1856–1939)*

1,908

The only paradise is paradise lost.

—*Marcel Proust (1871–1922)*

1,909

Historical reminder: always put Horace before Descartes.

—*Donald O. Rickter*

1,910

Most of our future lies ahead.

—*Denny Crum, Louisville basketball coach*

1,911

If there is another way to skin a cat, I don't want to know about it.

—*Steve Kravitz*

1,912

God created man, but I could do better.

—*Erma Bombeck (1927–1996)*

1,913

If there is a supreme being, he's crazy.

—*Marlene Dietrich (1901–1992)*

1,914

Only two things are infinite, the universe and human stupidity, and I'm not sure about the former.

—*Albert Einstein (1879–1955)*

1,915

We are here on earth to do good to others. What the others are here for, I don't know.

—*W. H. Auden (1907–1973)*

1,916

I don't know, I don't care, and it doesn't make any difference.

—*Jack Kerouac (1922–1969)*

1,917

There ain't no answer. There ain't going to be any answer.
There never has been an answer. That's the answer.
—*Gertrude Stein (1874–1946)*

1,918

The meek shall inherit the earth . . . if you don't mind.
—*Graffito*

1,919

If you don't count some of Jehovah's injunctions, there is
no humor in the Bible.
—*Mordecai Richler (1931–2001)*

1,920

Woe unto you who laugh now, for you shall mourn and
weep.
—*Jesus Christ (0?–32?), according to Luke 6:25*

1,921

I sometimes worry that God has Alzheimer's and has forgotten us.
—*Lily Tomlin and Jane Wagner*

1,922

God seems to have left the receiver off the hook.

—Arthur Koestler (1905–1983)

1,923

If God listened to every shepherd's curse, our sheep would all be dead.

—Russian proverb

1,924

What can you say about a society that says that God is dead and Elvis is alive?

—Irv Kupcinet

1,925

To Jesus Christ! A splendid chap!

—Toast by Sir Ralph Richardson (1902–1983)

1,926

If Jesus was Jewish, how come he has a Mexican name?

—Unknown

1,927

Churches welcome all denominations, but most prefer fives and tens.

—Unknown

1,928

The Vatican is against surrogate mothers. Good thing they didn't have that rule when Jesus was born.

—*Elayne Boosler*

1,929

A difference of opinion is what makes horse racing and missionaries.

—*Will Rogers (1879–1935)*

1,930

Do television evangelists do more than lay people?

—*Stanley Ralph Ross*

1,931

Sin is geographical.

—*Bertrand Russell (1872–1970)*

1,932

Even when I'm sick and depressed, I love life.

—*Artur Rubenstein (1887–1982)*

1,933

Life! Can't live with it, can't live without it.

—*Cynthia Nelms*

1,934

Life is something that happens when you can't get to sleep.

—*Fran Lebowitz*

1,935

There is no cure for birth or death except to try to enjoy the interval.

—*George Santayana (1863–1952)*

1,936

Why torture yourself when life will do it for you?

—*Laura Walker*

1,937

It may be that we have all lived before and died, and this is hell.

—*A. L. Prusick*

1,938

Life's a bitch, and then you meet one.

—*Unknown*

1,939

Always look out for Number One and be careful not to step in Number Two.

—*Rodney Dangerfield*

1,940

It's not what you are, it's what you don't become that hurts.

—*Oscar Levant (1906–1972)*

1,941

The ethical argument regarding abortion hinges on the question of exactly when life begins. Some believe that life begins at forty.

—*Kevin Nealon*

1,942

It is said that life begins when the fetus can exist apart from its mother. By this definition, many people in Hollywood are legally dead.

—*Jay Leno*

1,943

Some mornings it just doesn't seem worth it to gnaw through the leather straps.

—*Emo Philips*

1,944

Everything I did in my life that was worthwhile I caught hell for.

—*Earl Warren (1891–1974)*

1,945

It's a dog-eat-dog world, and I'm wearing Milk Bone shorts.

—*Kelly Allen*

1,946

You have to live life to love life, and you have to love life to live life. It's a vicious circle.

—*Unknown*

1,947

In a fight between you and the world, bet on the world.

—*Franz Kafka (1883–1924)*

1,948

Man was predestined to have free will.

—*Hal Lee Luyah*

1,949

Swallow a toad in the morning if you want to encounter nothing more disgusting the rest of the day.

—*Nicolas Chamfort (1741–1794)*

1,950

If you want a place in the sun, you must leave the shade of the family tree.

—*Osage saying*

1,951

In spite of the cost of living, it's still popular.

—*Kathleen Norris (1880–1966)*

1,952

If you're already in a hole, it's no use to continue digging.

—*Roy W. Walters*

1,953

The longer you stay in one place, the greater your chances of disillusionment.

—*Art Spander*

1,954

The optimist proclaims that we live in the best of all possible worlds, and the pessimist fears this is true.

—*James Branch Cabell (1879–1958)*

1,955

An optimist is someone who thinks the future is uncertain.

—*Unknown*

1,956

I always wanted to be somebody, but I should have been more specific.

—*Lily Tomlin and Jane Wagner*

1,957

Dawn! A brand new day! This could be the start of something average.

—*Ziggy (Tom Wilson)*

1,958

"That would be nice."

Charlie Brown on hearing that in life you win some and lose some.

—*Charles Schulz (1922–2000)*

1,959

The second half of the 20th Century is a complete flop.

—Isaac Bashevis Singer (1904–1991)

1,960

The more unpredictable the world becomes, the more we rely on predictions.

—Steve Rivkin

1,961

"Fred Astaire! If only I had modeled my life after him instead of Daffy Duck."

—Thomas Gifford (1937–2000)

1,962

Reality is a collective hunch.

—Lily Tomlin and Jane Wagner

1,963

Humankind cannot bear very much reality.

—T. S. Eliot (1888–1965)

1,964

You've got to take the bitter with the sour.

—Samuel Goldwyn (1882–1974)

1,965
Strife is better than loneliness.

—*Irish saying*

1,966
Truth is more of a stranger than fiction.

—*Mark Twain (1835–1910)*

1,967
It is annoying to be honest to no purpose.

—*Ovid (43 B.C.–A.D. 18)*

1,968

Truth is the safest lie.

—*Unknown*

1,969

I have seen the truth, and it doesn't make sense.

—*Unknown*

1,970

Never let a computer know you're in a hurry.

—*Unknown*

1,971

My theory of evolution is that Darwin was adopted.

—*Steven Wright*

1,972

Never try to walk across a river just because it has an average depth of four feet.

—*Martin Friedman*

1,973
Physics lesson: When a body is submerged in water, the phone rings.

—*Unknown*

1,974
I like trees because they seem more resigned to the way they have to live than other things do.

—*Willa Cather (1873–1947)*

1,975
I am at two with nature.

—*Woody Allen*

1,976
Men are nicotine-soaked, beer-besmirched, whiskey-greased, red-eyed devils.

—*Carry Nation (1846–1911)*

1,977

Many men die at twenty-five and aren't buried until they are seventy-five.

—*Benjamin Franklin (1706–1790)*

1,978

Men are superior to women. For one thing, they can urinate from a speeding car.

—*Will Durst*

1,979

Men are irrelevant.

—*Fay Weldon*

1,980

I require three things in a man. He must be handsome, ruthless, and stupid.

—*Dorothy Parker (1893–1967)*

1,981

His mother should have thrown him away and kept the stork.

—*Mae West (1892–1980)*

1,982

I have yet to hear a man ask for advice on how to combine marriage and a career.

—*Gloria Steinem*

1,983

When a man brings his wife flowers for no reason—
there's a reason.

—*Molly McGee*

1,984

Men! You can't live with them and you can't

    1. Dip them in batter for tempura,

    2. Use them for collateral on a loan,

    3. Put in new batteries.

—*"Sylvia" (Nicole Hollander)*

1,985

The main difference between men and women is that men
are lunatics and women are idiots.

—*Rebecca West (1892–1983)*

1,986

Any young man who is unmarried at the age of twenty-
one is a menace to the community.

—*Brigham Young (1801–1877)*

1,987

Talking with a man is like trying to saddle a cow. You
work like hell, but what's the point?

—*Gladys Upham*

1,988

Men read maps better than women because only men can
understand the concept of an inch equaling a hundred
miles.

—*Roseanne Barr*

1,989

A dork is a dork is a dork.

—*Judy Markey*

1,990

I have known more men destroyed by the desire to have
wife and child and to keep them in comfort than I have
seen destroyed by drink and harlots.

—*William Butler Yeats (1865–1939)*

1,991

I grew up to have my father's looks, my father's speech patterns, my father's posture, my father's opinions, and my mother's contempt for my father.

—*Jules Feiffer*

1,992

A woman who takes things from a man is called a girl-friend. A man who takes things from a woman is called a gigolo.

—*Ruthie Stein*

1,993

The main result of feminism has been the Dutch Treat.

—*Nora Ephron*

1,994

Men should think twice before making widowhood women's only path to power.

—*Gloria Steinem*

1,995

You make the beds, you do the dishes, and six months later you have to start all over again.

—*Joan Rivers*

1,996

Women have the feeling that since they didn't make the
rules, the rules have nothing to do with them.

—*Diane Johnson*

1,997

Women are cursed, and men are the proof.

—*Roseanne Barr*

1,998

When a woman behaves like a man, why doesn't she behave like a nice man?

—*Edith Evans (1888–1976)*

1,999

If a woman has to choose between catching a fly ball and
saving an infant's life, she will choose to save the infant's
life without even considering if there are men on base.

—*Dave Barry*

2,000

Woman in Hurricane Has Same Baby Three Times

—*Tabloid headline suggested by Tracey Ullman*

2,001

Women can do any job men can and give birth while doing it.

—*Allan Heavey*

2,002

Women complain about premenstrual syndrome, but I think of it as the only time of the month I can be myself.

—*Roseanne Barr*

2,003

My plastic surgeon told me my face looked like a bouquet of elbows.

—*Phyllis Diller*

2,004

She was so ugly she could make a mule back away from an oat bin.

—*Will Rogers (1879–1935)*

2,005

I don't consider myself bald. I'm simply taller than my hair.

—*Tom Sharp*

2,006

You're only as good as your last haircut.

—*Susan Lee*

2,007

I am my hair.

—*Woman overheard by Roy Blount, Jr.*

2,008

Every time I look at you I get a fierce desire to be lonesome.

—*Oscar Levant (1906–1972)*

2,009

I hate people. People make me pro-nuclear.

—*Margaret Smith*

2,010

Love is an exploding cigar we willingly smoke.

—*Lynda Barry*

2,011

You need someone to love while you're looking for someone to love.

—*Shelagh Delaney*

2,012

God is love, but get it in writing.

—*Gypsy Rose Lee (1914–1970)*

2,013

Abstinence makes the heart grow fonder.

—*Knox Burger*

2,014

It is better to have flunked your Wasserman than never to
have loved at all.

—*Jim Stark*

2,015

Boy meets girl. So what?

—*Bertolt Brecht (1898–1956)*

2,016

Men and women, women and men. It will never work.

—*Erica Jong*

2,017

If you want to catch a trout, don't fish in a herring barrel.

—*Ann Landers (1918–2002) on singles bars*

2,018

The animals most often encountered in the singles jungle
are pigs, dogs, wolves, skunks, slugs, and snakes. The fox
is imaginary.

—*Robert Byrne*

Robert Byrne should be gagged.

—*Tracy Chreene*

2,019

I go from stool to stool in singles bars hoping to get lucky, but there's never any gum under any of them.

—*Emo Philips*

2,020

A "Bay Area Bisexual" told me I didn't quite coincide with either of her desires.

—*Woody Allen*

2,021

PERSONALS:

Famous Writer needs woman to organize his life and spend his money. Loves to turn off Sunday football and go to the Botanical Gardens with that special someone. Will obtain plastic surgery if necessary.

—*Sure-fire singles ad by Joe Bob Briggs*

2,022

When I meet a man I ask myself, "Is this the man I want my children to spend their weekends with?"

—*Rita Rudner*

2,023

Oh God, in the name of Thine only beloved Son, Jesus Christ, Our Lord, let him phone me now.

—*Dorothy Parker (1893–1967)*

2,024

I enjoy dating married men because they don't want anything kinky, like breakfast.

—*Joni Rodgers*

2,025

Women with pasts interest men because they hope history will repeat itself.

—*Mae West (1892–1980)*

2,026

I turned down a date once because I was looking for someone a little closer to the top of the food chain.

—*Judy Tenuta*

2,027

Have you ever dated someone because you were too lazy to commit suicide?

—*Judy Tenuta*

2,028

Never date a woman you can hear ticking.

—*Mark Patinkin*

2,029

There is one thing I would break up over, and that is if she caught me with another woman. I won't stand for that.

—*Steve Martin*

2,030

My boyfriend and I broke up. He wanted to get married and I didn't want him to.

—*Rita Rudner*

2,031

I'm dating a woman now who, evidently, is unaware of it.

—*Garry Shandling*

2,032

Necessity is the mother of attraction.

—*Luke McKissack*

2,033

When confronted with two evils, a man will always choose the prettier.

—*Unknown*

2,034

Blondes have more fun because they're easier to find in the dark.

—*Unknown*

2,035

When I was giving birth, the nurse asked, "Still think blondes have more fun?"

—*Joan Rivers*

2,036

It is possible that blondes also prefer gentlemen.

—*Mamie Van Doren*

2,037

Gentlemen prefer bonds.

—*Andrew Mellon (1855–1937)*

2,038

Is sex better than drugs? That depends on the pusher.

—*Unknown*

2,039

For birth control I rely on my personality.

—*Milt Abel*

2,040

Condoms aren't completely safe. A friend of mine was wearing one and got hit by a bus.

—*Bob Rubin*

2,041

When the clerk tried to sell me condoms that were made of sheep intestines because they have a more natural feel, I said, "Not for northern women."

—*Elayne Boosler*

2,042

Some condoms are made of sheep intestines, but I was so scared the first time I wore the whole sheep.

—*Danny Williams*

2,043

Some condom packages are stamped "Reservoir." You mean those things can generate hydroelectric power?

—*Elayne Boosler*

2,044

National Condom Week is coming soon. Hey, there's a parade you won't want to miss.

—*Jay Leno*

2,045

This gum tastes funny.

—Sign on condom machine

2,046

"I don't know, I never looked."
Answer to the question: "Do you smoke after sex?"

—Unknown

2,047

I don't even masturbate anymore, I'm so afraid I'll give myself something. I just want to be friends with myself.

—Richard Lewis

2,048

The advantage of masturbation over intercourse is that it's less competitive.

—Robert Byrne

2,049

Before sleeping together today, people should boil themselves.

—Richard Lewis

2,050

Mr. Right is now a guy who hasn't been laid in fifteen years.

—*Elayne Boosler*

2,051

I finally had an orgasm, and my doctor told me it was the wrong kind.

—*Woody Allen*

2,052

My wife and I don't have mutual orgasms. We have State Farm.

—*Milton Berle (1908–2002)*

2,053

Erogenous zones are either everywhere or nowhere.

—*Joseph Heller (1923–1999)*

2,054

During sex I fantasize that I'm someone else.

—*Richard Lewis*

2,055

I don't mind sleeping on an empty stomach provided it isn't my own.

—*Philip J. Simborg*

2,056

"I don't know, what's the record?"
Answer to the question: "How horny can you get?"

—*Neil Simon*

2,057

The difference between sex and love is that sex relieves tension and love causes it.

—*Woody Allen*

2,058

I always thought of you as, at best, asexual, but maybe I was being kind.

—*From the television show* Slap Maxwell

2,059

The late porn star Johnny Wadd claimed to have been laid 14,000 times. He died of friction.

—*Larry Brown*

2,060

I'm not kinky, but occasionally I like to put on a robe and stand in front of a tennis ball machine.

—*Garry Shandling*

2,061

Kinky sex involves the use of duck feathers. Perverted sex involves the whole duck.

—*Lewis Grizzard*

2,062

One figure can sometimes add up to a lot.

—*Mae West (1892–1980)*

2,063

I wouldn't let him touch me with a ten-foot pole.

—*Mae West (1892–1980)*

2,064

Mae West had a voice like a vibrating bed.

—*John Kobal*

2,065

It's okay to laugh in the bedroom so long as you don't point.

—*Will Durst*

2,066

Sex is a powerful aphrodisiac.

—*Keith Waterhouse*

2,067

What do I know about sex? I'm a married man.

—*Tom Clancy*

2,068

Some are born to greatness, some achieve greatness, and some have greatness thrust within them.

—*Hal Lee Luyah*

2,069

Warning signs that your lover is bored:
1. Passionless kisses
2. Frequent sighing
3. Moved, left no forwarding address.

—*Matt Groening*

2,070

I once made love for an hour and fifteen minutes, but it was the night the clocks are set ahead.

—*Garry Shandling*

2,071

In the old days, women wore so many girdles, corsets, pantaloons, bloomers, stockings, garters, step-ins and God knows what all that you had to practically be a *prospector* to get to first base . . . to even *find* first base.

—*Danny McGoorty (1903–1970)*

2,072

Ooooh. Ahhhh. Get out.

　—*Andrew Dice Clay's impression of a one-night stand*

2,073

It is a gentleman's first duty to remember in the morning who it was he took to bed with him.

—*Dorothy L. Sayers (1893–1957)*

2,074

I would never go to bed with a man who had so little regard for my husband.

—*From a novel by Dan Greenburg*

2,075

Oysters are supposed to enhance your sexual performance, but they don't work for me. Maybe I put them on
too soon.

—*Garry Shandling*

2,076

My wife gives good headache.

—*Rodney Dangerfield*

2,077

Oral sex is like being attacked by a giant snail.

—*Germaine Greer*

2,078

Once while we were making love, a curious optical illusion occurred, and it almost looked as though she were moving.

—*Woody Allen*

2,079

He gave her a look you could have poured on a waffle.

—*Ring Lardner (1885–1933)*

2,080

In breeding cattle you need one bull for every twenty-five cows, unless the cows are known sluts.

—*Johnny Carson*

2,081

After making love I said to my girl, "Was it good for you, too?" And she said, "I don't think this was good for anybody."

—*Garry Shandling*

2,082

In sex as in banking there is a penalty for early withdrawal.

—*Cynthia Nelms*

2,083

The mirror over my bed reads: Objects appear larger than they are.

—*Garry Shandling*

2,084

I was a virgin till I was twenty, then again till I was twenty-three.

—*Carrie Snow*

2,085

Losing my virginity was a career move.

—*Madonna*

2,086

Sex after ninety is like trying to shoot pool with a rope. Even putting my cigar in its holder is a thrill.

—*George Burns (1896–1996)*

2,087

Sometimes a cigar is just a cigar.

—*Sigmund Freud (1856–1939)*

2,088

This is my last year to fool around. Then I'm going to settle down and marry a rock star.

—*From the 1986 movie* Modern Girls

2,089

Dating means doing a lot of fun things you will never do
again if you get married. The fun stops with marriage because you're trying to save money for when you split up
your property.

—*Dave Barry*

2,090

There's nothing like a Catholic wedding to make you wish
that life had a fast forward button.

—*Dan Chopin*

2,091

I married the first man I ever kissed. When I tell my children that, they just about throw up.

—*Barbara Bush*

2,092

Until I got married, I was my own worst enemy.

—*Unknown*

2,093

The poor wish to be rich, the rich wish to be happy, the single wish to be married, and the married wish to be dead.

—*Ann Landers (1918–2002)*

2,094

Marriage is like paying an endless visit in your worst clothes.

—*J. B. Priestley (1894–1984)*

2,095

Marriage is like a besieged fortress. Everyone outside wants to get in, and everyone inside wants to get out.

—*P. M. Quitard (c. 1842)*

2,096

The chains of marriage are so heavy it takes two to carry them, and sometimes three.

—*Alexandre Dumas (1802–1870)*

2,097

Marriage is ridiculous.

—*Goldie Hawn*

2,098

Instead of getting married again, I'm going to find a woman I don't like and give her a house.

—*Lewis Grizzard*

2,099

Love is blind, and marriage is a real eye-opener.

—*Unknown*

2,100

My divorce came as a complete surprise to me. That will happen when you haven't been home in eighteen years.

—*Lee Trevino*

2,101

The secret of a happy marriage is to tell your spouse everything but the essentials.

—*Cynthia Nelms*

2,102

All men make mistakes, but married men find out about them sooner.

—*Red Skelton (1913–1997)*

2,103

In marriage a man becomes slack and selfish and under-
goes a fatty degeneration of the spirit.
—*Robert Louis Stevenson (1850–1894)*

2,104

Conrad Hilton was very generous to me in the divorce set-
tlement. He gave me 5,000 Gideon Bibles.
—*Zsa Zsa Gabor*

2,105

The only thing that holds a marriage together is the husband being big enough to step back and see where the wife
is wrong.
—*Archie Bunker*

2,106

I've been married so long I'm on my third bottle of
Tabasco sauce.
—*Susan Vass*

2,107

There is nothing like living together for blinding people to
each other.
—*Ivy Compton Burnett (1884–1969)*

2,108

Always get married early in the morning. That way, if it doesn't work out, you haven't wasted a whole day.

—*Mickey Rooney*

2,109

There are pigtails on the pillow in the morning that weren't there before.

—*Martin Luther (1483–1546) on marriage*

2,110

I'm going to marry a Jewish woman because I like the idea of getting up on Sunday morning and going to the deli.

—*Michael J. Fox*

2,111

That married couples can live together day after day is a miracle the Vatican has overlooked.

—*Bill Cosby*

2,112

My wife and I were happy for twenty years. Then we met.

—*Rodney Dangerfield*

2,113

My husband said he needed more space, so I locked him outside.

—*Roseanne Barr*

2,114

You may marry the man of your dreams, but fifteen years later you're married to a reclining chair that burps.

—*Roseanne Barr*

2,115

I grew up in a very large family in a very small house. I never slept alone until after I was married.

—*Lewis Grizzard*

2,116

My parents stayed together for forty years, but that was out of spite.

—*Woody Allen*

2,117

If it weren't for marriage, men and women would have to fight with total strangers.

—*Unknown*

2,118

Monogamous is what one partner in every relationship wants to be.

—*Strange de Jim*

2,119

Monogamous and monotonous are synonymous.

—*Thaddeus Golas*

2,120

Monogamy leaves a lot to be desired.

—Unknown

2,121

If you want monogamy, marry a swan.

—From the movie Heartburn, *1987*

2,122

When Sears comes out with a riding vacuum cleaner, then I'll clean the house.

—Roseanne Barr

2,123

My mom was fair. You never knew whether she was going to swing with her right or her left.

—Herb Caen

2,124

As a housewife, I feel that if the kids are still alive when my husband gets home from work, then hey, I've done my job.

—Roseanne Barr

2,125

My mother always phones me and asks, "Is everything all wrong?"

—*Richard Lewis*

2,126

I'd get pregnant if I could be assured I'd have puppies.

—*Cynthia Nelms*

2,127

Giving birth is like trying to push a piano through a transom.

—*Alice Roosevelt Longworth (1884–1980)*

2,128

When I was born I was so surprised I didn't talk for a year and a half.

—*Gracie Allen (1906–1964)*

2,129

I have never understood the fear of some parents about babies getting mixed up in the hospital. What difference does it make as long as you get a good one?

—*Heywood Broun (1888–1939)*

2,130

A soiled baby with a neglected nose cannot be conscientiously regarded as a thing of beauty.

—*Mark Twain (1835–1910)*

2,131

Babies don't need vacations, but I still see them at the beach.

—*Steven Wright*

2,132

When childhood dies, its corpses are called adults.

—*Brian Aldiss*

2,133

Adults are obsolete children.

—*Dr. Seuss (1904–1991)*

2,134

It's a dull child that knows less than its father.

—*Unknown*

2,135

Before I was married I had three theories about raising children. Now I have three children and no theories.

—*John Wilmot, Earl of Rochester (1647–1680)*

2,136

When my kids become wild and unruly, I use a nice, safe playpen. When they're finished, I climb out.

—*Erma Bombeck (1927–1996)*

2,137

My children love me. I'm like the mother they never had.

—*Roseanne Barr*

2,138

The highlight of my childhood was making my brother laugh so hard that food came out of his nose.

—*Garrison Keillor*

2,139

We had a quicksand box in our back yard. I was an only child, eventually.

—*Steven Wright*

2,140

I was the kid next door's imaginary friend.

—*Emo Philips*

2,141

As parents, my wife and I have one thing in common. We're both afraid of children.

—*Bill Cosby*

2,142

My father was frightened of his father, I was frightened of my father, and I am damned well going to see to it that my children are frightened of me.

—*King George V (1865–1936)*

2,143

If a child shows himself to be incorrigible, he should be decently and quietly beheaded at the age of twelve lest he grow to maturity, marry, and perpetuate his kind.

—*Don Marquis (1878–1937)*

2,144

I reached puberty at age thirty. At age twelve I looked like a fetus.

—*Dave Barry*

2,145

My niece was in *The Glass Menagerie* at school. They used Tupperware.

—*Cathy Ladman*

2,146

Reasoning with a child is fine if you can reach the child's reason without destroying your own.

—*John Mason Brown (1900–1969)*

2,147

There is nothing wrong with teenagers that reasoning with them won't aggravate.

—*Unknown*

2,148

If Abraham's son had been a teenager, it wouldn't have been a sacrifice.

—*Scott Spendlove*

2,149

If you want to recapture your youth, cut off his allowance.

—*Al Bernstein*

2,150

Anybody who has survived his childhood has enough information about life to last him the rest of his days.

—*Flannery O'Connor (1925–1964)*

2,151

Ask your child what he wants for dinner only if he's buying.

—*Fran Lebowitz*

2,152

If you must hold yourself up to your children, hold yourself up as an object lesson and not as an example.

—*George Bernard Shaw (1856–1950)*

2,153

My parents were too poor to have children, so the neighbors had me.

—*Buddy Hackett*

2,154

Have children while your parents are still young enough to take care of them.

—*Rita Rudner*

2,155

Children despise their parents until the age of forty, when they suddenly become just like them, thus preserving the system.

—*Quentin Crewe*

2,156

Roses are reddish
Violets are bluish
If it weren't for Christmas
We'd all be Jewish.

—*Benny Hill (1925–1992)*

2,157

I stopped believing in Santa Claus when my mother took me to see him in a department store, and he asked for my autograph.

—*Shirley Temple*

2,158

The three stages of a man's life:
1. He believes in Santa Claus;
2. He doesn't believe in Santa Claus;
3. He is Santa Claus.

—*Unknown*

2,159

You can't beat the gentiles in December. We were stupid to make Hanukkah then.

—*Ralph Schoenstein's grandfather*

2,160

Santa Claus has the right idea: Visit people once a year.

—*Victor Borge (1909–2000)*

2,161

Thanksgiving comes *after* Christmas for people over thirty.

—*Peter Kreeft*

2,162

Christmas is Christ's revenge for the crucifixion.

—*Unknown*

2,163

Setting a good example for children takes all the fun out of middle age.

—*William Feather*

2,164

There is no such thing as fun for the whole family.

—*Jerry Seinfeld*

2,165

In order to influence a child, one must be careful not to be that child's parent or grandparent.

—*Don Marquis (1878–1937)*

2,166

The time not to become a father is eighteen years before a war.

—*E. B. White (1899–1985)*

2,167

A married man with a family will do anything for money.

—*Charles Maurice de Talleyrand-Perigord (1754–1838)*

2,168

To be a successful father, there's one absolute rule: When you have a kid, don't look at it for the first two years.

—*Ernest Hemingway (1899–1961)*

Hemingway was a jerk.

—*Harold Robbins (1916–1997)*

Harold Robbins doesn't sound like an author, he sounds like a company brochure.

—The New Yorker

2,169

You should have seen what a fine-looking man he was before he had all those children.

—*Arapesh tribesman*

2,170

Parenthood remains the greatest single preserve of the amateur.

—*Alvin Toffler*

2,171

I have over 42,000 children, and not one comes to visit.

—*Mel Brooks as*
The 2000-Year-Old Man

2,172

It behooves a father to be blameless if he expects his son to be.

—*Homer (c. 1000 B.C.)*

2,173

Any father whose son raises his hand against him is guilty of having produced a son who raised his hand against him.

—Charles Péguy (1873–1914)

2,174

Parents are not interested in justice, they are interested in quiet.

—Bill Cosby

2,175

My parents only had one argument in forty-five years. It lasted forty-three years.

—Cathy Ladman

2,176

My parents have been visiting me for a few days. I just dropped them off at the airport. They leave tomorrow.

—Margaret Smith

2,177

I've been promoted to middle management. I never thought I'd sink so low.

—*Tim Gould*

2,178

Do it my way or watch your butt.

—*Management philosophy from the movie* Raising Arizona, *1987*

2,179

No man ever listened himself out of a job.

—*Calvin Coolidge (1872–1933)*

2,180

Canadians shouldn't come down to Southern California and take jobs away from our Mexicans.

—*Stanley Ralph Ross*

2,181

There ain't no rules around here! We're trying to accomplish something!

—*Thomas Edison (1847–1931)*

2,182

A career is a job that has gone on too long.

—*Cartoon caption by Jeff MacNelly*

2,183

I used to work at The International House of Pancakes. It was a dream, and I made it happen.

—*Paula Poundstone*

2,184

Tell your boss what you think of him, and the truth shall set you free.

—*Unknown*

2,185

A holding company is a thing where you hand an accomplice the goods while the policeman searches you.

—*Will Rogers (1879–1935)*

2,186

A criminal is a person with predatory instincts without sufficient capital to form a corporation.

—*Howard Scott*

2,187

The economy of Houston is so bad right now that two prostitutes the police arrested turned out to be virgins.

—*Bill Abeel*

2,188

Success isn't permanent, and failure isn't fatal.

—*Mike Ditka*

2,189

Success has many fathers, failure is a mother.

—*Jeanne Phillips*

2,190

The worst part of success is trying to find someone who is happy for you.

—*Bette Midler*

2,191

Success is women you don't even know walking around your house.

—*From* Saturday Night Live

2,192

If at first you don't succeed, find out if the loser gets anything.

—*Bill Lyon*

2,193

Success in life means not becoming like your parents.

—*Louise Bowie*

2,194

To make a small fortune, invest a large fortune.

—*Bruce Cohn*

2,195

Formula for success: Rise early, work hard, strike oil.

—*J. Paul Getty (1892–1976), allegedly*

2,196

The penalty of success is to be bored by the people who used to snub you.

—*Nancy, Lady Astor (1879–1964)*

2,197

Talk is cheap until you hire a lawyer.

—*Unknown*

2,198

I've never been in love. I've always been a lawyer.

—*Unknown*

2,199

There are three reasons why lawyers are replacing rats as laboratory research animals. One is that they're plentiful, another is that lab assistants don't get attached to them, and the third is that there are some things rats just won't do.

—*Unknown*

2,200

A tragedy is a busload of lawyers going over a cliff with an empty seat.

—*Unknown*

2,201

Lawyer Drowning in Bay Rescued
—*Headline nominated by George de Shazer*
as the saddest of the year

2,202

Lawsuit, n. A machine you go into as a pig and come out of as a sausage.

—*Ambrose Bierce (1842–1914?)*

2,203

Is it a bigger crime to rob a bank or to open one?

—*Ted Allan*

2,204

Two can live as cheaply as one. Take the bird and the horse, for example.

—*Unknown*

2,205

I don't like money, but it quiets my nerves.

—*Joe Louis (1914–1981)*

2,206

I wish Karl would accumulate some capital instead of just writing about it.

—*Karl Marx's mother, allegedly*

2,207

Money can't buy friends, but it can get you a better class of enemy.

—*Spike Milligan*

2,208

Money won is twice as sweet as money earned.

—*From the movie* The Color of Money, *1986*

2,209

Alimony is always having to say you're sorry.

—*Philip J. Simborg*

2,210

Never get deeply in debt to someone who cried at the end of *Scarface*.

—*Robert S. Wieder*

2,211

The rule is not to talk about money with people who have much more or much less than you.

—*Katherine Whitehorn*

2,212

The way to make money is to buy when blood is running in the streets.

—*John D. Rockefeller (1839–1937)*

2,213

I don't know much about being a millionaire, but I'll bet I'd be darling at it.

—*Dorothy Parker (1893–1967)*

2,214

I don't have a bank account, because I don't know my mother's maiden name.

—*Paula Poundstone*

2,215

I had plastic surgery last week. I cut up my credit cards.

—*Henny Youngman (1906–1998)*

2,216

Consequences, shmonsequences, as long as I'm rich.

—*Daffy Duck*

2,217

A foundation is a large body of money surrounded by people who want some.

—*Dwight Macdonald (1906–1983)*

2,218

The upper crust is a bunch of crumbs held together by dough.

—*Joseph A. Thomas (1906–1977)*

2,219

I no longer prepare food or drink with more than one ingredient.

—*Cyra McFadden*

2,220

Eternity is two people and a roast turkey.

—*James Dent*

2,221

Do you hunt your own truffles or do you hire a pig?

—*Conversational icebreaker suggested by Jean McClatchy*

2,222

I refuse to spend my life worrying about what I eat. There is no pleasure worth forgoing just for an extra three years in the geriatric ward.

—*John Mortimer*

2,223

I asked the clothing store clerk if she had anything to make me look thinner, and she said, "How about a week in Bangladesh?"

—*Roseanne Barr*

2,224

Diets are mainly food for thought.

—*N. Wylie Jones*

2,225

Avoid fruits and nuts. You are what you eat.

—*Garfield (Jim Davis)*

2,226

I'm on a grapefruit diet. I eat everything but grapefruit.

—*Chi Chi Rodriguez*

2,227

In two decades I've lost a total of 789 pounds. I should be hanging from a charm bracelet.

—*Erma Bombeck (1927–1996)*

2,228

The toughest part of being on a diet is shutting up about it.

—*Gerald Nachman*

2,229

My idea of heaven is a great big baked potato and someone to share it with.

—*Oprah Winfrey*

2,230

If it tastes good, it's trying to kill you.

—*Roy Qualley*

2,231

Everything I want is either illegal, immoral, or fattening.

—*Alexander Woollcott (1887–1943)*

2,232

Eating an anchovy is like eating an eyebrow.

—*Unknown*

2,233

A favorite dish in Kansas is creamed corn on a stick.

—*Jeff Harms*

2,234

Meat is murder, but fish is justifiable homicide.

—*Jeremy Hardy*

2,235

I smell a rat. Did you bake it or fry it?

—*Bill Hoest*

2,236

Why should we take up farming when there are so many mongongo nuts in the world?

—*African Bushman quoted by Jared Diamond*

2,237

You'll be hungry again in an hour.

—*Fortune cookie opened by Ziggy (Tom Wilson)*

2,238

Your request for no MSG was ignored.

—*Fortune cookie opened by Merla Zellerbach*

2,239

A vegetarian is a person who won't eat meat unless someone else pays for it.

—*Al Clethen*

2,240

Cannibals aren't vegetarians, they're humanitarians.

—*Unknown*

2,241

I'm not a vegetarian because I love animals; I'm a vegetarian because I hate plants.

—*A. Whitney Brown*

2,242

Never order anything in a vegetarian restaurant that ordinarily would have meat in it.

—*Tom Parker*

2,243

Where there's smoke, there's toast.

—*Unknown*

2,244

Never eat anything whose listed ingredients cover more than one-third of the package.

—*Joseph Leonard*

2,245

I don't eat snails. I prefer fast food.

—*Strange de Jim*

2,246

It's okay to be fat. So you're fat. Just be fat and shut up about it.

—*Roseanne Barr*

2,247

Come in, or we'll both starve

—*Sign in restaurant window*

2,248

I hate to eat and eat and eat and run.

—*Neila Ross*

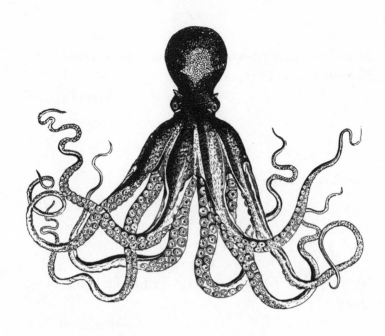

2,249
Some people like to eat octopus. Liberals, mostly.
—*Russell Baker*

2,250
Do not make a stingy sandwich
Pile the cold-cuts high
Customers should see salami
Coming through the rye.
—*Allan Sherman (1924–1973)*

2,251

Plant carrots in January, and you'll never have to eat carrots.

—*Unknown*

2,252

Ask not what you can do for your country, ask what's for lunch.

—*Orson Welles (1915–1985)*
on reaching 300 pounds

2,253

Continental breakfasts are very sparse. My advice is to go right to lunch without pausing.

—*Miss Piggy*

2,254

Miss Piggy is a boar.

—*Ed Lucaire*

2,255

The key to a successful restaurant is dressing girls in degrading clothes.

—*Michael O'Donoghue*

2,256

The food in Yugoslavia is either very good or very bad. One day they served us fried chains.

—*Mel Brooks*

2,257

Good health makes the practice of virtue more difficult.

—*John Bunyan (1628–1688)*

2,258

If you don't take care of your body, where will you live?

—*Unknown*

2,259

Your medical tests are in. You're short, fat, and bald.

—*Ziggy (Tom Wilson)*

2,260

How can I get sick? I've already had everything.

—*George Burns (1896–1996)*

2,261

When I told my doctor I couldn't afford an operation, he offered to touch up my X rays.

—*Henny Youngman (1906–1998)*

2,262

I quit therapy because my analyst was trying to help me behind my back.

—*Richard Lewis*

2,263

The art of medicine, like that of war, is murderous and conjectural.

—*Voltaire (1694–1778)*

2,264

Winston Churchill's habit of guzzling a quart or two a day of good cognac is what saved civilization from the Luftwaffe, Hegelian logic, Wagnerian love-deaths, and potato pancakes.

—*Charles McCabe (1915–1983)*

2,265

I feel sorry for people who don't drink, because when they get up in the morning, they're not going to feel any better all day.

—*Frank Sinatra (1915–1998)*

2,266

I drink too much. Last time I gave a urine sample there was an olive in it.

—*Rodney Dangerfield*

2,267

I never took hallucinogenic drugs because I never wanted my consciousness expanded one unnecessary iota.

—*Fran Lebowitz*

2,268

Politics is a means of preventing people from taking part in what properly concerns them.

—*Paul Valéry (1871–1945)*

2,269

Politics consists of choosing between the disastrous and the unpalatable.

—*John Kenneth Galbraith*

2,270

Democracy is the name we give to the people when we need them.

—*Robert Pellevé, Marquis de Flers*
(1872–1927)

2,271

There has never been a good government.

—*Emma Goldman (1869–1940)*

2,272

No more good must be attempted than the public can bear.

—*Thomas Jefferson (1743–1826)*

2,273

Thomas Jefferson's slaves loved him so much they called him by a special name: Dad.

—*Mark Russell*

2,274

When they asked George Washington for his ID, he just took out a quarter.

—*Steven Wright*

2,275

George Bush is Gerald Ford without the pizzazz.

—*Pat Paulsen*

2,276

A promising young man should go into politics so that he can go on promising for the rest of his life.

—*Robert Byrne*

2,277

A politician is a man who approaches every problem with an open mouth.

—*Adlai Stevenson (1900–1965)*

2,278

A politician can appear to have his nose to the grindstone while straddling a fence and keeping both ears to the ground.

—*Unknown*

2,279

My grandmother's brain was dead, but her heart was still beating. It was the first time we ever had a Democrat in the family.

—*Emo Philips*

2,280

No matter what your religion, you should try to become a government program, for then you will have everlasting life.

—*U.S. Representative Lynn Martin*

2,281

Most isms are wasms.

—*Philosophy professor Gerald Vision*

2,282

We've upped our standards. Up yours.

—*Campaign slogan by Pat Paulsen*

2,283

If I had known that my son was going to be president of Bolivia [in the 1940s], I would have taught him to read and write.

—*Enrique Penaranda's mother*

2,284

Being head of state is an extremely thankless job.

—*Bokassa I (1921–1996), former emperor of the Central African Republic, while on trial for infanticide, cannibalism, and torture*

2,285

If Roosevelt were alive today, he'd turn over in his grave.

—*Samuel Goldwyn (1882–1974)*

2,286

When they circumcised Herbert Samuel, they threw away the wrong part.

—*David Lloyd George (1863–1945) on a rival*

2,287

Early today the senator called a spade a spade. He later issued a retraction.

—*Joe Mirachi*

2,288

Voters want a fraud they can believe in.

—*Will Durst*

2,289

A penny saved is a Congressional oversight.

—*Hal Lee Luyah*

2,290

Are the people who run for president really the best in a country of 240 million? If so, something has happened to the gene pool.

—*Bob McKenzie*

2,291

Nonviolence is a flop. The only bigger flop is violence.

—*Joan Baez*

2,292

Nonviolence is fine as long as it works.

—*Malcolm X (1925–1965)*

2,293

You're not famous until my mother has heard of you.

—*Jay Leno*

2,294

The nice thing about being a celebrity is that, if you bore people, they think it's their fault.

—*Henry Kissinger*

2,295

A celebrity is a person known to many people he is glad he doesn't know.

—H. L. Mencken (1880–1956)

2,296

They want me on all the television shows now because I did so well on "Celebrity Assholes."

—Steve Martin

2,297

People hate me because I am a multifaceted, talented, wealthy, internationally famous genius.

—Jerry Lewis

2,298

In her last days, Gertrude Stein resembled a spoiled pear.

—Gore Vidal

2,299

I don't like Diane Keaton anymore. She's had way too much therapy.

—Patricia Wentz

2,300

It's sweeping the country like wildflowers.

—*Samuel Goldwyn (1882–1974)*

2,301

Nominations in Most Boring Headline contest, sponsored
by *The New Republic,* 1986:

Worthwhile Canadian Initiative *(New York Times)*
University of Rochester Decides to Keep Name
(New York Times)
Surprises Unlikely in Indiana *(Chicago Tribune)*
Economist Dies *(Wisconsin State Journal)*

2,302

Every hero becomes a bore at last.

—*Ralph Waldo Emerson (1803–1882)*

2,303

When I played pro football, I never set out to hurt anybody deliberately . . . unless it was, you know, important,
like a league game or something.

—*Dick Butkus*

2,304

Baseball is what we were, football is what we have become.

—*Mary McGrory*

2,305

Go Braves! And take the Falcons with you.

—*Bumper sticker in Atlanta*

2,306

Cal quarterback Joe Kapp used to call audibles that were just obscenities directed at the other team. I like that.

—*Stanford quarterback Greg Ennis*

2,307

Yell for a losing football team:
Let's all jump and scream
For the lavender and cream.

—*Tom Batiuk*

2,308

Baseball would be a better game if more third basemen got hit in the mouth by line drives.

—*Dan Jenkins*

2,309

George Steinbrenner is the salt of the earth, and the Yankee players are open wounds.

—*Scott Osler*

2,310

That's getting a little too close to home.

—*Bob Feller on hearing that
a foul ball hit his mother*

2,311

I'm not going to buy my kids an encyclopedia. Let them walk to school like I did.

—*Another thing never said by Yogi Berra*

2,312

Pro basketball has turned into Wrestlemania, which is why I like college basketball and high school basketball. Actually, it's why I like baseball.

—*Frank Layden*

2,313

No comment.

—*Doug Moe on hearing that he had
been voted the most quotable coach
in the National Basketball Association*

2,314

If you are caught on a golf course during a storm and are afraid of lightning, hold up a 1-iron. Not even God can hit a 1-iron.

—*Lee Trevino*

2,315

Skiing combines outdoor fun with knocking down trees with your face.

—*Dave Barry*

2,316

If you are going to try cross-country skiing, start with a small country.

—*From* Saturday Night Live

2,317

Yell for a Virginia high school:

We don't drink!
We don't smoke!
Norfolk!

—*Unknown*

2,318

Fishing is a delusion entirely surrounded by liars in old clothes.

—*Don Marquis (1878–1937)*

2,319

I bet on a horse at ten to one. It didn't come in until half-past five.

—*Henny Youngman (1906–1998)*

2,320

A good sport has to lose to prove it.

—*Unknown*

2,321

As for bowling, how good can a thing be if it has to be done in an alley?

—*John Grigsby's ex-wife*

2,322

When I feel athletic, I go to a sports bar.

—*Paul Clisura*

2,323

Curiosity killed the cat, but for a while I was a suspect.

—*Steven Wright*

2,324

It took me an hour to bury the cat, because it wouldn't stop moving.

—*From* The Monty Python Show

2,325

Being a newspaper columnist is like being married to a nymphomaniac. It's great for the first two weeks.

—*Lewis Grizzard*

2,326

As a novelist, I tell stories, and people give me money. Then financial planners tell me stories, and I give them money.

—*Martin Cruz Smith*

2,327
The cure for writer's cramp is writer's block.

—*Inigo DeLeon*

2,328
A painter can hang his pictures, but a writer can only hang himself.

—*Edward Dahlberg (1900–1977)*

2,329
The multitude of books is a great evil. There is no limit to this fever for writing.

—*Martin Luther (1483–1546)*

2,330

As she fell face down into the black muck of the mud-wrestling pit, her sweaty 300-pound opponent muttering soft curses in Latin on top of her, Sister Marie thought, "There is no doubt about it; the Pope has betrayed me."

—*Richard Savastio*
Entry in San Jose State's bad writing contest, 1983

2,331

Desiree, the first female ape to go up in space, winked at me slyly and pouted her thick, rubbery lips unmistakably—the first of many such advances during what would prove to be the longest, most memorable space voyage of my career.

—*Martha Simpson*
Entry in San Jose State's bad writing contest, 1985

2,332

Jake liked his women the way he liked his kiwi fruit; sweet yet tart, firm-fleshed yet yielding to the touch, and covered with short brown fuzzy hair.

—*Gretchen Schmidt*
Entry in San Jose State's bad writing contest, 1989

2,333

Nice guys can't write.

—*Literary agent Knox Burger*

2,334

If the doctor told me I had only six minutes to live, I'd type a little faster.

—*Isaac Asimov (1920–1992)*

2,335

Writing books is certainly a most unpleasant occupation. It is lonesome, unsanitary, and maddening. Many authors go crazy.

—*H. L. Mencken (1880–1956)*

2,336

A blank page is God's way of showing you how hard it is to be God.

—*Unknown*

2,337

Either a writer doesn't want to talk about his work, or he talks about it more than you want.

—*Anatole Broyard*

2,338

In Ireland, a writer is looked upon as a failed conversationalist.

—*Unknown*

2,339

To call Richard Brautigan's poetry doggerel is an insult to the entire canine world.

—*Lazlo Coakley*

2,340

I am here to live out loud.

—*Emile Zola (1840–1902)*

2,341

I sound my barbaric yawp from the rooftops of the world.

—*Walt Whitman (1819–1892)*

2,342

Nothing stinks like a pile of unpublished writing.

—*Sylvia Plath (1932–1963)*

2,343

No passion in the world is equal to the passion to alter someone else's draft.

—*H. G. Wells (1866–1946)*

2,344

Having your book turned into a movie is like seeing your oxen turned into bouillon cubes.

—*John Le Carré*

2,345

Writing is a profession in which you have to keep proving your talent to people who have none.

—*Jules Renard (1864–1910)*

2,346

The relationship of editor to author is knife to throat.

—*Unknown*

2,347

If I had more time, I would write a shorter letter.

—*Blaise Pascal (1623–1662)*

2,348

Reading this book is like waiting for the first shoe to drop.

—*Ralph Novak*

2,349

A book must be an ice ax to break the frozen sea within us.

—*Franz Kafka (1883–1924)*

2,350

The New York Times Book Review is alive with the sound of axes grinding.

—*Gore Vidal*

2,351

JFK—The Man and the Airport

—*Somebody's suggested book title*

2,352

Nine-tenths of all existing books are nonsense.

—*Benjamin Disraeli (1804–1881)*

2,353

Books for general reading always smell bad; the odor of common people hangs about them.

—*Friedrich Nietzsche (1844–1900)*

Nietzsche was stupid and abnormal.

—*Leo Tolstoy (1828–1910)*

[Tolstoy's *War and Peace* and *Anna Karenina* are] loose, baggy monsters.

—*Henry James (1843–1916)*

Henry James writes fiction as if it were a painful duty.

—*Oscar Wilde (1854–1900)*

2,354

I hate books, for they only teach people to talk about what they don't understand.

—*Jean-Jacques Rousseau (1712–1778)*

2,355

Books should be tried by a judge and jury as though they were crimes.

—*Samuel Butler (1835–1902)*

2,356

Has the net effect of the invention of printing been good or bad? I haven't the slightest idea and neither has anyone else. As well ask whether it was a good or a bad plan to give over so much of the world's space to oceans.

—H. L. Mencken (1880–1956)

2,357

Autobiography is a preemptive strike against biographers.

—Barbara Grizzuti Harrison

2,358

I haven't read any of the autobiographies about me.

—Elizabeth Taylor

2,359

I always read the last page of a book first so that if I die before I finish I'll know how it turned out.

—Nora Ephron

2,360

I'm thirty years old, but I read at the thirty-four-year-old level.

—Dana Carvey

2,361

When you watch television, you never see people watching television. We love television because it brings us a world in which television does not exist.

—*Barbara Ehrenreich*

2,362

Hear no evil, speak no evil, see no evil, and you'll never be a television anchorman.

—*Dan Rather*

2,363

Imagine what it would be like if TV actually were good. It would be the end of everything we know.

—*Marvin Minsky*

2,364

America is a mistake, a giant mistake.

—*Sigmund Freud (1856–1939)*

2,365

Making duplicate copies and computer printouts of things no one wanted even one of in the first place is giving America a new sense of purpose.

—Andy Rooney

2,366

Americans will put up with anything provided it doesn't block traffic.

—Dan Rather

2,367

Tips for Americans traveling abroad:
—Carry the Koran
—Paint a red dot on your forehead
—Wear sandals
—Never ask how the Mets are doing.

—Mark Russell

2,368

The shortest distance between two points is usually under repair.

—Unknown

2,369

If all the cars in the United States were placed end to end, it would probably be Labor Day Weekend.

—*Doug Larson*

2,370

Parking is such street sorrow.

—*Herb Caen*

2,371

The guy who invented the first wheel was an idiot. The guy who invented the other three, *he* was a genius.

—*Sid Caesar*

2,372

A hick town is one in which there is no place to go where you shouldn't be.

—*Alexander Woollcott (1887–1943)*

2,373

All creative people should be required to leave California for three months every year.

—*Gloria Swanson (1899–1983)*

2,374

In some parts of the world, people still pray in the streets. In this country they're called pedestrians.

—*Gloria Pitzer*

2,375

Nebraska is proof that Hell is full, and the dead walk the earth.

—*Liz Winston*

2,376

You can always tell a Texan, but not much.

—*Unknown*

2,377

Texans are proof that the world was populated by aliens.

—*Cynthia Nelms*

2,378

Canada is the vichyssoise of nations—it's cold, half French, and difficult to stir.

—*Stuart Keate*

2,379

I moved to Florida because you don't have to shovel water.

—*James "The Amazing" Randi*

2,380

In Buffalo, suicide is redundant.

—From A Chorus Line

2,381

Why don't some people just shoot themselves in the head the day they are born?

—Arkady Renko

2,382

In Green Bay, Wisconsin, ten bowling shirts are considered a great wardrobe.

—Greg Koch

2,383

Not as bad as you might have imagined.

—Motto suggested for New Jersey by Calvin Trillin

2,384

Preferable to Youngstown.

—Motto suggested for Akron, Ohio, by Calvin Trillin

2,385

A person who speaks good English in New York sounds like a foreigner.

—*Jackie Mason*

2,386

New York is an exciting town where something is happening all the time, most of it unsolved.

—*Johnny Carson*

2,387

An interesting thing about New York City is that the subways run through the sewers.

—*Garrison Keillor*

2,388

On a New York subway you get fined for spitting, but you can throw up for nothing.

—*Lewis Grizzard*

2,389

New York City is filled with the same kind of people I left New Jersey to get away from.

—*Fran Lebowitz*

2,390

On New Year's Eve, people in New Jersey stay up till midnight and watch their hopes drop.

—*Richard Lewis*

2,391

If you want to be safe on the streets at night, carry a projector and slides of your last vacation.

—*Helen Mundis*

2,392

The top TV shows in Russia are "Bowling for Food" and "Wheel of Torture."

—*Yakov Smirnoff*

2,393

The Russians love Brooke Shields because her eyebrows remind them of Leonid Brezhnev.

—*Robin Williams*

2,394

Art is about making something out of nothing and selling it.

—*Frank Zappa*

2,395

I do not seek, I find.

—*Pablo Picasso (1881–1973)*

2,396

A thing of beauty is a joy for a while.

—*Hal Lee Luyah*

2,397

I am a critic—as essential to the theater as ants to a picnic.

—*Joseph Mankiewicz (1909–1992)*

2,398

Without music, life would be a mistake.
—*Friedrich Nietzsche (1844–1900)*

2,399

I have played over the music of that scoundrel Brahms.
What a giftless bastard!
—*Peter Ilyich Tchaikovsky (1840–1893)*

2,400

If Beethoven had been killed in a plane crash at the age of
twenty-two, it would have changed the history of music
. . . and of aviation.

—*Tom Stoppard*

2,401

Bach in an hour. Offenbach sooner.
—*Sign on music store door*

2,402

I was involved in the Great Folk Music Scare back in the
sixties, when it almost caught on.

—*Martin Mull*

2,403

We aren't worried about posterity; we want it to sound good right now.

—*Duke Ellington (1899–1974)*

2,404

SONG TITLES:

"I Can't Get Over a Man Like You, So You'll Have to Answer the Phone."

—*Melody Anne*

"You're the Only Thing That's Rising in the Sour Dough of Life."

—*Maxine Edwards*

"If I Had to Do It All Over Again, I'd Do It All Over You."

—*Abe Burrows*

"Don't Sit Under the Apple Tree with Anyone Else but Me."

—*Isaac Newton (1642–1727), perhaps?*

"I Gave Her a Ring, and She Gave Me the Finger."

—*Unknown*

"I Can't Fall Asleep Since You Sat on My Pillow Last Night."

—*David E. Ortman*

2,405

If it weren't for the Japanese and Germans, we wouldn't have any good war movies.

—*Stanley Ralph Ross*

2,406
Old soldiers never die, just young ones.

—*Graffito*

2,407
War is the unfolding of miscalculations.
—*Barbara Tuchman (1912–1989)*

2,408
The war situation has developed not necessarily to Japan's advantage.

—*Emperor Hirohito (1901–1989),
after losing two cities to atom bombs*

2,409
Violence never solved anything.
—*Genghis Khan (1162–1227), according to Bob Lee*

2,410

A doctor could make a million dollars if he could figure out a way to bring a boy into the world without a trigger finger.

—*Arthur Miller*

2,411

When a thing is funny, search it carefully for a hidden truth.

—*George Bernard Shaw (1856–1950)*

2,412

It's hard to be funny when you have to be clean.

—*Mae West (1892–1980)*

2,413

I never had a sense of humor. What started me in a theatrical direction was finding at a very early age that I had a talent. I could impersonate chickens. Buk buk buk bacagh.

—*Jonathan Miller*

2,414

You don't stop laughing because you grow old; you grow old because you stop laughing.

—*Michael Pritchard*

2,415

Old age comes at a bad time.

—*Sue Banducci*

2,416

After a certain age, if you don't wake up aching in every joint, you are probably dead.

—*Tommy Mein*

2,417

If you survive long enough, you're revered—rather like an old building.

—*Katharine Hepburn*

2,418

You know you're getting old when you stoop to tie your shoes and wonder what else you can do while you're down there.

—*George Burns (1896–1996)*

2,419

Old age means realizing you will never own all the dogs you wanted to.

—*Joe Gores*

2,420

Children are a great comfort in your old age—and they help you reach it faster, too.

—*Lionel Kauffman*

2,421

My grandmother started walking five miles a day when she was sixty. She's ninety-seven now, and we don't know where the hell she is.

—*Ellen DeGeneres*

2,422

When I was young, the Dead Sea was still alive.

—*George Burns (1896–1996)*

2,423

My health is good; it's my age that's bad.

—*Ray Acuff (1903–1992) at 83*

2,424

An old man in love is like a flower in winter.

—*Portuguese proverb*

2,425

My parents didn't want to move to Florida, but they turned sixty, and it was the law.

—*Jerry Seinfeld*

2,426

Never ask old people how they are if you have anything else to do that day.

—*Joe Restivo*

2,427

Death is not the end; there remains the litigation.

—*Ambrose Bierce (1842–1914?)*

2,428

If you don't go to other people's funerals, they won't go to yours.

—*Unknown*

2,429

Death is nature's way of saying, "Your table is ready."

—*Robin Williams*

2,430

Grave, n. A place in which the dead are laid to await the coming of the medical student.

—*Ambrose Bierce (1842–1914?)*

2,431

The old neighborhood has changed. Hurley Brothers Funeral Home is now called Death 'n' Things.

—*Elmore Leonard*

2,432

No matter how rich you become, how famous or powerful, when you die the size of your funeral will still pretty much depend on the weather.

—*Michael Pritchard*

2,433

Death sneaks up on you like a windshield sneaks up on a bug.

—*Unknown*

2,434

The wages of sin are death, but by the time taxes are taken out, it's just sort of a tired feeling.

—*Paula Poundstone*

2,435

Get out of here and leave me alone. Last words are for fools who haven't said enough already.

—*Last words of Karl Marx (1818–1883), allegedly*

2,436

Errol Flynn died on a seventy-foot yacht with a seventeen-year-old girl. Walter's always wanted to go that way, but he's going to settle for a seventeen-footer and a seventy-year-old.

—*Mrs. Walter Cronkite*

2,437

I don't want to achieve immortality by being inducted into baseball's Hall of Fame. I want to achieve immortality by not dying.

—*Leo Durocher (1905–1991) at 81*

2,438

LAST WILL AND TESTAMENT:
I owe much, I have nothing, the rest I leave to the poor.

—*Rabelais (1494–1553)*

2,439

Exercise daily. Eat wisely. Die anyway.

—*Unknown*

2,440

I really didn't say everything I said.

—*Yogi Berra*

2,441

Next to the originator of a great quote is the first quoter of it.

—*Ralph Waldo Emerson (1803–1882)*

2,442

A committee is a group of important individuals who singly can do nothing but who can together agree that nothing can be done.

—*Fred Allen (1894–1956)*

2,443

Diplomacy is the art of letting someone else have your way.

—*Unknown*

2,444

Palm Springs University—more than one hundred degrees available.

—*Unknown*

2,445

The trouble with England is that it's all pomp and no circumstance.

—*From the 1954 movie* Beat the Devil

2,446

You can be sincere and still be stupid.

—*Unknown*

2,447

I felt sorry for myself because I had no hands until I met a man who had no chips.

—*Kent G. Andersson*

2,448

Make a bet every day, otherwise you might walk around
lucky and never know it.

—*Jimmy Jones*

2,449

I bear no grudges. I have a mind that retains nothing.

—*Bette Midler*

2,450

Go to the zoo and enlist. Shave your neighbor's dog. Yo!
Dump your spaghetti on that guy's head.

—*Inside the ears of crazy people*
with cartoonist Gary Larson

2,451

Two leaps per chasm is fatal.

—*Chinese proverb*

2,452

People who sell macramé should be dyed a natural color and hung out to dry.

—*Calvin Trillin*

2,453

The only thing standing between you and a watery grave is your wits, and that's not my idea of adequate protection.

—*From the movie* Beat the Devil, *1954*

2,454

If the rich could hire people to die for them, the poor could make a wonderful living.

—*Jewish proverb*

2,455

My karma ran over your dogma.

—*Unknown*

2,456

Flying is hours and hours of boredom sprinkled with a few seconds of sheer terror.

—*Gregory "Pappy" Boyington (1912–1988)*

2,457

There is nothing worse than a "now" look with a "then" face.

—*Dave Falk*

2,458

Prejudices save time.

—*Robert Byrne*

2,459

The prime purpose of eloquence is to keep other people from talking.

—*Louis Vermeil*

2,460

There are some things only intellectuals are crazy enough to believe.

—*George Orwell (1903–1950)*

2,461

People performing mime in public should be subject to citizen's arrest on the theory that the normal First Amendment protection of free speech has in effect been waived by someone who has formally adopted a policy of not speaking.

—*Calvin Trillin*

2,462

If you shoot at mimes, should you use a silencer?

—*Steven Wright*

2,463

It is easier for a camel to pass through the eye of a needle if it is lightly greased.

—*John Nesvig*

2,464

Time flies like an arrow.
Fruit flies like a banana.

—*Lisa Grossman*

2,465

She had the Midas touch. Everything she touched turned into a muffler.

—*Lisa Smerling*

2,466

I've always found paranoia to be a perfectly defensible position.

—*Pat Conroy*

2,467

The early worm gets caught.

—*John Igo*

2,468

Familiarity breeds contempt, but you can't breed without familiarity.

—*Maxim Kavolik*

2,469
Familiarity breeds children.

—*Mark Twain (1835–1910)*

2,470
Two heads are better than none.

—*Jean Green*

2,471
The best car safety device is a rear-view mirror with a cop in it.

—*Dudley Moore (1935–2002)*

2,472
Leroy is a self-made man, which shows what happens when you don't follow directions.

—*Cartoon caption by Bill Hoest*

2,473

If Noah had been truly wise
He would have swatted those two flies.

—*H. Castle*

2,474

The fuchsia is the world's most carefully spelled flower.

—*Jimmy Barnes*

2,475

I had a prejudice against the British until I discovered that
fifty percent of them were female.

—*Raymond Floyd*

2,476

Washington Irving.
Answer to the question "Who was the first president,
Max?"

—*Steve Allen's Question Man*

2,477

Any other last requests?
Answer to the question "Would you mind not smoking?"

—*Unknown*

2,478

Wise men talk because they have something to say; fools talk because they have to say something.

—*Plato (427?–348? B.C.)*

Plato was a bore.

—*Friedrich Nietzsche (1844–1900)*

2,479

Nietzsche is pietsche,
But Sartre is smartre.

—*Unknown*

Nietzsche was stupid and abnormal.

—*Leo Tolstoy (1828–1910)*

2,480

Help! I'm being held prisoner by my heredity and environment!

—*Dennis Allen*

2,481

Drawing on my fine command of the English language, I said nothing.

—*Robert Benchley (1889–1945)*

2,482
GREAT MOMENTS IN HISTORY:
January 17, 1821: First recorded incident of a bird mistaking a civil servant for a statue.

Second Recorded Incident

2,483

The days of the digital watch are numbered.

—*Tom Stoppard*

2,484

I have never seen a situation so dismal that a policeman couldn't make it worse.

—*Brendan Behan (1923–1964)*

2,485

A clear conscience is often the sign of a bad memory.

—*Unknown*

2,486

Praise does wonders for the sense of hearing.

—*Unknown*

2,487

If I die, I forgive you; if I live, we'll see.

—*Spanish proverb*

2,488

A pedestrian is a man whose son is home from college.

—*Unknown*

2,489

Most conversations are simply monologues delivered in the presence of witnesses.

—*Margaret Millar*

2,490

She's descended from a long line her mother listened to.

—*Gypsy Rose Lee (1914–1970)*

2,491

Confusion is always the most honest response.

—*Marty Indik*

2,492

I'm not confused, I'm just well-mixed.

—*Robert Frost (1874–1963)*

2,493

Does the name Pavlov ring a bell?

—*Unknown*

2,494

If at first you don't succeed, you're about average.

—*Unknown*

2,495

Who's Bob?
What to reply to a person who says, "I'm so confused,
Bob."

—*John Grimes*

2,496

I was walking down the street wearing glasses when the
prescription ran out.

—*Steven Wright*

2,497

When I can no longer bear to think of the victims of broken homes, I begin to think of the victims of intact ones.

—*Peter De Vries (1910–1943)*

2,498

Have you always been a Negro or are you just trying to be
fashionable?

—*From the television series* Julia

2,499

If I had permission to do everything, I wouldn't want to do
anything.

—*The one best thing Joe Palen ever said*

2,500

Thou shalt not admit adultery.

—*Hal Lee Luyah*

2,501

There's a deception to every rule.

—*Hal Lee Luyah*

2,502

Easy Street is a blind alley.

—*Unknown*

2,503

To disagree with three-fourths of the British public is one of the first requisites of sanity.

—*Oscar Wilde (1854–1900)*

2,504

There are two kinds of complainers, men and women.

—*Unknown*

2,505

There are two kinds of people, those who finish what they start and so on.

—*Robert Byrne*

2,506

A hat should be taken off when you greet a lady and left off for the rest of your life. Nothing looks more stupid than a hat.

—*P. J. O'Rourke*

2,507

Toys are made in heaven, batteries are made in hell.

—*Tom Robbins*

2,508

I bought some batteries, but they weren't included.

—*Steven Wright*

2,509

There's never enough time to do all the nothing you want.

—*Bill Watterson*

2,510

Quote me if I'm wrong.

—*Unknown*

2,511

The only thing I can't stand is discomfort.

—*Gloria Steinem*

2,512

Oh, well, half of one, six dozen of the other.

—*Joe Garagiola*

2,513

The trouble with dawn is that it comes too early in the day.

—*Susan Richman*

2,514

When I think over what I have said, I envy dumb people.

—*Seneca (4 B.C.–A.D. 65)*

2,515

What kills a skunk is the publicity it gives itself.

—*Abraham Lincoln (1809–1865)*

2,516

If you have any problems at all, don't hesitate to shut up.

—*Robert Mankoff*

2,517

Fear is that little darkroom where negatives are developed.

—*Michael Pritchard*

2,518

Last night somebody broke into my apartment and replaced everything with exact duplicates. When I pointed it out to my roommate, he said, "Do I know you?"

—*Steven Wright*

2,519

The town where I grew up has a zip code of E-I-E-I-O.

—*Martin Mull*

2,520

They should put expiration dates on clothes so we would know when they go out of style.

—*Garry Shandling*

2,521

Confidence is always overconfidence.

—*Robert Byrne*

2,522

Lucy: Do you think anybody ever really changes?
Linus: I've changed a lot in the last year.
Lucy: I mean for the better.

—*Charles Schulz (1922–2000)*

2,523

The major concerns of Emily Litella:
    1. Conservation of national race horses
    2. Violins on television
    3. Soviet jewelry
    4. Endangered feces.

—*Gilda Radner (1946–1989)*

2,524

Let a smile be your umbrella, because you're going to get
soaked anyway.

—*Unknown*

2,525

Gravity isn't easy, but it's the law.

—*Unknown*

2,526
Queen Elizabeth is the whitest person in the world.

—*Bette Midler*

2,527
Everybody is who he was in high school.

—*Calvin Trillin*

2,528
I got kicked out of ballet class because I pulled a groin muscle, even though it wasn't mine.

—*Rita Rudner*

2,529
Open your mouth only to change feet.

—*Stanley Ralph Ross*

2,530
Gentiles are people who eat mayonnaise for no reason.

—*Robin Williams*

2,531
Some guy hit my fender, and I said to him, "Be fruitful and multiply," but not in those words.

—*Woody Allen*

2,532

The turn of the century will probably be made by a woman.

—*Unknown*

2,533

Isn't Muamar Khadafy the sound a cow makes when sneezing?

—*Dave Barry*

2,534

All Ireland is washed by the Gulf Stream, except my wife's family.

—*Brendan Behan (1923–1964)*

2,535

Keep things as they are—vote for the Sado-Masochistic Party.

—*Unknown*

2,536

He who lives far from neighbors may safely praise himself.

—*Erasmus (1466–1536)*

2,537

Astrology is not an art, it is a disease.

—*Maimonides (1135–1204)*

2,538

The closest anyone ever comes to perfection is on a job application form.

—*Unknown*

2,539

Capital punishment is our society's recognition of the sanctity of human life.

—*Senator Orrin Hatch of Utah*

2,540

So much work, so few women to do it.

—*Unknown*

2,541

I'm not a Jew. I'm Jew*ish*. I don't go the whole hog.

—*Jonathan Miller*

2,542

On Golden Blond.

—*Porn video title*

2,543

I locked my keys in the car and had to break the windshield to get my wife out.

—*Red Skelton (1913–1997)*

2,544

Prostitution, like acting, is being ruined by amateurs.

—*Alexander Woollcott (1887–1943)*

2,545

A good husband is healthy and absent.

—*Japanese proverb*

2,546

WYMI—the all-philosophy radio station.

—*Mike Dugan*

2,547

No man should plant more garden than his wife can hoe.

—*Old saying*

2,548

If you have something of importance to say, for God's sake start at the end.

—*Sarah Jeannette Duncan*

SOURCES, REFERENCES, AND NOTES

That this is primarily a book of humor rather than scholarship doesn't mean that credit shouldn't be given where it is due. Unfortunately, my notebooks of "Remarks Worth Remembering," and my memory are spotty on documentation, as are most of the published collections of quotations I have turned to for help. If you know an author or source I failed to give, please write to me in care of the publisher (see copyright page). With help from readers there will be fewer partial and missing ascriptions in the next edition.

I would particularly like to hear from the professional writers of comedy and gags whose handiwork is no doubt credited here and elsewhere to their celebrity clients.

The principal secondary sources I consulted are listed in order of size, each with an identifying letter that will be referred to in the citations that follow.

A. *A New Dictionary of Quotations on Historical Principles,* selected and edited by H. L. Mencken; Alfred A. Knopf, New York, 1952.

B. *The Quotable Woman,* compiled and edited by Elaine Partnow; Anchor Press/Doubleday, New York, 1978.

C. *Familiar Quotations,* by John Bartlett; Little, Brown, Boston, 1955.

D. *The Crown Treasury of Relevant Quotations,* by Edward F. Murphy; Crown Publishers, New York, 1978.

E. *The Great Quotations,* compiled by George Seldes; Lyle Stuart, New York, 1960.

F. *Peter's Quotations,* by Laurence J. Peter; William Morrow, New York, 1977.

G. *The Hamlyn Pocket Dictionary of Quotations,* edited by Jonathan Hunt; The Hamlyn Publishing Group, London, 1979.

H. *The Penguin Dictionary of Modern Quotations,* J. M. and M. J. Cohen; Penguin Books, Harmondsworth, England, 1976.

I. *A Dictionary of Wit, Wisdom & Satire,* by Herbert V. Prochnow and Herbert V. Prochnow, Jr.; Harper & Row, New York, 1962.

J. *The Pocket Book of Quotations,* edited by Henry Davidoff; Pocket Books, New York, 1952.

K. *The Book of Quotes,* by Barbara Rowes; E. P. Dutton, New York, 1979.

L. *The Quotable Quotations Book,* compiled by Alec Lewis; Simon & Schuster, New York, 1980.

M. *The Viking Book of Aphorisms,* by W. H. Auden and Louis Kronenberger; Viking Press, New York, 1966.

N. *Popcorn in Paradise, The Wit and Wisdom of Hollywood,* edited by John Robert Colombo; Holt, Rinehart and Winston, New York, 1980.

O. *Nobody Said It Better,* by Miriam Ringo; Rand McNally, Chicago, Ill., 1980.

P. *Proverbs and Epigrams;* Ottenheimer Publishers, Baltimore, Md., 1954.

Q. *Quotations of Wit and Wisdom,* John W. Gardner and Francesca Gardner Reese; W. W. Norton, New York, 1975.

R. *The Book of Insults,* compiled by Nancy McPhee; St. Martin's Press, New York, 1978.

S. *The Writer's Quotation Book,* edited by James Charlton; Pushcart Press, Yonkers, N.Y., 1980.

T. *Morrow's International Dictionary of Contemporary Quotations,* compiled by Jonathan Green; William Morrow and Company, New York, 1982.

U. *The Oxford Book of Aphorisms*, compiled by John Gross; Oxford University Press, Oxford, England, 1983.

V. *3,500 Good Quotes for Speakers*, Gerald F. Lieberman; Doubleday & Company, New York, 1983.

W. *Was It Good for You Too? Quotations on Love and Sex*, Bob Chieger; Atheneum, New York, 1983.

X. *The Book of Political Quotes*, compiled by Jonathon Green; McGraw Hill, New York, 1982.

Y. *Joe Franklin's Encyclopedia of Comedians*, Joe Franklin; Citadel Press, Secaucus, N.J. 1979.

Z. *More Funny People*, Steve Allen; Stein and Day, New York, 1982.

Quotation
Number

1. As given in R.

2. "Selections From the Allen Notebooks," in *Without Feathers*, 1975.

5. *Sisyphus*.

6. *Twilight of the Idols*, 1889.

7. *Mackeral Plaza*, 1958.

14. *Anthony Adverse*, 1933.

17. *Soldier, Sage, Saint*, 1978.

18. *One Fat Englishman*, 1963.

19. Possibly a corruption of something Thoreau said about fishing.

21. The *San Francisco Chronicle*, July 20, 1981.

24. *A Certain Slant of Light*, 1980.

25. A *Peanuts* comic strip.

26. As given in L.

27. From a *Peanuts* comic strip, January 1982.

28. *Coop*, 1978.

29. See 270.

30. As given in I.

32. *A Book About Myself*, 1922.

33. As given in M.

Quotation
Number

34. *The Tragedy of Pudd'nhead Wilson,* 1894.

35. Quoted in *On Being Funny,* by Eric Lax. 1975.

38. *Newsweek,* June 23, 1975.

39. *Seattle Times.*

41. As given in J.

42. *Metropolitan Life,* 1978.

47. *Barrett Wendell and His Letters,* 1924.

49. *The Ginger Man,* 1965.

51. First sentence of the short story "An Imperfect Conflagration."

52. *Death, A Poem.*

53. *Murder Considered As One of the Fine Arts,* 1827.

54. As given in A. It has been suggested that some of the quotes ascribed to Anonymous in Mencken's great work were written by Mencken himself. This could be one of them.

55. *A Day at the Races,* 1936.

58. Quoted by Anatole Broyard in a *New York Times* book review, 1980.

59. *San Francisco Chronicle,* June 5, 1981.

60. *The Pushcart Prize V,* 1980.

65. Quoted in *Omni.*

70. *Rhetoric II.*

72. *A Glass Eye at the Keyhole,* 1938.

73–75. *The Devil's Dictionary,* 1906; all have been shortened.

82. *The Devil's Dictionary,* 1906.

83. As quoted in the *San Francisco Chronicle,* April 12, 1981.

84. As given in M.

88. *Notebooks.*

89. *You Don't Have to Be in Who's Who to Know What's What,* 1980.

90. As given in K.

95. *Nature,* 1841.

98. Quoted in the *San Francisco Chronicle,* November 11, 1979.

101. *The Rules of Christian Manners and Civility,* 1695.

105. *Conversations with Gore Vidal,* 1981.

107. As given in B.

108. *Books of the Times,* Vol. II. no. 7, p. 333.

Quotation
Number

110. As given in N.

111. *My Early Life*, 1930.

113. Quoted in "The Verbal Karate of Florynce Kennedy," by Gloria Steinem, *Ms.*, March 1973.

114. *Man in the Holocene*, 1980.

121. *Miss Tallulah Bankhead*, by Lee Israel, 1972.

122. *Karl Kraus*, by Harry Zohn, 1980.

124. *Reasons of the Heart*, 1965.

125. *The Most of Malcolm Muggeridge*, 1966.

126. *Vile Bodies*, 1930

129. *Soliloquies I.*

135. As given in Q.

140. As given in Q.

141. *The Picture of Dorian Gray*, 1891.

143. *Reflections of a Bachelor Girl*, 1903.

144. *The Way of All Flesh*, 1903.

147. See 82.

148. As given in A.

150. Quoted by Sara Mayfield in *The Constant Circle*, 1968.

153. Quoted by *The New York Times*, April 29, 1956.

156. Quoted in *Womanlist*, by Weiser and Arbeiter, 1981.

159. Quoted in *Funny People*, by Steve Allen, 1981.

161. TS to RB.

163. From *Happy to Be Here*, 1982. Mr. Keillor uses the third person.

164. Quoted in L. M. Boyd's syndicated newspaper column, *The Grab Bag.*

168. As given in A.

170. As given in E.

174. As given in Q.

175. As given in D.

177. *Don Quixote*, 1605.

179. Sasuly is the author of *Bookies and Bettors*, 1982.

180. Quoted by RB in *McGoorty, The Story of a Billiard Bum*, 1970.

182. Quoted by Charles McCabe in the *San Francisco Chronicle*, June 30, 1978.

186. *The Decline and Fall of Practically Everybody*, 1950.

187. See 186.

188. WH to RB.

196. *Tropic of Cancer*, 1934.

Quotation
Number

197. As given in I.

198. *Maxims for Revolutionaries,* 1903.

201. *Everybody's Political What's What.*

202. SD is a San Francisco disc jockey.

204. *Legend: Tolstoy's Letters,* 1978.

205. As given in O.

210. As given in Q.

211. In an interview.

217. Quoted by Herbert Mitgang in *The New York Times Book Review,* July 1980.

218. Quoted by William Buckley in *The New York Times Book Review,* April 24, 1977.

219. *New York Times Book Review,* September 16, 1979.

222. As given in S.

223. From his *Journal.*

224. As given in E.

225. As given in E.

226. As recalled by Richard Sasuly (see 179).

230. Also ascribed to others.

238. Slightly shortened.

239. TS to RB.

243. See 42.

247. As given in A.

249. Unnamed "philosopher" quoted by Ron Butler in *San Francisco Examiner,* July 12, 1981.

250. *You Might As Well Live.*

253. *Poor Richard,* Act I, 1963.

254. Quoted in *Variety.*

255. See 150.

256. Quoted in *Reader's Digest,* November 1960.

257. Can anyone identify the creator of this, the greatest spoonerism of all time?

258. Quoted in *Life,* January 1981.

259. As given in K.

263. ARL was Teddy Roosevelt's daughter. For more see *Mrs. L. Conversations with Alice Roosevelt Longworth,* by Michael Teague, 1981.

269. Verbatim transcript, press conference.

270. Quoted by Leo Rosten in *Infinite Riches,* 1978.

271. From the White House tapes.

272. As given in K.

Quotation
Number

274. Quoted by Jack Anderson, May 1979.

278. Quoted in *Life*, January 1981.

280. In Jeff Davis's column in the *San Francisco Examiner,* October 12, 1980.

284. Quoted by Herb Caen in his *San Francisco Chronicle* column, January 28, 1981.

285. Quoted in the *Pacific Sun,* March 21, 1981.

288. See 269.

290. As given in H.

294. Quoted in *Life*, August 5, 1946.

295. From a letter quoted by Charles McCabe in his *San Francisco Chronicle* column, October 24, 1980.

297. *The Decay of Lying,* 1891.

298. Quoted by Peter De Vries in *The New York Times Book Review,* December 6, 1981.

299. As given in R.

300. *The Smart Set,* November 1920, p. 140.

301. *The Good Word,* 1978.

307. Attorney AH to RB.

311. Quoted by Herb Caen in the *San Francisco Chronicle,* June 1980. AL is the former basketball coach at the University of Texas.

314. RO is a professional gag writer who markets his work to a wide variety of celebrities and politicians, enabling them to feign wit where none exists.

315. Needlepoint sampler recalled by Debi McFarland for RB.

316. *Miss Piggy's Guide to Life,* 1981, by Henry Beard.

317. *The Picture of Dorian Gray,* 1891.

318. As given in Q.

319. *Rhetoric,* c. 322 B.C.

322. As given in K.

323. As given in K.

326. On *The Dick Cavett Show,* July 21, 1981.

327. As given in R.

336. From his *Letters.*

339. *Life on the Mississippi,* 1883.

343. CM is a *San Francisco Chronicle* columnist.

Quotation
Number

344. *Murphy's Law,* by Arthur Block, 1977.

345. *The Official Rules,* Paul Dickson, 1978.

346. *Down Shoe Lane.*

347. See 345.

348. *Journal,* February 3, 1860.

350. See 164.

361. *Brevia.*

362. As recalled by Charles Champlin.

363. *A Night at the Opera,* 1935.

364. Quoted in *The Observer,* August 28, 1949.

365. *The Goon Show,* with Peter Sellers, Spike Milligan, and others, ran on BBC radio from 1951 to 1958.

366. As given in H.

367. *The Comments of Moung Ka.*

368, 369. *The Catcher in the Rye,* 1951.

370. *Nausea,* January 1932.

372. *New York Times Magazine,* 1953.

374. *Best Sports Stories,* 1978.

378. "A Guide to Some of the Lesser Ballets," in *Without Feathers,* 1975.

379. As given in I.

381. In concert at the Hungry i in San Francisco, July 1965.

384. Ascribed to Katharine Hepburn in N.

387. As given in R.

388. *Who's Nobody in America,* by Fulwiler and Evans, 1981.

390. Reported by Herb Caen in the *San Francisco Chronicle,* April 24, 1980.

392. As given in N.

395. In various newspapers, 1978.

396. Quoted in Terence O'Flaherty's column, the *San Francisco Chronicle,* March 18, 1980.

398. Rewritten to conform to current postal rates.

404. Also said of other people.

405. *Newsweek,* March 28, 1960.

406–407. See 263.

412. *Duck Soup,* 1933.

416. As given in N.

418. See 34.

424. *The Case of Wagner.*

425. *A View From a Broad,* 1980.

427. As given in N.

Quotation
Number

428. *Chips Off the Old Benchley,* 1949.

432. *The Constant Wife,* 1926.

433. *Our Betters,* 1923.

434. See 113.

435. *Inside Mr. Enderby,* 1968.

436. *Farewell, My Lovely,* 1940.

437. 1962.

440. In an interview with Barbara Walters.

441. JC was a writer for the *New York Post.*

443. *Unreliable Memoirs,* 1981.

444. The author probably is Paul Valéry (1871–1945) and not Arthur C. Clarke.

446. BH to RB.

447. As given in Q.

450. As recalled by Andre Previn and quoted by Herb Caen, *San Francisco Chronicle,* February 1982.

451. The line "Forgive your enemies, but do not forget them," appears in the 1927 silent movie *Napoleon,* written and directed by Abel Gance.

453. *Finishing Touches,* Act III, 1973.

454. *Soon To Be a Major Motion Picture,* 1980.

456. As given in E.

457. Quoted in *A Thinking Man's Guide to Baseball,* 1967, by Leonard Koppet.

464. Quoted by Anatole Broyard in *The New York Times Book Review,* June 7, 1981.

465. *The Cat and the King,* 1981.

466. From an article on parental advice by Anthony Brown, distributed by the *Los Angeles Times* Syndicate.

467. *Rowing Toward Eden,* 1981.

469. As quoted by the *PG&E Progress,* January 1981.

474. Quoted by Dave Kindred in *The Washington Post.*

477. RL to RB.

478. In his syndicated newspaper column.

483. In an article on the death of *Scanlon's Magazine, Harper's,* April 1981.

485. In a letter to Sir Frederick Pollock.

488. In the story "Tlon, Uqbar, Orbis Tertius."

Quotation
Number

489. *The Young Immigrants,*
1920.

493. *The Medusa and the Snail,*
1979.

497. *Consenting Adults,* 1981.

504. And not his countryman,
Hermann Goering.

507. See 270.

508. See 270.

509. A slightly different version
appears in Herb Caen's column in the *San Francisco
Chronicle,* May 1978. Mr.
Wegner can be found at Trin-
ity University in San Antonio,
Texas.

512. Quoted by Merla Zellerbach
in the *San Francisco Chronicle,* December 31, 1980.

515. *Dialogues in Limbo,* 1925.

516. *The Winter's Tale.*

521. *New York Times Book Review,* May 8, 1979.

523, 524. MH was a professor of
Greek and Latin at Columbia.

530. *How to Prosper in the Coming Bad Years,* 1979.

534. Quoted in *Funny People,* by
Steve Allen, 1981.

536. *San Francisco Chronicle,* February 9, 1981.

538. *Household Hints,* 1966.

541. As given in M.

542. *Write If You Get Work,*
1975.

543. As given in F.

544. From a letter dated 1796.

545. *The Fall,* 1957.

546. *The Flying Inn,* 1912.

548. In a letter to Charles Green
Shaw.

549. Quoted by Aldous Huxley in
Heaven and Hell, 1956.

550. *San Francisco Chronicle,*
January 21, 1982.

551. Quoted by Herb Caen, the
San Francisco Chronicle, February 14, 1982.

552. By Erskine & Moran, 1981.

553. As given in N.

555. Quoted in *The Wall Street
Journal.*

559. *The Model Millionaire,*
1887.

560. *The Love Nest,* 1963.

561. *The Myth makers,* 1979.

569. *Faust,* 1808.

570. *The Last Word.*

Quotation
Number

571. *Why I Am Not a Christian,* 1950.

574. *The Capitalist Handbook.*

576. From her *Letters.*

577. *The History of the French Revolution,* 1837.

579. June 26, 1979.

580. See 488.

581. Compiled from various interviews.

583. As given in K.

585. See 583.

586. *The Tonight Show,* February 7, 1979.

588. See 180.

590. From a poem titled "Put Back Those Whiskers, I Know You," in *Good Intentions,* 1942.

591. *Many Long Years Ago,* 1945.

592. Quoted by George Bernard Shaw in the preface to *Androcles and the Lion,* 1912.

593. *The House of the Seven Gables,* 1851.

598. *My Ten Years in a Quandary,* 1936.

599. See 598.

600. Quoted by Leacock in *Humor: Its Theory and Technique,* 1935.

601. *Too Much College,* 1941.

602. "Gertrude the Governess," in *Nonsense Novels,* 1914.

605. As given in F.

606. As given in F.

607. "Selections From the Allen Notebooks," in *Without Feathers,* 1975.

609. *Versus,* 1949.

611. JH to RB about a television talk-show host, 1970.

612. As given in K.

613. See 140.

614. See 34.

615. *Polite Conversation,* 1738.

619. *New York Times Book Review.*

620. As given in B.

622. Before his retirement in 1981, KHA was in charge of the San Francisco Opera Company.

624. *Dialogues,* 1954.

626. As given in F.

628. To C. A. Dana, April 1865.

629. *Euphues,* 1579.

Quotation
Number

633. As quoted by Allison Silver in *The New York Times Book Review,* February 28, 1982.

636. As given in K.

639. As given in U.

640. *Notebooks,* 1912.

641. As given in H.

642. Quoted in *The New York Times Book Review,* October 30, 1983.

645. Linda Festa to RB.

646. As given in *Peter's Quotations* (New York: William Morrow and Company, 1977).

647. *The Tonight Show,* September 31, 1982.

649. As given in U.

651. *The Tonight Show,* August 11, 1982.

652. Thanks to Ms. Christopher B. Eubanks.

653. As given in V.

655. Thanks to Robert Machuta.

656. As given in W.

657. As given in U.

659. From *The Ladies Guide* (Battle Creek, Mich.: Modern Medicine Publishing Company, 1895). Dr. Kellogg helped invent cornflakes and peanut butter. In addition to denouncing masturbation, he believed that smoking caused cancer and that certain ailments could be cured by rolling a cannonball on the stomach.

660. As quoted by John Molloy in a San Francisco lecture in 1982.

661. A slightly different version is in V.

664. From the movie *Sleeper.*

665. As given in *Quotations for Writers and Speakers,* by A. Andrews.

666. As given in T.

669. Thanks to George Dushek.

672. As given in *Wilhelm Meisters Lehrjahre,* 1795.

674. As given in A.

675. Linda Festa to RB.

676. Quoted in the *San Francisco Chronicle,* August 14, 1982.

677. As given in Walter Wagner, *You Must Remember This.*

678. As given in W.

Quotation
Number

748. As given in Newbern and Rodebaugh, *Proverbs of the World.*

749. As given in *Vital Parts.* Thanks to Gerald Howard.

750, 751. As given in V.

752. As given in *The British Museum Is Falling Down.*

753. As given in *The Lonely Life.*

755. Robert Orben is a professional joke writer who publishes a newsletter called *Orben's Current Comedy* that is airmailed to subscribers. This is from the November 2, 1983, edition. The address is 700 Orange Street, Wilmington, Delaware 19801.

756. As given in V.

757. As given in *Last Words*, 1933.

760. As given in *The Measure of My Days*, 1972.

762. As given in *Newsweek*, 1978.

763. As given in T.

765. As given in Frank Muir, *The Frank Muir Book.*

766. As given in *The Old Woman.*

767. As recalled by Arlene Heath.

768. As given in *Time*, December 28, 1970.

770. As given in *Living It Up.*

771. From the movie *Annie Hall.*

772. As given in *Reginald in Russia*, 1910.

775. Thanks to Cyra McFadden.

776. Quoted by Georgia Hesse in the *San Francisco Chronicle.* Hesse added that Dom Pérignon was blind at the time.

781. As given in Herb Caen's *San Francisco Chronicle* column, November 24, 1983.

782. As given in T.

784, 785. As given in Y.

786. As given in Gary Herman, comp., *The Book of Hollywood Quotes* (London: Omnibus Press, 1979). Thanks to Chris Arnold.

787. Quoted by Jimmy Breslin in his syndicated column, April 1983.

788. As given in T.

790. From *Rhinoceros*, Act II.

791. Bill Musselman is a basketball coach.

Quotation
Number

794. From the movie *Sleeper*.

797. As given in the *Observer*, April 19, 1957.

798. From *Death of a Salesman*.

799. From Larry Gelbart's introduction to Z.

800. As given in *Funny, but Not Vulgar*, 1944.

801, 802. From Mordecai Richler's introduction to *The Best of Modern Humor* (New York: Alfred A. Knopf, 1983).

804. As given in Calvin Trillin's San Francisco lecture, January 18, 1984.

805. From a cable TV special called "Homage to Steve," 1984.

808. As given in *Sisterhood Is Powerful*.

811. As given in T.

812. As given in V.

813. As given in *Metropolitan Life*.

814. As given in V.

815. As given in *Kiss and Tell*.

816. As given in *Quote and Unquote*.

817. As given in T.

821. As given in *Esquire*, 1970.

826. See note 729.

827. As given in *The Saturday Evening Post*, 1952.

828. A slightly different version is given in W.

830. As given in *Ms.* (November 1983).

831. As given in the movie *The Culture of Narcissism* (1979).

832. As given in *I'm No Angel*.

833. From Gerald Nachman's column in the *San Francisco Chronicle*, August 1982.

834. As given in T.

838. As given in *The Big Book of Jewish Humor*.

840. As given by S. M. Ulam. *Adventures of a Mathematician* (New York: Charles Scribner's Sons, 1976).

844. As given in *The Conquest of Happiness*.

847. As given in T.

855. As given in *Jackie Mason's America* (Lyle Stuart, Inc., 1983).

856. As given in *The Painted Lady*.

857. Thanks to Linda Festa.

Quotation
Number

859. As given in *Careers for Women.*

864. See note 729.

869. Quoted by Herb Caen in the *San Francisco Chronicle,* May 17, 1983.

870. *New Yorker,* January 2, 1984.

871. As given in V.

873. As given in *The Village Voice,* April 1983.

875. As given in X.

877. As given in Joseph Heller, *Catch-22.*

879. As given in V.

880. As given in X.

881. From Will Rogers, *Autobiography.*

884. From *The Tonight Show,* February 8, 1984.

885. At The Punch Line, San Francisco, January 1984.

886. Herb Caen's column, *San Francisco Chronicle,* August 19, 1983.

888. From an article in the *San Francisco Paper,* February 1984.

889. As given in U.

890. As given in J. Green, *The Book of Rock Quotes.*

894. As given in A.

896. See note 855.

902. See note 855.

904. As given in *Orben's Current Comedy,* October 19, 1983.

905. See note 729.

909. Recalled by Calvin Trillin.

911. Thanks to Arlene Heath.

912. As given in T.

913. As given in Y.

915. As given in the *Daily Herald,* October 5, 1962.

916. Quoted by Paul Burka in *Esquire* (April 1983).

917. As given in Andy Rooney, *And More by Andy Rooney.*

918. See note 729.

920. *The Tonight Show,* September 26, 1983.

921. Gerald Nachman is a columnist for the *San Francisco Chronicle.*

922. As given in *The Hole.*

923. Quoted by Sir Laurence Olivier on the BBC.

927. See note 729.

929, 930. See note 804.

Quotation
Number

931. As given in T.

933. As given in Herb Caen's column, *San Francisco Chronicle,* December 2, 1982.

934. As given in *The Letters of Edna St. Vincent Millay.*

935. As given in *The Men's Club.*

936. Quoted by Richard Condon in *Prizzi's Honor.*

940. Quoted by Paul Fussell in *Class.*

941. See note 729.

942. As given in U.

943. As given in *The Observer,* April 20, 1958.

944. As given in H.

947. As given in X.

948. The novel *The Third Man* was written by Graham Greene.

950. From the TV show *Late Night with David Letterman,* January 6, 1984.

951. From his nightly commentary on Channel 4 (NBC), San Francisco, September 29, 1982.

952. From her San Francisco lecture, November 4, 1983.

953. From *Late Night with David Letterman,* February 9, 1984.

954. From a letter to Goodman Ace.

957. Will Durst won the 1983 San Francisco Standup Comedy Competition.

959. See note 885.

961. *The Tonight Show,* September 14, 1983.

964. As given in Y.

965. As given in U.

970. As given in V.

974. As given in U.

979. Thanks to Tom Stewart.

986. As given in *The Critic as Artist,* 1891.

987. Written for a competition among the paper's sub-editors for "the world's most boring headline." Described by Claud Cockburn in his *Autobiography.*

988. Cecilia Bartholomew writes and teaches writing in the San Francisco area.

989. Quoted by George Will in his syndicated column, December 20, 1983.

Quotation
Number

990. In *The New York Times Book Review,* January 1, 1984.

992. As given in T.

997. As given in *The Nature and Aim of Fiction.* Thanks to Gerald Howard.

1,000. As given in *The New York Times Book Review,* June 6, 1982.

1,001. *Afterthoughts,* 1931.

1,002. As given in *The Observer,* October 14, 1951.

1,004. As given in *The Guardian,* March 21, 1973.

1,006. As given in F. Scott Fitzgerald, *The Last Tycoon.*

1,008. As given in the *Sunday Times* (London), October 16, 1977.

1,009. As given in *Time,* 1957.

1,010. Quoted by W. H. Auden in *A Certain World.*

1,015, 1,016, 1,017. See note 788.

1,018. As given in *The New York Times Book Review,* 1971.

1,019. As given in *The Observer* October 8, 1961.

1,020. As given in Y.

1,035. From the movie *All About Eve,* 1950.

1,037. As given in *San Francisco Chronicle,* December 21, 1982.

1,038. As given in *San Francisco Chronicle,* January 2, 1983.

1,039. Arthur Gingold wrote *Items from Our Catalog.*

1,040. Quoted by Gerald Nachman in the *San Francisco Chronicle,* September 22, 1983.

1,041. Quoted by Gerald Nachman in the *San Francisco Chronicle,* July 18, 1983.

1,042. Quoted by Gerald Nachman in the *San Francisco Chronicle,* December 21, 1983.

1,044. As given in *The New York Times Magazine,* January 9, 1966.

1,045. As given in T.

1,049. As given in V.

1,050. Martin Cruz Smith to RB.

1,052. As given in W.

1,053. As given in H.

Quotation
Number

1,056. Thanks to Maureen Connolly.

1,064. See note 716.

1,065. From a Hallmark card.

1,072. As given in *A Madman's Diary*.

1,073. Inge was dean of St. Paul's.

1,074. As given in *More in Anger*, 1958.

1,075. See note 716.

1,076. From the radio show *The Prairie Home Companion*, June 1983.

1,079. As given in *Cat Scan* (New York: Atheneum, 1983).

1,081. Thanks to Leslie Sheridan.

1,083. As given in *The Diary of Alice James*.

1,085. As given in Z.

1,086. As given in V.

1,087. As given in *Jeeves and the Hard-boiled Egg*.

1,089. Quoted by Harry Zohn, *Karl Kraus*.

1,090. As given in the *Observer*, July 19, 1975.

1,092. *The Tonight Show*, February 10, 1984.

1,093. As given in the *Atlantic Monthly*, 1981.

1,096. As given in A. Schlesinger, Jr., *A Thousand Days*.

1,097, 1,098. As given in G.

1,099. As given in Y.

1,101. As given in T.

1,104. *The Tonight Show*, November 17, 1982.

1,107. See note 952.

1,116. Thanks to Charles T. DeShong.

1,122. As given in *The Book of Laughter and Forgetting*.

1,124. Thanks to Dick Werthimer.

1,125. Thanks to Robert Machuta.

1,127. Thanks to Charles T. DeShong.

1,128. Darrin Weinberg to RB.

1,130. See note 885.

1,132. John Rostoni to Teressa Skelton to RB.

1,136. Often called Sturgeon's Law.

1,137. *Improvisation*.

1,140. As given in *The Naked Civil Servant*.

1,141. See note 698.

Quotation
Number

1,144. As given in U.

1,145. As given in *Psychology in the Wry*.

1,151. Dan Quisenberry is a baseball pitcher.

1,154. Teressa Skelton to RB.

1,155. Thanks to Bob Hudson.

1,157. See note 729.

1,158. Quoted by Herb Caen in the *San Francisco Chronicle*, May 22, 1983.

1,160. As given in *Orben's Current Comedy*, September 21, 1983. See note 755.

1,162. As given in Z.

1,163. As given in *My Saber Is Bent*, 1983. See note 755.

1,167. As given in *The Bald Twit Lion*.

1,169. As given in *Epistles*.

1,180. As given in *How to Become a Virgin*.

1,182. As given in *They and I*.

1,187. As given in *Present Laughter*, Act I.

1,189. As given in *Orben's Current Comedy*, November 17, 1983. See note 755.

1,193. As given in X.

1,194. See slightly different wording in U.

1,195. As given in H.

1,196. As given in Z.

1,200. As given in *The Wall Street Journal*, 1975.

1,202. See note 788.

1,207. *Maxims*, 1665.

1,209. As given in George Robey, *Looking Back on Life*.

1,210. *The Tonight Show*, September 14, 1983.

1,214. As given in *Unkempt Thoughts*.

1,218. As given in *Night Thought Book*, 1834.

1,223. Linda Festa to RB.

1,227. As given in *Ugly Trades*.

1,229. Jerry Bundsen is a former aide to Herb Caen, who quoted this line in his column in the *San Francisco Chronicle* in October 1983.

1,231. As given in Y.

1,233. In the introduction to *Mother Night*.

1,234. As given in *Class*.

1,236. As given in Z.

Quotation
Number

1,239. Quoted in the magazine *Friendly Exchange* (Winter 1982).

1,242. As given in *The Densa Quiz.*

1,243. As given in the *Observer,* 1974.

1,244. Thanks to Arlene Heath.

1,246. See note 788.

1,248. As given in *Social Studies.*

1,249, 1,250. As given in T.

1,252. Thanks to George Dushek.

1,255. As given in W.

1,259. As given in *Quality Street,* Act III.

1,260. As given in William Fifield, *In Search of Genius.*

1,261. As given in *The Devil's Dictionary.*

1,262. As given in *Poor Richard's Almanac.*

1,263. As given in *Speedboat.* Thanks to Gerald Howard.

1,266. Thanks to George Dushek.

1,268. As given in *On Reading and Books,* 1851.

1,271. As given in letter to T. J. Hogg, 1821.

1,272. As given in Stanton Dela-plane's column in the *San Francisco Chronicle,* March 7, 1934.

1,273. *The Tonight Show,* March 13, 1984.

1,276. BS in a letter to RB.

1,277. JDM in the *Bulletin,* 1974

1,279. LT in *What Is Religion?* 1902.

1,282. HLM in an Associated Press interview, 1941.

1,283. RM in *The Towers of Trebizond,* 1956.

1,284. Quoted by G. M. Thomson in *Vote of Censure,* 1968.

1,285. BM in a speech in Lausanne, 1904.

1,287. CK is a standup comedian.

1,288. From the television series *All in the Family.* Thanks to George Aronek.

1,290. Quoted in the *San Francisco Chronicle,* December 17, 1985.

1,291. According to William Safire in his syndicated column, December 8, 1985.

1,292. FN in *Thus Spake Zarathustra.*

Quotation
Number

1,293. EH in a letter.

1,294. HR as quoted in Leslie Halliwell's *The Filmgoer's Companion,* 1984.

1,296. RS is a standup comedian.

1,299. From *The Cynic's Lexicon,* compiled by Jonathon Green, 1982.

1,300. Thanks to David Huard.

1,301. FN in *Thus Spake Zarathustra,* 1891.

1,302. Quoted in *3500 Good Quotes for Speakers,* compiled by Gerald F. Lieberman, 1983.

1,304. NW quoted in *Was It Good for You, Too?* compiled by Bob Chieger, 1983.

1,305. WA in *Play It Again, Sam,* 1969.

1,307. Quoted in the *San Francisco Sunday Chronicle-Examiner,* September 1, 1985.

1,309. O in *Ars Amatoria.*

1,310. J in *Satires,* A.D. 110.

1,311. From *A New Dictionary of Quotations on Historical Principles,* compiled by H. L. Mencken, 1952.

1,313. SR in the *San Francisco Chronicle,* August 2, 1985.

1,318. Taken from the jacket of MP's 1985 book *Shoes Never Lie.*

1,319. AC is a standup comedian.

1,321. Quoted in the comedy trade paper *Just for Laughs,* August 1985.

1,325. Quoted in *Forbes,* September 16, 1985.

1,327. JM in *Miss Manners' Guide to Excruciatingly Correct Behavior,* 1985.

1,328. JV is a standup comedian.

1,329. MD in *Dogs Are Better Than Cats,* 1985.

1,330. RB in the *Atlantic Monthly,* February 1985.

1,331. EB is a standup comedian.

1,332. MP is a standup comedian.

1,336. Quoted in the *San Francisco Chronicle,* December 31, 1984.

1,337. *The Tonight Show,* January 10, 1985.

1,338. RO in *Orben's Current*

Quotation
Number

Comedy, a weekly newslet-
ter of topical gags, November 6, 1985.

1,339. JM in *Common Courtesy*,
1985.

1,340. ARC was interviewed by
The New York Times in
December 1985. He was
quoted further as saying
that he didn't rule out the
possibility that the honor
bestowed on him was political smear.

1,342. See note 1,311.

1,344. Quoted by HG in his auto-
biographical novel *Family*.

1,346. Thanks to H. Peter Metzger.

1,347. From *Miss Piggy's Guide to
Life*, 1981, as told to HB.

1,348. From *Quote*, November 1,
1985.

1,349. MS to RB.

1,350. From the Peanuts comic
strip, April 1984.

1,352. KW is a popular columnist
in Great Britain.

1,354. GK on his radio show *A
Prairie Home Companion*.
July 21, 1985.

1,357. AH in the *San Francisco
Chronicle*, November 25,
1985.

1,358. Quoted in *The Cynic's Lexicon*, compiled by Jonathon
Green, 1982.

1,359. AC in *The New York
Times*, February 18, 1968.

1,360. MW at the San Francisco
Standup Comedy Competi-
tion, 1979.

1,362. GG in a letter to the *Journal
of Irreproducible Results*.

1,363. RY in *Family Weekly*, 1977.

1,366. Thanks to Marty Indik.

1,369. GS is a standup comedian.

1,371. GS on *The Tonight Show*,
August 17, 1985.

1,372. Seen in London by Herb
Caen.

1,373. WD won the 1983 San
Francisco Standup Comedy
Competition.

1,374. Given in *Was It Good for
You, Too?* compiled by Bob
Chieger, 1983.

1,375. JK is a standup comedian.

1,378. MM is a standup comedian.

Quotation
Number

1,379. Quoted by Peter Stack in the *San Francisco Chronicle,* October 4, 1985. RL is a standup comedian.

1,380. GL is publisher of *High Society.*

1,381. AB in *Rolling Stone,* July 14, 1977.

1,386. PD in his 1955 novel *Major Thompson Lives in France and Discovers the French.*

1,388. LB in *Don Juan,* 1819.

1,390. BN is a standup comedian. Thanks to Pete Harley.

1,391. Thanks to Lee Simon.

1,392. GS is a standup comedian.

1,393. WT is a standup comedian.

1,395. MD to RB.

1,398. From the movie *She Done Him Wrong* (1933), screenplay by MW.

1,403. MS in *The New York Times Book Review,* November 6, 1985.

1,406. GN is a columnist and critic for the *San Francisco Chronicle.*

1,408. *Out of Africa,* screenplay by Kurt Luedtke based on books by and about Isak Dinesen.

1,409. SB in *Men: An Owner's Manual,* 1984.

1,410. CS is a standup comedian.

1,412. GN in the *San Francisco Chronicle,* February 26, 1985.

1,413. GK in his San Francisco lecture, December 13, 1984.

1,415. Thanks to Susan Richman.

1,416. Thanks to Arlene Heath.

1,417. RM in *The Towers of Trebizond,* 1956.

1,419. Quoted in *Was It Good for You, Too?* compiled by Bob Chieger, 1983.

1,421. Thanks to Merla Zellerbach.

1,423. Thanks to Susan Richman.

1,424. Quoted by Herb Caen in the *San Francisco Chronicle,* December 23, 1983.

1,425. DS on *The Tonight Show,* 1972.

1,430. See note 1,338.

1,432. PP is a standup comedian.

1,433. See note 1,338.

1,435. SP is a standup comedian.

Quotation
Number

1,439. In *Letters and Journals* (New York: Viking, 1985).

1,440. LPS in *Afterthoughts,* 1934.

1,441. EP is a standup comedian.

1,448. WS is a standup comedian.

1,449. MS to RB.

1,454. LH on *Freeman Reports,* November 30, 1985.

1,455. Thanks to Joe Gores.

1,458. In RB's biography *Mc-Goorty,* 1972, and 1984.

1,460. JG in *Esquire,* April 1983.

1,461. Thanks to Knox Burger.

1,465. LPS in *All Trivia,* 1949.

1,467. See note 1,338.

1,468. RM at a San Francisco press conference, May 21, 1985.

1,473. Quoted by Merla Zellerbach in the *San Francisco Chronicle,* March 7, 1984.

1,474. Quoted in the *Little Dublin News,* March 1985, published in Dubuque, Iowa.

1,482. LB in the *San Francisco Examiner,* July 15, 1984.

1,494. HC in the *San Francisco Chronicle,* April 28, 1985.

1,500. FML to RB.

1,502. GK in his San Francisco lecture, December 13, 1984.

1,505. JC on *The Tonight Show,* November 20, 1984.

1,506. HC in the *San Francisco Chronicle,* December 11, 1985.

1,508–1,509. RB in his syndicated *New York Times* column, September 22, 1985.

1,510. DTW to RB.

1,512. LT in her one-woman Broadway show, 1985.

1,513. HAS in *Let the Crabgrass Grow,* 1960.

1,515. GC in *The Widow's Tears,* 1612.

1,516. RS is a standup comedian.

1,519. CK won the Pulitzer Prize for poetry in 1985.

1,520. Quoted in *Hot News,* published periodically by Lyle Stuart.

1,525. Thanks to David Huard.

1,526. Thanks to Marty Indik.

1,527. BS in *What Makes Sammy Run?* 1941.

1,530. CT in *American Fried,* 1979.

Quotation
Number

1,533. ML in the *Pacific Sun,* November 15, 1985.

1,534. FL in *Social Studies,* 1981.

1,535. DEW in *A Likely Story,* 1984.

1,537. EB on *The Tonight Show,* September 25, 1985.

1,538. Quoted by Herb Caen in the *San Francisco Chronicle,* May 6, 1985.

1,539. WA in *Please Don't Drink the Water,* 1967.

1,540. Quoted by Herb Caen in the *San Francisco Chronicle,* December 13, 1984.

1,542. CT in *American Fried,* 1979.

1,545. BM in *Idiots First,* 1963.

1,546. JS is a standup comedian.

1,549. JE is a San Francisco radio talk-show host.

1,551. CS is a standup comedian.

1,553. CB in his San Rafael, California, lecture, February 1985.

1,557. Thanks to H. Peter Metzger.

1,558. GM is a standup comedian.

1,563. RS is a standup comedian.

1,564. MP on the BBC World Service.

1,566–1,567. Delivered on Comedy Celebration Day, July 20, 1985, when sixty standup comedians performed for a total of seven hours in San Francisco's Golden Gate Park.

1,570. RB in his syndicated *New York Times* column, August 27, 1985.

1,571. See note 1,338.

1,572. Quoted by Herb Caen in the *San Francisco Chronicle,* March 7, 1985.

1,573. Thanks to Dr. Stephen F. Goodman.

1,574. JJG to RB in jest; RB didn't need a root canal.

1,576. Thanks to Collin Wilcox.

1,579. Thanks to Audrey Stanley, KARN, Little Rock.

1,581. EB is a standup comedian.

1,582. YS is a Soviet comedian who emigrated to the United States in 1981. He also said that in the United States you watch television,

Quotation
Number

but in Russia television watches you.

1,583. GN in the *San Francisco Chronicle,* August 27, 1985.

1,587. HC in the *San Francisco Chronicle,* December 29, 1985. The quote is out of context, for it appeared in a column in which HC argued that drunk jokes aren't really funny and vowed to use fewer of them in his widely read column.

1,589–1,592. Many quotes of this sort can be found in *The Lexicon of Musical Invective,* compiled by Nicolas Slonimsky, 1969.

1,593. From the Question Man segment of the old *Steve Allen Show*

1,594. Thanks to Kitty Sprague.

1,596. AH to RB.

1,601. MB in *Playboy,* 1979.

1,602. SL in *The Mariposa Bank Mystery,* 1912.

1,604. SP is a standup comedian.

1,605. GS in *The Life of Reason,* 1954.

1,606. Thanks to Leonard Tong.

1,607. As quoted by RB in *McGoorty,* 1972 and 1984.

1,611. Quoted by Bob Greene in *Cheeseburgers.* Thanks to Tom Winston.

1,612. RR to the New York State Boxing Commission, May 23, 1962.

1,613. Quoted by Patricia Holt in the *San Francisco Chronicle,* November 13, 1985.

1,615. Thanks to Marty Indik.

1,616. BU on *Larry King Live,* September 17, 1985.

1,619. EG is a standup comedian.

1,620. BM in the *San Francisco Examiner,* February 10, 1985.

1,623. EB was the grand marshal of the 1986 Rose Bowl Parade.

1,627. FD on Cable News Network, November 4, 1985.

1,631. Quoted by Barnaby Conrad III in the *San Francisco Chronicle,* November 24, 1985.

Quotation
Number

1,636–1,637. Thanks to Arlene Heath.

1,640. Quoted in the *San Francisco Chronicle*, August 10, 1985.

1,643. GT in *Punch*, June 18, 1958.

1,644. From a sketch titled *Fern Ock Veek, Sickly Whale Oil Processor*, reprinted in *The New! Improved! Bob and Ray Book*, 1985.

1,645. Quoted by Stephanie von Buchau in the *Pacific Sun*, February 8, 1985.

1,646. FL in *Social Studies*, 1981.

1,647. From *Conversations with Capote*, by Lawrence Grobel.

1,649. RM in *The Drowning Pool*, 1951.

1,650. NS in *Playboy*, February 1979.

1,651. Letter to RB.

1,653. Letter to Groucho Marx, June 12, 1953.

1,657. Thanks to Susan Richman.

1,660. MF in *The New York Times*, April 16, 1975.

1,661. BS is a standup comedian.

1,662. HDT in *Journal*, January 3, 1861.

1,665. From *The Journal of Irreproducible Results*. Thanks to D. O. Rickter.

1,671. SD in the *San Francisco Chronicle*, July 11, 1984.

1,672. AM is the author of *The Canadians*, 1985.

1,673. JC on *The Tonight Show*, November 20, 1984.

1,678. Thanks to Gary Muldoon.

1,680. Thanks to Harry Roach.

1,684. SP is a standup comedian.

1,686. Quoted by Leah Garchik in the *San Francisco Chronicle*, December 6, 1985.

1,694–1,695. Quoted in *The Hollywood Hall of Shame* by Harry and Michael Medved, 1984.

1,696. Screenplay by Billy Wilder, Lesser Samuels, and Walter Newman.

1,697. Quoted in *The Jewish Mother's Hall of Fame*, by Fred Bernstein, 1986.

Quotation
Number

1,702. Thanks to Mary Indik.

1,704. SW on *The Tonight Show,* February 28, 1985.

1,711. BM is a standup comedian.

1,716. Wording by RB.

1,725. JP in a letter to RB.

1,730. EK at the opening of an exhibition of jade in January 1985.

1,736. CC to Ethel Barrymore, according to *Time,* March 6, 1955.

1,737. Screenplay by Jim Abrahams and Jim and Jerry Zucker.

1,738. Thanks to Tom Stewart.

1,739. RN during an interview on CBS in 1984.

1,744. See note 1,373.

1,747. Al Ordover is a close personal friend of Knox Burger.

1,748. RS is former chairman of the Democratic party.

1,751. FD in *Sports Illustrated,* July 9, 1984.

1,752. From *The Cynic's Lexicon,* compiled by Jonathon Green, 1982.

1,754. Quoted by Richard Nixon to Barbara Walters, May 8, 1985.

1,761. JM in the introduction to Hemingway's *The Most Dangerous Summer,* 1985.

1,769. CC is book editor of the *San Jose Mercury-News.*

1,770. GV in *Oui,* April 1975.

1,773. GF in a letter to Ivan Turgenev, November 8, 1879.

1,774. Quoted by Shay Duffrin in his one-man show *Confessions of an Irish Rebel,* 1984.

1,778. TJ in a letter, 1819.

1,779. TL was the coach of the Los Angeles Dodgers.

1,781. OW in *The Critic as Artist,* 1890.

1,783. LA in the *Sunday Times,* (London), February 28, 1962.

1,785. IC in her 1981 novel *The Shooting Party.*

1,787. Quoted by Thomas Fleming in *The New York Times Book Review,* January 6, 1985.

Quotation
Number

1,788. Thanks to Hugh Parker.

1,789. Quoted by Merla Zellerbach in the *San Francisco
Chronicle,* December 21,
1982.

1,792. Quoted in *New York* magazine, July 8, 1974.

1,793. PA reviewing *The Other
637 Best Things Anybody
Ever Said* in the *San Rafael
Independent Journal,*
March 21, 1985.

1,795. RD is chiefly known as the
former roommate of Marty
Indik, who himself is not
particularly well known.

1,798. GV in *The New York
Times,* February 4, 1973.

1,799. RB in *The New York
Times,* June 18, 1968.

1,801. RR in the *San Francisco
Examiner,* July 1, 1984.

1,805. Thanks to Harry Roach.

1,806. JH as quoted in the *Pacific
Sun,* November 28, 1985.

1,807. GK in *Lake Wobegone
Days,* 1985.

1,808. FL in *Metropolitan Life,*
1978.

1,814. AHW in *The New York
Times,* 1968.

1,816. From *The Cynic's Lexicon,*
compiled by Jonathon
Green, 1982.

1,817. JB in *Affurisms,* 1869.

1,819. Thanks to Lee Simon.

1,820. WMH in a letter to RB.

1,826. Quoted by Rob Morse in
the *San Francisco Exam-
iner,* January 5, 1986.

1,828. JP in *Aphorisms,* privately
printed in 1985.

1,830. Thanks to Arlene Heath.

1,832. Thanks to Marty Indik.

1,834. WS in *The Merchant of
Venice.*

1,839. KEG in *The Well-Tempered
Sentence,* 1984.

1,840. LMB in his syndicated column, May 5, 1985.

1,842. Thanks to David L. Huard.

1,843. GBS as quoted by Ulick
O'Connor in *All the
Olympians,* 1984.

1,844. GBS in a letter to H. G.
Wells.

1,847. Quoted by Herb Caen
in the *San Francisco Chron-*

Quotation
Number

icle, November 17, 1985.

1,851. Thanks to Robert Gordon.

1,853. BB as quoted by Shay Duffrin in his one-man show *Confessions of an Irish Rebel.*

1,855. Cartoon caption in *The New Yorker,* January 6, 1986.

1,856. WT is a professional ventriloquist.

1,858. Thanks to Jim Eason.

1,860. Steve Allen remembers this line from the 1930s. Letter to RB.

1,861. SK is a standup comedian.

1,862. SP is a standup comedian.

1,864. Thanks to Marty Indik.

1,868. As given in *The Dictionary of Humorous Economics.*

1,871. AC in *Notebooks,* 1965.

1,872. Quoted by Herb Caen in the *San Francisco Chronicle,* February 2, 1985.

1,875. AE as quoted in *The Book of Political Quotes,* compiled by Jonathon Green, 1982.

1,880. JB as quoted by Joe Franklin in his *Encyclopedia of Comedy,* 1979.

1,883. ERM as quoted by Harry Reasoner.

1,887. JS as quoted in *The Book of Political Quotes,* compiled by Jonathon Green, 1982.

1,890. JL is a standup comedian.

1,891. See note 1,373.

1,892. HLM in a letter. Thanks to Mary Indik.

1,893. Quoted by Herb Caen in the *San Francisco Chronicle,* May 19, 1983.

1,895. Thanks to Bob Engan.

1,898. WT is a ventriloquist.

1,900. From the movie *Gentlemen Prefer Blondes,* 1953.

1,901. SB in a lecture in San Francisco, November 1984.

1,908. Thanks to Oakley Hall.

1,911. SK is a standup comedian.

1,912. EB as quoted by Charles Roos in the *Rocky Mountain News,* August 31, 1986.

1,913. MD as quoted in *Rave* magazine, November 1986.

Quotation
Number

1,914. AE as quoted by Herb Caen in the *San Francisco Chronicle,* May 16, 1989.

1,915. WHA as quoted by Dear Abby in her column, May 16, 1988.

1,919. MR in the Introduction to his *The Best of Modern Humor,* Knopf, 1983.

1,921. LT and JW in *The Search for Intelligent Life in the Universe.*

1,923. Russian proverb quoted by R. W. Payne in *A Stress Analysis of a Strapless Evening Gown,* 1963.

1,925. RR as quoted by Alec Guinness in his autobiography, 1986.

1,926. Unknown, thanks to Rothwell D. Mason.

1,927. Unknown, as quoted in the *Hayward Daily Review,* February 18, 1986.

1,936. LW in a letter to RB.

1,938. Unknown, thanks to Marqua Lee Brunette.

1,941. KN on *Saturday Night Live.*

1,943. EP, thanks to R. G. Fisher.

1,944. EW as quoted in the *San Francisco Chronicle,* April 8, 1989.

1,946. Unknown, thanks to Eliza Sunneland.

1,947. FK as quoted by Leah Garchick in the *San Francisco Chronicle,* August 21, 1988.

1,950. Osage saying thanks to Bob Lee.

1,951. KN as quoted by Herb Caen in the *San Francisco Chronicle,* August 10, 1985.

1,952. RWW as quoted in *The Journal of Irreproducible Results,* 1985.

1,953. AS in the *San Francisco Examiner.*

1,960. SR, thanks to C. Wesley Eicole, M.D.

1,962. LT and JW in *The Search for Intelligent Life in the Universe.*

1,964. SG as quoted by A. Scott Berg in *Goldwyn,* 1989.

1,965. Irish saying, thanks to Richard Meehan.

Quotation
Number

1,969. Unknown, thanks to Stephan Adams.

1,972. MF as quoted in *The Journal of Irreproducible Results*, 1985.

1,979. FW in *Down Among the Women*.

1,981. MW in the movie *Belle of the Nineties*, 1934.

1,986. BY thanks to Robert C. Smith.

1,987. GU, thanks to Johnson Letellier.

1,989. JM in the *Chicago Sun-Times*, November 9, 1986.

1,992. RS in the *San Francisco Chronicle*, August 15, 1988.

1,999. DB is a syndicated columnist for the *Miami Herald*.

2,000. From TU's television show, May 5, 1989.

2,001. AH is a standup comedian.

2,003. PD as quoted by Milton Berle in *B.S. I Love You*, McGraw-Hill, 1988.

2,005. TS is a standup comedian.

2,006. SL, thanks to Emily Smith.

2,007. RB as quoted by Jon Carroll in the *San Francisco Chronicle*, April 1, 1986.

2,013. KB in a letter from the front, 1943.

2,014. JS, thanks to John Diones.

2,017. AL, thanks to John Grigsby.

2,020. WA in *The Lunatic's Tale*, 1986.

2,021. JBB is a syndicated columnist.

2,022. RR is a standup comedian.

2,023. DP in *A Telephone Call*.

2,024. JR is a standup comedian.

2,026. JT is a standup comedian.

2,028. MP writes for the *Providence Journal*.

2,045. Thanks to Dr. Win Bottom.

2,051. WA in the movie *Manhattan*, 1979.

2,053. JH in *Good as Gold*, 1979.

2,056. NS in *Brighton Beach Memoirs*, 1986.

2,057. WA in the movie *A Midsummer Night's Sex Comedy*, 1982.

2,058. From the show that aired October 7, 1987.

2,059. LB is a standup comedian.

Quotation
Number

2,061. LG in *Elvis Is Dead and I Don't Feel So Good Myself*, 1987.

2,063. Censors cut this MW line from *Every Day's a Holiday*, 1937.

2,064. JK in *People Will Talk*, 1986.

2,065. WD is a standup comedian.

2,066. KW in *Billy Liar on the Moon*, 1975.

2,069. From MG's cartoon strip *Life Is Hell*.

2,072. AC is a standup comedian.

2,077. GG in *Playboy*, June 1989.

2,078. WA in *The Lunatic's Tale*, 1986.

2,088. Screenplay by Laurie Craig.

2,089. DB in *Florida* magazine.

2,090. DC is a standup comedian.

2,095. Q is a French writer quoted by Peter De Vries in *Into Your Tent I'll Creep*, 1971.

2,099. Unknown, thanks to Robert G. Smith.

2,103. RLS, thanks to Susan Trott.

2,105. From the television show *All in the Family*.

2,106. SV is a standup comedian.

2,109. ML as quoted by Jeanne Wearing on KPOF, Denver, October 1986.

2,110. MJF as quoted by Leah Garchick in the *San Francisco Chronicle*, January 27, 1988.

2,111. BC in *Love and Marriage*, 1989.

2,112. RD in *Rave*, November 1986.

2,116. WA in *The Lunatic's Tale*, 1986.

2,118. SJ as quoted by Herb Caen in the *San Francisco Chronicle*, February 3, 1986.

2,119. TG as quoted by Herb Caen in the *San Francisco Chronicle*, February 3, 1986.

2,123. HC in the *San Francisco Chronicle*, June 13, 1986.

2,138. GK in a lecture at College of Marin (Kentfield, California), January 12, 1989.

2,140. EP as quoted by Guy Trebay in *The Village Voice*, January 7, 1985.

2,145. CL is a standup comedian.

Quotation
Number

2,150. FO'C as quoted by Mark Childress in *The New York Times Book Review,* May 21, 1989.
2,153. BH on *The Tonight Show,* January 2, 1987.
2,154. RR is a standup comedian.
2,158. Unknown, thanks to Henry Crossfield.
2,159. RS's grandfather as quoted in RS's *Yes, My Darling Daughter,* 1976.
2,161. PK as quoted by J. Bryan III in *Hodgepodge Two,* Atheneum, 1989.
2,162. Unknown, as quoted by Herb Caen in the *San Francisco Chronicle,* December 22, 1987.
2,169. Tribesman quoted by Margaret Mead in *Male and Female,* 1949.
2,175. CL is a standup comedian.
2,176. MS is a standup comedian.
2,179. CC, thanks to Bill McCollough.
2,181. TE as quoted by D. Fischer in *Historians' Fallacies,* 1970.

2,182. JM in the *Rocky Mountain News.*
2,183. PP is a standup comedian.
2,184. Unknown, as quoted by Ray Orrock in the *Hayward Daily Review,* February 28, 1986.
2,187. BA as quoted by Herb Caen in the *San Francisco Chronicle,* May 6, 1986.
2,188. MD, thanks to John Grigsby.
2,192. BL is a sports columnist for the *Philadelphia Inquirer.*
2,194. BC as quoted by Rob Morse in the *San Francisco Examiner,* June 1, 1986.
2,200. Unknown, thanks to Lee Simon.
2,201. GS as quoted by Herb Caen, the *San Francisco Chronicle,* December 22, 1987.
2,203. From TA's 1975 movie *Lies My Father Told Me.*
2,210. RSW in the *San Francisco Chronicle,* June 5, 1986.
2,216. DD, thanks to Marty Indik.

Quotation
Number

2,217. DM as quoted in *The New York Times Book Review*, December 29, 1985.

2,219. CM in the *San Francisco Examiner*, July 20, 1986.

2,221. JM in the *San Francisco Chronicle*, November 30, 1988.

2,224. NWJ in a letter to RB.

2,228. GN in the *San Francisco Chronicle*, May 18, 1989.

2,229. OW in *People*, March 6, 1989.

2,230. RQ, Cyra McFadden's former stepfather, as quoted in her *Rain or Shine*, 1986.

2,231. AW, thanks to Robert G. Smith.

2,233. JH is a standup comedian.

2,234. JH, thanks to Marty Indik.

2,236. Tribesman quoted by Jared Diamond in *Discover*, May 1987.

2,239. AC is a standup comedian.

2,241. AWB is a standup comedian.

2,244. JL as quoted by Herb Caen in the *San Francisco Chronicle*, March 3, 1986.

2,245. SJ as quoted by Herb Caen in the *San Francisco Chronicle*, July 10, 1988.

2,253. MP as quoted in *Miss Piggy's Guide to Life*, as told to Henry Beard, 1981.

2,254. EL to RB.

2,255. MO'D as quoted by Paul Slansky in *Playboy*, 1989.

2,256. MB as quoted in *Playboy*, 1975.

2,257. JB as quoted by Edward S. Gifford, Jr., in *He's My Boy*, 1962.

2,258. Unknown, thanks to Jim Eason.

2,269. JKG in *Ambassador's Journal*, 1969.

2,270. RP in *L'Habit Vert*, 1912.

2,279. EP as quoted by Guy Trebay in *The Village Voice*, January 7, 1985.

2,280. On Cable News Network, April 26, 1988.

2,281. GV, thanks to Stefan D. Koch, who was his student at Temple University.

2,283. As quoted by Carlos Fuentes in *The New York*

Quotation
Number

Times Book Review, April 6, 1986.

2,284. As quoted by Dale McFeathers of the Scripps Howard News Service.

2,287. Cartoon caption by JM in *The New Yorker,* April 3, 1989.

2,290. BM is a television newsman in Oakland, California.

2,293. JL as quoted in *Esquire,* December 1986.

2,294. HK as quoted in the *Miami Herald,* January 3, 1987.

2,297. JL as quoted in *Esquire,* December 1986.

2,298. GV, thanks to Bill Weiss.

2,299. PW-D to RB.

2,300. SG as quoted in *The Moguls* by Norman Zierold, 1969.

2,303. DB, thanks to Johnson Letellier.

2,304. MM as quoted by Herb Caen in the *San Francisco Chronicle,* January 1, 1985.

2,306. GE as quoted by Jake Curtis in the *San Francisco Chronicle,* August 31, 1987.

2,307. TB in his cartoon strip *Funky Winkerbean.*

2,308. DJ as quoted in *Boring Stuff* by Alan Caruba.

2,309. SO in the *Los Angeles Times,* November 1988.

2,310. From a column by Art Rosenbaum in the *San Francisco Chronicle,* January 20, 1988.

2,314. LT on *The Tonight Show,* January 1985.

2,317. I remember this pep yell from the 1950s.

2,319. HY as quoted by Milton Berle in *B.S. I Love You,* 1988.

2,320. Unknown, thanks to Jason Olive.

2,322. PC as quoted by Herb Caen in the *San Francisco Chronicle,* July 11, 1988.

2,325. LG, thanks to Susan Richman.

2,326. MCS to RB.

2,327. ID as quoted by Herb Caen in the *San Francisco Chronicle,* August 15, 1988.

2,329. ML in *Table Talk.*

Quotation
Number

2,335. HLM at the 1940 convention of the American Booksellers Association.

2,336. Unknown, as quoted by Milton Berle in *B.S. I Love You*, 1988.

2,337. AB in *The New York Times Book Review*, May 21, 1989.

2,339. LC in a letter to the *San Francisco Chronicle*, February 9, 1988.

2,343. HGW as quoted by Macdonald Carey in the *Writers Guild of America News*, May 1986.

2,344. JL, thanks to Karl Fulves.

2,346. Unknown, thanks to Karl Fulves.

2,348. RN in *People* reviewing a book by Judith Michael.

2,349. FK in a letter written when he was twenty.

2,350. GV as quoted by David Show in the *Los Angeles Times*, December 12, 1985.

2,352. BD in *Lothair*, 1870.

2,353. FN in *Beyond Good and Evil*.

2,354. JJR in *Emile*.

2,355. SB in *Note Books*.

2,356. HLM at the 1940 convention of the American Booksellers Association.

2,357. BGH on the television program *Bookmark*, April 2, 1989.

2,358. LT on *The Donahue Show*, February 12, 1988.

2,359. A line from the movie *When Harry Met Sally*, 1989, screenplay by NE.

2,361. BE in *Mother Jones*.

2,362. DR as quoted in the *National Enquirer*, January 7, 1987.

2,363. MM as quoted in *The New York Times Book Review*, September 27, 1987.

2,366. DR, thanks to Bob Cudmore.

2,368. Unknown, as quoted by Ray Orrock in the *Hayward Daily Review*.

2,371. SC as quoted by Milton Berle in *B.S. I Love You*, 1988.

2,374. GP, thanks to John Grigsby.

Quotation
Number

2,376. Unknown, thanks to Jim Eason.

2,379. JR as quoted in *Money* magazine, September 1986.

2,381. AR is a character in *Gorky Park* (1981) and *Polar Star* (1989), novels by Martin Cruz Smith published by Random House.

2,382. GK made the remark after being traded by the Green Bay Packers to the Miami Dolphins.

2,386. JC on his 25th Anniversary Show, September 25, 1986.

2,387. From a lecture by GK at College of Marin (Kentfield, California), January 12, 1989.

2,389. FL as quoted in *Rave,* November 1986.

2,392. YS as quoted in *Rave,* November 1986.

2,394. FZ in *Money* magazine, September 1986.

2,397. From JM's 1950 screenplay for *All About Eve,* a movie based on a short story by Mary Orr.

2,401. As quoted by Joseph Gallagher in the *Baltimore Sun,* October 12, 1988.

2,406. Graffito, thanks to Stefan D. Koch.

2,408. H as quoted by John Toland in *The Rising Sun;* thanks to Robert Gordon.

2,413. JM quoted in *The New Yorker,* April 17, 1989.

2,414. MP, thanks to Jim Eason.

2,415. SB as quoted by Herb Caen in the *San Francisco Chronicle,* April 9, 1989.

2,416. TM as quoted by Herb Caen in the *San Francisco Chronicle,* January 6, 1986.

2,421. ED is a standup comedian.

2,431. EL in *Glitz.*

2,433. Unknown, thanks to Stefan D. Koch.

2,435. KM, thanks to Jason Olive.

2,437. LD as quoted in the *San Francisco Chronicle.* July 27, 1989.

2,440. YB as quoted by George Will in *Newsweek,* April 14, 1986.

Quotation
Number

2,442. FA as quoted by J. Bryan, III in *Merry Gentlemen (and One Lady)*, 1985.

2,443. Unknown, thanks to Susan Richman.

2,445. Screenplay by Truman Capote and John Huston.

2,448. JJ is a horse trainer quoted by William Murray in *When the Fat Man Sings*, 1987.

2,451. Chinese proverb thanks to Michele Plunkett.

2,453. Screenplay by Truman Capote and John Huston.

2,456. GB shot down twenty-four Japanese planes in WWII.

2,457. DF as quoted by Herb Caen in the *San Francisco Chronicle*, December 6, 1987.

2,459. LV as quoted in *Forbes*, April 17, 1987.

2,460. GO as quoted by Alexander Bloom in *Prodigal Sons*, Oxford University Press, 1986.

2,461. CT in *The New Yorker*, May 15, 1989.

2,463. JN, thanks to Johnson Letellier.

2,465. LS, thanks to Kris Chotzinoff.

2,466. PC, from his novel *Prince of Tides*, 1986.

2,468. MK as quoted in *Perfect Pitch* by Nicolas Slonimsky, 1988.

2,470. JG, thanks to Susan Richman.

2,473. HC, thanks to John Grigsby.

2,474. JB as quoted by Herb Caen in the *San Francisco Chronicle*, August 9, 1988.

2,478. P, thanks to Bill McCollough.

2,480. DA in a letter to RB.

2,492. RF as quoted by Charles Roos in the *Rocky Mountain News*, September 26, 1986.

2,493. Unknown, thanks to Jason Olive.

2,498. Screenwriter: Alvin Sargent. Thanks to Jack Mingo.

Quotation
Number

2,502. Unknown, thanks to Jason Olive.

2,506. PJO'R in *Modern Manners*, 1988.

2,507. TR as quoted in the *San Francisco Examiner*, September 28, 1987. Thanks to Michael O. Stearns.

2,511. GS, thanks to Blair Chotzinoff.

2,522. From a *Peanuts* comic strip, March 28, 1989.

2,523. GR on *Saturday Night Live*.

2,528. RR is a standup comedian.

2,532. The quote is sometimes credited to the late film star Alan Ladd.

2,533. DB as quoted by Herb Caen in the *San Francisco Chronicle*, April 22, 1986.

2,536. E in *In Praise of Folly*.

PRINCIPAL SOURCES
OF ARTWORK

Harter's Picture Archives for Collage and Illustration, edited by Jim Harter and containing over 300 nineteenth-century cuts.

Music, A Pictorial Archive of Woodcuts & Engravings, selected by Jim Harter and containing 841 illustrations.

Men, A Pictorial Archive from Nineteenth-Century Sources, selected by Jim Harter and containing 412 illustrations.

Women, A Pictorial Archive from Nineteenth-Century Sources, selected by Jim Harter and containing 391 illustrations.

Picture Sourcebook for Collage and Decoupage, edited by Edmund V. Gillon, Jr., and containing over 300 illustrations.

The above five titles are published by Dover Publications.

INDEX OF AUTHORS

(*Note:* Numbers refer to quotations, not pages.)

INDEX OF SUBJECTS AND KEY WORDS

(*Note:* Numbers refer to quotations, not pages.)